# AMERICA
# IN THE SIXTIES

# AMERICA
# IN THE SIXTIES

## An Intellectual History

RONALD BERMAN

*THE FREE PRESS*, New York
COLLIER-MACMILLAN LIMITED, *London*

*First Printing*

_Barbara, Andy, Julie, and Kathy_

# Acknowledgments

The Committee on Research of the University of California, San Diego has generously supported this book. The library of UCSD has been extraordinarily helpful, and I am obligated to it. Mr. John Parrack of The Free Press has done a fine job of seeing a difficult book into print. Portions of this book have appeared in *The Kenyon Review.*

In addition, I am indebted to the following magazines and publishers for permission to quote copyrighted material, specific credit for which appears within: The Activist Publishing Company; Basic Books; Beacon Press; Citadel Press; *Commentary; The Correspondent;* The Devon-Adair Company; Diablo Press; Dial Press; *Dissent;* Doubleday and Company; *Encounter;* Grove Press; Harcourt, Brace and World; Harvard University Press; *Judaism;* Alfred A. Knopf; *Liberation;* The Macmillan Company; The M.I.T. Press; William Morrow and Company; New Directions; *The New Leader; New Politics; New York Review of Books;* Oxford University Press; *Partisan Review;* S. G. Phillips; Frederick A. Praeger; G. P. Putnam's Sons; *Ramparts;* Random House; *The Realist;* Henry Regnery Company; Charles Scribner's Sons; *Studies on the Left;* University of Chicago Press; Viking Press.

# CONTENTS

*     *     *

*A*s there were many reformers, so likewise many reformations; every country proceeding in a particular way and method, according as their national interest, together with their constitution and clime, inclined them: some angrily and with extremity; others calmly and with mediocrity, not rending, but easily dividing, the community;—which, though peaceable spirits do desire, and may conceive that revolution of time and the mercies of God may effect, yet that judgment that shall consider the present antipathies between the two extremes—their contrarieties in conditions, affection, and opinion—may, with the same hopes, expect a union in the poles of heaven.

SIR THOMAS BROWNE, *Religio Medici*

# 1.

# ENTERING THE SIXTIES

For the intellectual, certain historical periods begin as metaphors of change. He looks at the past, characteristically, with the animus of modernity. Eventually the past includes the present; it is part of the doubleness of modern intellectual life that yesterday's hope should be today's irony. To be part of the past is to judge one's self, and the modern intellectual feels both pride and a certain shame in having survived his ideas. If he goes back to the Thirties for his justification he may view it as the great age of commitment but it is equally probable that his affections will be tempered by remorse. He may sense, as Robert Warshow did in a notable essay on that experience,[1] that the complex independence of intellectual life surrendered itself to a form of certainty and therefore

1. Robert Warshow, *The Immediate Experience* (New York, 1962), pp. 33–48.

of vulgarity. The intellectuals then began their campaign for existence as a public force, but their examination of the culture around
them failed to include their own assumptions. They became dis-
ingenuous, ideological. Their readiness to accept the standards of
politics as if they could apply to the entire life of the mind was,
finally, disabling. It led to the central problem of the modern
intellectual: How, in Warshow's phrase, he could "define his own
position in the whole world of culture."

The Forties had their own momentum and carried American
intellectuals along with it. But they ended with the confrontation
of Alger Hiss and Whittaker Chambers, two men with all the
crippling strengths of the opposition they embodied. It was a
baffling encounter: "the Third Perioder, still pursuing the absolute,
makes a tragic final appearance as the scorned squealer; the Popular
Fronter can only exit in the role of the hopeless liar." [2] That is how
Leslie Fiedler put it, in a much debated end to our innocence.
From that time until the Sixties the intellectuals, particularly those
on the left, acknowledged that they lived in a kind of limbo. They
were roused from their inertia by McCarthyism—but their pleasure in the conflict was qualified by a sense that they had become
differentiated to a very great degree from the culture in which
they found themselves. They relinquished for a time the vision of
a culture in which the intellectual had found not only his own
identity but his role as a public figure.

The Fifties were for many intellectuals a captivity in Babylon.
They were the bloated Fifties in which a nation became trapped
by its own affluence. As one book saw it, they were *The Haunted
Fifties*,[3] a decade that existed as if the Thirties had not preceded
them. The "style" of Dulles and Eisenhower was provincial Christian and necessarily Republican. It was a new gilded age. Neither
as public symbols nor as an effective class did intellectuals have
the status they believed themselves to have earned. The resentment
they cultivated turned into suspicion of themselves; in an important essay that appeared in 1960, C. Wright Mills wrote that
"our major orientations—liberalism and socialism—have virtually

---

2. Leslie A. Fiedler, *An End To Innocence* (Boston, 1955), p. 23.
3. I. F. Stone, *The Haunted Fifties* (New York, 1963).

collapsed as adequate explanations of the world and of ourselves." [4]
Another essay of 1960, both apologetic and ironic, implied that intellectuals had brought their own fate upon themselves:

> What a nine years it has been! What an unholy, inactive lot we were during that time. Bitter, cynical, indifferent, supine, momentous events proceeded without us, the world advanced in spite of us, life ebbed and flowed in vast movements while we loafed on beaches and in television rooms. How sad for most of us, who rode out our nation's unconnection, remaining unconnected, solitary, alien, complacent.[5]

Any change that would come must, the intellectuals saw, include themselves.

It appeared unlikely, as we were entering the Sixties, that this would occur. The most important book at that time, Daniel Bell's *The End of Ideology*, foresaw that the idea of change no longer had philosophical roots:

> Thus one finds, at the end of the fifties, a disconcerting caesura. In the West, among the intellectuals, the old passions are spent. The new generation, with no meaningful memory of these old debates, and no secure tradition to build upon, finds itself seeking new purposes within a framework of political society that has rejected, intellectually speaking, the old apocalyptic and chiliastic visions.[6]

*The End of Ideology* was a powerful argument against the pretensions of an intellectual class. Socialism was, as an operative belief, quite finished. Liberalism had not regenerated itself—and, as Bell rightly suspected, would not be persuasive in a new dialectic

4. C. Wright Mills, "On Reason and Freedom," in *Identity and Anxiety*, Maurice Stein, Arthur Vidich, and David White, ed. (Glencoe, 1960), p. 111.

5. Harvey Breit, "A Second Novel," *Partisan Review* (Summer 1960), p. 561. © 1960 by *Partisan Review;* quoted with permission of the publisher and the author.

6. Daniel Bell, *The End of Ideology* (New York, 1960), p. 374. Copyright © 1960, 1961 by The Free Press, A Corporation; copyright © 1962 by the Free Press. Quoted with permission.

of generations. The man whose career he outlined as a paradigm of intellectual fortunes, Dwight MacDonald, was seen to have gravitated from one form of politics to another, exhausting all hopes without discovering any. We are reminded of William Buckley's observation that MacDonald's political career looked as if it had been painted by Jackson Pollack; it was the kind of irony that held together too much truth. *The End of Ideology* was a seminal book, but it faced the dangers of all prediction. It could foresee neither the new left nor the new conservatism; it was not aware of those international eruptions that would permanently alter our domestic intellectual life. On one very important point it lost no validity at all with the passage of time: The liberal mainstream of American life had become solidified. If the tradition of the new proved unattractive that was true, in part, because the liberal community was satisfied with its status.

The new decade opened with a presidential election that had more overtones than those of religion; it was perceived by many intellectuals as the end of something, and another, more liberalizing, movement into the future. Yet there were many abstainers. In looking over the now-ancient journals of 1960 we can see how bitter the intellectuals were over the choice of candidates and philosophies, how sure they were that the ages of McKinley, Coolidge, and Eisenhower had put their unequivocal stamp on the American culture. For Kenneth Rexroth the new confrontation was purely a symbolic drama, and the title of his essay in *The Nation*, "I'll Sit This One Out," gave public notice of his disillusion.[7] For Gerald Johnson it was "Burroughs Against IBM,"[8] a case of candidates armed not with mighty philosophies but with the same weapons of class and cultural interest. One notes parenthetically that, in 1960, liberals were infuriated by the sameness of the candidates, while in 1964 they were enraged by the difference. Dwight MacDonald wrote that there were simply no issues in the election—the nation, in 1960, was evidently satis-

---

7. Kenneth Rexroth, "I'll Sit This One Out," *The Nation* (24 September 1960), pp. 172–176.

8. Gerald Johnson, "Burroughs Against IBM," *The New Republic* (August 8, 1960), p. 12.

fied with itself to the point of stupefaction.[9] He reviewed the great senility that had overcome us—the fall of Adlai Stevenson, the resemblance of one party to another, the fact of a country rich beyond the dreams of Marx—and concluded that there was no real divisiveness abroad. For him, although history was to indicate otherwise, the Sixties were to be years of intellectual attrition.

Those who welcomed the Sixties were sure that a revolution in American culture had occurred. In the first year of the decade Walter Lippmann wrote that "we're at the end of something that is petering out and aging and about finished." [10] He sensed that the problems of the future were different, and that, politically, there was a new generation abroad. Arthur Schlesinger, Jr. foretold "a new epoch" and unloaded upon it the omnibus virtues of "vitality," "identity," and "new values . . . straining for expression and for release." [11] The American people he found weary and drained by the Fifties (it was convenient to believe that mass culture enjoyed the same state of mind that he did) and he indicted the times for being self-centered. His utopian view of the Sixties was, in the pejorative sense of the word, political; he announced that the Kennedy years would supply new jobs, new values, and a totally positive social being. It would certainly be wrong to assume that only liberals were hypnotized by the time of change—in "Hope For The '60's," Frank Meyer wrote that they promised "to reverse the whole trend of American intellectual history from the days of Lincoln to those of Franklin Roosevelt." [12] There would be an end not to ideology, but to collectivism, unfreedom, and secularism. Yet, for Amitai Etzioni,[13] the new politics indicated "nothing less than the end of a neo-conserva-

9. Dwight MacDonald, "The Candidates and I," *Commentary* (April, 1960), pp. 287–294.

10. Walter Lippmann, "Walter Lippmann as Interviewed by Howard K. Smith," *The New Republic* (25 July 1960), pp. 19–24.

11. Arthur Schlesinger, Jr., *The Politics of Hope* (Boston, 1962), pp. 81–93.

12. Frank Meyer, "Hope For The '60's," *National Review* (14 January 1961), p. 19.

13. Amitai Etzioni, "Neo-liberalism—The Turn of the 60's," *Commentary* (December, 1960), pp. 473–479.

tive decade and the beginning of a neo-liberal one." It was a varied choice.

*America In The Sixties* attempts to trace the satisfactions and disappointments attendant on great hopes. The intellectuals have been at their most self-conscious and many notable attempts have been made toward the definition of their identity and social function. Almost universally these definitions have disregarded older ideas about intellectual life, i.e., it was not meditation, privacy, and inner development that engaged those who located the man of thought, but action, public immersion, and power. It is one of the great themes of the Sixties that intellectuals as a group feel they should themselves supply to a democracy those public virtues not accounted for by mere electoral representation; all kinds of demands have been made, not the least of which is that intellectuals should embody our moral impulses.

Even when the public role of the intellectual was assumed there were no sureties. The intellectual realizes that he exists in history—but to what extent can he identify with the values of the Enlightenment, and to what extent is he a prisoner of the modern? My conclusion has been that this dialectic has been framed but hardly resolved. It is part of the mythology of the mind that the Enlightenment is our great ancestor, but our ignorance of the meaning of the Enlightenment—to say nothing of the determinism inherent in Marxian and Freudian thought—couples oddly with rationalist freedom. There are the sociological difficulties: Some of the major writing of this decade has not received the public attention it deserves, and we remain far too ignorant of the intellectual as déclassé. The most compelling studies of intellectuals abroad reveal to us a stage through which we may be passing: The intellectual is at the same time assumed to be a public figure and a destroyer of those traditions which make possible the concept of a polity. In this decade his destructive attitude toward himself has had serious consequences in terms of personal identity; translated into political terms it has brought to bear entirely new conceptions of possibility. Whether in the Third World or in the newly energized academic world, the intellectual of the Sixties found himself with the power to build and to tear down. Finally, when he did come to terms, on rare occasions, with his own sense of self and the public sense of his function, he found the ineluctable barriers of cultural office. The more intellectuals came to governmental responsibility the more they found themselves in the grip of process and bureaucracy. What I have called the literature of disappointment is that great body of commentary which ironically compares the ideology of the mind to the action it may generate.

When I have considered the intellectual and religion I have tried to point out how the idea of the iconic has passed from the church to the body politic. I have been especially concerned with the demoralization this has wrought upon Jews, and with the incipient rebellion this decade has witnessed among those who refuse to link Judaism and liberalism. The new Jewish radicalism is conservative, and the worship of politics has, for Jews, become a subject of intense and conscious rejection. For Christians the subject is more open—American Protestantism has not made demands upon intellectuals equal to those demands they have made upon it. My sense of it is that the Protestant intellectual has followed a path well traveled in this century, and has consecrated politics even as he has deconsecrated the "mythology" of the gospel.

It has been necessary to go over the entire matter of civil rights, not to justify or attack the movement, but simply to see how the Negro has become, to himself and others, a cultural object. I have reviewed the major Negro strategies, but I have found that this is not enough. It is only in the work of individual intellectuals like LeRoi Jones, James Baldwin, and especially Malcolm X that the Negro condition may be understood. It is of enormous importance that we separate the Negro as individual from the Negro as symbol; that we see how ideas like that of negritude inhibit and finally destroy our sense of truth. And it has been necessary to trace the absorbing history of Negro and liberal antagonism, a history that dilated in feeling and importance as the age of the demonstration subsided.

I have gone over the history of the new left with much detail and some severity. It is my thesis that in this movement intellectuals of the Sixties tried most directly to assume public power. They perceived this power as being in the hands of a class antagonistic to intellect—and in any case unworthy of exercising power for the greatest good. The new left movement has involved great energies and vast errors. Its central demand—that the cultural *via media* in which we live be viewed as an objective form of fascism—could never hope for any acknowledgment but that of contempt or resentful sympathy. Its existential bias reduced all political demands to a desire for vitality, and its famous distinction between "form" and "essence" permitted it to compare democratic uncertainties unfavorably with totalitarian directness. Its culture heroes were adopted, the men of the left who, in the exemplary Third World, had finally imposed the force of rationality on the protean body of history. Whether in terms of ideology or activism the new left failed in its objectives. It could not justify the political supremacy of an intellectual minority, and it could not shape the academic institution to its own demands. Indeed, the whole experience of the new left has been divisive, and perhaps the most notable effect it has had was to make the moderate left conscious of its own conservatism.

In dealing with the writer I have taken the figure par excellence of the modern culture hero. The writer has tried not for direct power but, as in the cases of Mailer and Burroughs, for a kind of moral supremacy. His famous alienation has been voluntary and not unprofitable; it is a case of wiping out the assets of his liberal culture and replacing them with values of quite another kind. Consciousness has been made into an ethical value and sexuality into an ideological weapon. The most alarming thing about modern sexuality is not its heightened sensuality; indeed, it is frigid, academic, and symbolic. The strained rendition of homosexual ecstasy—like the less ambivalent but equally didactic love of man and woman—has been in the largest sense political. Whether in the pages of the novelists or in the handbooks of the bohemian left, sexuality has been unjoyous and serious. It has been racialized, so that we may see it as the sole property of the deserving Negro. It has been politicized, so that we may see it as the natural characteristic of the emancipated left. Perhaps most ironically, it has been held up as the standard of natural relationship and realism even as it has been turned into a kind of religious formalism. In dealing with the fiction of homosexuality, I have noted the great contradiction of a fiction—and an accompanying criticism—which treats the exhibition of homosexual love as a triumph of the scientific and novelistic while relying on attitudes entirely appropriate to the soapiest Oscar Wilde.

In short, *America in the Sixties* reviews the ideas of our time and their fate. There are a great many quotations in the pages that follow which I have retained because they are superior to paraphrase. My object has been to transmit the tone of the decade, and to make this book a kind of repository of information.

# 2.

# THE INTELLECTUAL

## Definitions

The intellectual in search of his own identity is also known to us as Julien Sorel, Stephen Dedalus, and Daniel Deronda. His modern incarnations have tended to be less overpowering—a Herzog for a Hamlet is good, but seems a diminution. Nevertheless, he is with us and exerts a certain authority in recent fiction. Fiction offers the supreme statement of the condition of the intellectual, but the definition may be approached more directly through the language of science. The argument from status is often appealed to, and is an evident starting point. But however tempting it may be to define the intellectual by vocation this has been a mode avoided by sociologists. Robert Merton, for example, indicated that this approach would have to be qualified if only to accommodate the truism that not every person being paid for the use of his mind had the interest or capacity to be an intellectual.[1] And, when the bona fide intellectual (to presume his existence) exercises "advisory and technical functions within a bureaucracy" he may well cease to act as an intellectual. Perhaps the safest approach to the matter of status is the descriptive, and this has been well used in Seymour Martin Lipset's *Political Man*. For Lipset, intellectuals are those who "create, distribute, and apply *culture*, that is, the symbolic world of man, including art, science, and religion."[2] A distinction follows between creators and retailers— performers as opposed to composers; teachers as opposed to scholars; most reporters as opposed to, one imagines, Walter Lippmann. One of the better moments in Lipset's essay is his acceptance of *Facts Forum* as a source of definition. This publication had, of course, made the famous accusation that lawyers, doctors, bankers, teachers, professors, preachers, writers, and publishers were the natural dupes of Communism. *Facts Forum* and the late senator from Wisconsin were, Lipset notes, not too far off the mark in perceiving the historic leftism of American intellectuals. That, Lipset suggests, is by now an integral part of their status. It is built into patterns of voting, thought, and even occupation—as in the matter of academic liberalism. This is not unexpected, for the probability that intellectuals cohere in a "homogeneous medium" was stated by Karl Mannheim in *Ideology and Utopia*.[3] The value of definition by status as practiced by Lipset is its statistical probability of accuracy. It is useful to see intellectuals examined on the concrete issues of their profession and their politics. The limits of such study are apparent—the matter of the quality of beliefs is not posed.

There is, of course, a moral problem embedded in the issue of intellectual status: Who can *become* an intellectual? Is entrance into this group, which is self-evidently exclusive by reason of

1. Robert K. Merton, "Role of the Intellectual in Public Bureaucracy," *Social Theory and Social Structure* (Glencoe, 1949), pp. 163–165.
2. Seymour Martin Lipset, "American Intellectuals: Their Politics and Status," *Political Man* (New York, 1960), p. 311.
3. Karl Mannheim, "Prospects of Scientific Politics," *Ideology and Utopia* (London, 1954), p. 138.

mental standards, limited also by social character? Max Lerner asserts that the creative elite is the true intelligentsia.[4] What he calls "a natural aristocracy" free of "the irrelevances [sic] of color, birth, religious belief, or income" is, however, precisely the kind of Platonic ideal which sociologists are, with great regret, in the act of abandoning. Whatever "talents" are, and Lerner shows not much awareness of their character, they seem now to be inseparable from the status producing them. Such, at least, is the burden of Nathan Glazer's research into Negro and Jewish cultures, which are evidently productive in ratio to their utilization of ethnic differences.[5] Glazer writes that pluralism has its concrete social form in private and distinctive associations based on ethnic grouping. While these are undeniably "exclusive and discriminatory" they yet constitute the bedrock of status from which individual accomplishments arise.[6] Glazer puts it flatly and historically when he says we do not live in a culture in which "heredity, ethnicity, religion and race are only incidental and accidental personal characteristics." [7] That world exists only in ideology. How far we are evolving from the position of Lerner may be measured by the proposal of Jacques Barzun in *The House of Intellect* that admission to the good colleges (and hence fairly automatically into the intellectual class) be partially governed by family profession and cultural status. This statement caused, of course, a *succés de scandale*.

A definition including both status and function is offered by Christopher Lasch, who sees the intellectual "as a person for whom thinking fulfills at once the function of work and play; more specifically, as a person whose relationship to society is defined, both in his eyes and in the eyes of the society, principally by his presumed capacity to comment upon it with greater detachment"

4. Max Lerner, "The Education of a Democratic Elite," *The Age of Overkill* (New York, 1962), pp. 219–230.

5. Nathan Glazer and Daniel Patrick Moynihan, *Beyond the Melting Pot* (Cambridge, Mass., 1963), pp. 1–23.

6. Nathan Glazer, "The Peoples of America," *The Nation* (20 Sept. 1965), p. 141.

7. Nathan Glazer, "Negroes and Jews: The New Challenge to Pluralism," *Commentary* (December, 1964), p. 34. Used with permission of the publisher and the author.

than those who actually operate the culture.[8] This ought to be viewed alongside the statements of Raymond Aron and H. Stuart Hughes, both of whom discuss the betrayal by intellectuals of their function. Aron differentiates between scribes, experts, and men of letters, all of whom are subject to pressures of the kind that confirm status while eroding function. The first of these categories is the natural prey of bureaucracies, which require annual inputs of literacy; the second is managerial; the third may supply engineers of the soul for totalitarianism.[9] For both Aron and Hughes the least admirable type is the mental technician, an intellectual who has given up his independence of thought and his social duty for the rewards of public administration. Built into the very nature of the intellectual, as Hughes sees it, is the defining obligation to be free. And, Hughes recognizes something often left out in the discussion of this issue. The freedom of intellectuals is not, as Sartre would have it, to be restricted to the role of implacable critic of his culture. There is a possibility of the intellectual being the "defender and rationalizer of existing institutions"—and this, Hughes admits, is more nearly the historical posture of intellectuals than we imagine.[10]

Those who attempt to define the intellectual on the grounds of his status and function recognize, as we see in Hughes, Aron, and Lasch, that the intellectual is both apart from and attached to the culture at large. Mannheim emphasized the "determined" character of the educated man, but these writers center on the peculiar freedom of intellectuals, and imply that their ideas ought to be directed by moral purposes. If we are to read the meaning of intellectual status as it is put by these men (and especially as it is implicit in *Political Man*), we must acknowledge that, contrary to much recent opinion, the intellectual is scarcely a revolutionary by nature. Indeed, insofar as he is "engaged" he may modify liberal

8. Christopher Lasch, *The New Radicalism in America* (New York, 1965), p. ix. Used with permission of the publisher, Alfred A. Knopf, and the author.

9. Raymond Aron, *The Opium of the Intellectuals* (New York, 1962), pp. 203–212.

10. H. Stuart Hughes, "Is the Intellectual Obsolete," *An Approach to Peace* (New York, 1962), pp. 160–162.

ideological commitment by the inherently conservative imperatives of maintaining his status. The liberal intellectual is the natural enemy of the activist.

A second group of definitions rests on the qualitative character of beliefs. In a famous statement Julien Benda insisted on the opposition of mind to ideology: The *"clerks"* are "all those whose activity essentially is *not* the pursuit of practical aims, all those who seek their joy in the practice of an art or a science or metaphysical speculation, in short in the possession of nonmaterial advantages, and hence in a certain manner say: 'My kingdom is not of this world'." Benda's *Betrayal of the Intellectuals,* with its brilliant attack on French and German nationalist ideologues, has become the *locus classicus* for intellectual disinterestedness. His statement on the treason of the clerks bears repeating: ". . . We have to admit that the 'clerks' now exercise political passions with all the characteristics of passion—the tendency to action, the thirst for immediate results, the exclusive preoccupation with the desired end, the scorn for argument, the excess, the hatred, the fixed ideas." [11] It is by no means a dead issue, as we see in the mordant studies of intellectuals in *The Captive Mind* and *The New Class.*

Aron has commented of ideologues that they are for Man and Reason but not in the disinterested sense. In France, at least, the intellectual is not often the Socratic figure praised by Benda. He is rationalist and futurist, cultivating a mandatory hostility toward the "arbitrary work of the centuries" as opposed to the culture born of a plan. The American intellectual may have the same sympathies, but they are tempered by realism. Much recent work takes for granted that ideology is a bad thing for intellectuals, and attempts to establish a view of the intellectual as an agent of moral suasion. Edward Shils writes that intellectuals exhibit "an unusual sensitivity to the sacred, an uncommon reflectiveness about the nature of their universe, and the rules which govern their society." [12] Lewis Coser maintains that they "provide moral stand-

---

11. Julien Benda, *The Betrayal of the Intellectuals,* Richard Aldington, trans. (Boston, 1959), p. 32. Copyright © 1928, by William Morrow and Company, Inc.; used with permission.

12. Edward Shils, "The Intellectuals and the Powers," *Comparative Studies in Society and History,* I (October, 1958), p. 5.

ards" and are priestly in function.[13] C. Wright Mills believed that
it was the first duty of intellectuals to provide "values." [14] Finally,
in his extended treatment of the subject, Richard Hofstadter wrote
of intellect that it "examines, ponders, wonders, theorizes, criti-
cizes, imagines . . . . evaluates evaluations, and looks for the
meaning of situations." If simple intelligence is something of an
animal virtue, intellect derives from human dignity.[15]

These definitions are limited but not without the power to convince. Yet they are oddly abstract when compared to experience.
In our modern tradition they seem already to be archaic. Here is a
description which may bring this out:

> When Ginsberg reads he is great. From behind owlish intellectual
> specs, in soiled dungarees and lumberjack shirt, with thick lips and
> shaggy but balding head Ginsberg hunches forward like some fan-
> tastic rabbi, thrashing a long arm pointed straight at his audience,
> harangueing [sic], weeping, caressing as he builds and builds his
> poem, his oddly boyish coarse grating NY voice hammering at you
> until, suddenly, magically, something explodes in your head and
> you feel transported—something rare, worth it, a fragment of the
> good raw truth.[16]

The point is not that a new definition of the intellectual is being
offered but that we have the capacity to modify the old ones so
radically. It is all here—the sense of being in on a spiritual drama,
the ritual exorcism by a priestly figure, the exhibition of Truth
rather than Beauty. But it is a simulacrum. And if the old definitions strain rather hard to keep up with their new spokesman, what
are we to make of the newest set of theories? The intellectual as
Turner of Consciousness,[17] as maintainer of world peace, as apoca-

13. Lewis Coser, *Men of Ideas* (New York, 1965), p. viii.

14. Quoted by Irving Louis Horowitz in "The Unfinished Writings
of C. Wright Mills," *Studies on the Left*, III (Fall, 1963), p. 10.

15. Richard Hofstadter, *Anti-Intellectualism in American Life* (New
York, 1963), p. 25. Used by permission of the publisher, Alfred A.
Knopf.

16. Paul Carroll, "Five Poets in Their Skins," *Big Table*, I, 4 (1960),
p. 137.

17. The term is Benjamin De Mott's, referring to Norman Mailer. In
"Reading They've Liked," *Hudson Review* (Spring, 1960), pp. 143 ff.

lypst,[18] as originator of a new cult of sexuality or narcosis [19]—in all these forms he is outside the definitions yet certainly inside the culture. Perhaps this book can look at the issues more closely.


## Intellectuals and History

Carl Becker's *Heavenly City of the Eighteenth-Century Philosophers* has a passage worth dwelling upon: ". . . If we would discover the little backstairs door that for any age serves as the secret entranceway to knowledge, we will do well to look for certain unobtrusive words with uncertain meanings that are permitted to slip off the tongue or the pen without fear and without research; words which, having from constant repetition lost their metaphorical significance, are unconsciously mistaken for objective realities." [20] In this context the words are "Nature" and "Reason"; in ours they are the opposed terms "medieval" and "enlightened," "progressive" and "reactionary," "liberal" and its various antonyms. I would like to examine the first pairing, for it gives us a sense of how intellectuals at present are conscious of their identities.

The opposition between medieval and enlightened is one of first principles. For example, we continually come across references to the latter which strike us as being historically illegitimate. Those who use this word about themselves are equivocally descended from the *philosophes*. On the issue of reason they may be Freudians. In ethics they are determinists. They are likely to take pleasure in oratorios, to tour cathedrals, to be engaged in the professional

18. The reference is to James Baldwin's *The Fire Next Time* (New York, 1963).

19. The claims made on behalf of Henry Miller or William Burroughs.

20. Carl Becker, *The Heavenly City of the Eighteenth-Century Philosophers* (New Haven, 1961), p. 47.

study of allegories. Yet they use the word often, and apply it to themselves and to their culture with the evident purpose of making distinctions in values. They do this in a way that makes plain that for them world history begins in the mid-eighteenth century. The magnitude of pre-Enlightenment culture is never really apprehended, although a good many of its more visible concretions may be used for the purposes of entertainment. So far as values are sought in the study of history, it is characteristic that the American intellectual turns to the Enlightenment. For him as for Voltaire the time between Rome and the Renaissance offers only the barren prospect of a thousand years of stupidity and barbarism.

The point of course is that whether one assumes the Christian or secular consensus should be a matter of complete indifference. What matters is that intellectuals of the Sixties continue to fight a battle that should, according to the expectations raised since the rise of the modern secular state, long have been concluded. What is remarkable is that we are in a state of ambivalence, committed explicitly to the Enlightenment, yet drawn to the irrational and mysterious attraction of belief. Two generations ago this great battle was fought by the Protestant thinkers—Eliot, Santayana, Niebuhr. Today this battle is being fought by Catholics and Jews. The Sixties will, I think, come to be known as the decade in which the Jewish intellectual, freed of the distractions of thirty years of political radicalism, fought out his relationship to the Enlightenment. This needs its own chapter, and will for the moment be deferred. At this time it will be useful to sketch in the conflicting claims of Enlightenment and anti-Enlightenment thought on modern intellectuals.

When Peter Gay's *The Party of Humanity* appeared,[21] it became the occasion for a certain reorientation of thought on the meaning of the Enlightenment. The reception of this book by J. H. Plumb [22] was important because the reviewer intentionally

---

21. Peter Gay, *The Party of Humanity* (New York, 1963). Used by permission of the publisher, Alfred A. Knopf.
22. In the *New York Review of Books* (23 January 1964), pp. 6–7. Copyright © 1964, The New York Review; used with permission.

left the field of history to argue on that of culture. He raised the issue of whether or not intellectuals owed to the Enlightenment a kind of allegiance which had its roots in sympathy. And he specifically raised the issue of the viability of Enlightenment thought outside of its historical context. Plumb's beginning shows his awareness of the problems involved: "Voltaire, Rousseau, Diderot, they have been so easy to discredit! Hitler, Hiroshima, the gas ovens, nationalism, tyrannies, and revolutions of this, our century mock the claims of Reason. How much saner seem those philosophers who concern themselves with the irrational, with man's violence and greed, and put their trust in the wisdom, charity, and mysterious purpose of God." Plumb adds an important qualification to what is to develop into a defense of the Enlightenment, i.e., since reality is objectively *not* as it was seen by the *philosophes* what we now aim at is a new Enlightenment based on "qualified confidence" and expressed in the terms of "a hope, rather than a belief, in man's capacity to secure social and political forms" befitting his intelligence. These are important qualifications, but no more meaningful than the principal idea in Gay of which he approves: The *philosophes* must now be seen not as unqualified and unrealistic optimists, but as thinkers conscious of the "bestial" side of man's nature. In other words, the importance of the Enlightenment rests no longer on its complete difference from what preceded it, but on a certain resemblance.

A notable part of Plumb's essay concerns a passage in Condorcet to which Gay had drawn attention. Both Gay and Plumb praise it extravagantly, and see in it the justification of Enlightenment social thought. The passage bears repetition.

> Civilization occupies only a small part of the globe [and the] number of those who are really civilized disappears before the mass of men delivered over to prejudice and ignorance. We see vast countries groaning in slavery; in one place we see nations degraded by the vices of a civilization whose corruption impedes progress; in another, nations still vegetating in the infancy of its first epochs. We see that the labors of these last ages have done much for the human spirit, little for the perfection of the human species; much for the glory of man, something for his liberty, but as yet almost

nothing for his happiness. . . . The mind of the philosopher rests with satisfaction on a small number of objects; but the spectacle of stupidity, slavery, extravagance, barbarity, afflicts him still more often; and the friend of humanity can enjoy unmixed pleasure only by surrendering to the sweet hopes of the future.

It would appear that any revisionist view of the Enlightenment, while sympathetic to the hope underlying this passage, would yet necessarily observe that it is impossible to make it serve as the underpinning of a new realism. Condorcet is a captive of the sterile dialectic of "corruption" versus "progress"; he is alienated from history, and from the possibility that "prejudice and ignorance" are inherent. In short, his view of human misery is founded on the assumption that it is external. The Freudian will be as suspicious of this passage as the Fundamentalist. Yet both Gay and Plumb emphasize the centrality of this passage to the case for the *philosophe's* knowledge "of the darker side of man's nature."

There follows an attack on the Christian churches which is so generalized and so devoid of evidence that to quote it would simply be embarrassing. This sally is concluded with a passage that indicates why the word "enlightened" has such a heavy residue of nonobjective meaning: "The forces of oppressive authority, in Church and State, still subdue and confound the human spirit; and the forces of dialogue, which the Enlightenment released, are still locked with them in an unequal struggle." If this is meant to apply to England since the seventeenth century there are some rather large exceptions to be made. If it is intended to apply to America one may wish to recall that, as Lionel Trilling has said, the liberal heirs of the Enlightenment constitute the only tradition in power. Plumb, of course, does not mean it to *apply* to anything. He uses certain words as Becker suggests, in order to express sympathies rather than meanings. What he is trying to say is that modern liberal intellectuals do have confidence in man's fate, that they do look to the authority of the secular savants to justify that faith, and that the faith itself demands criticism tempered by ideology. Most important, from the point of view of diagnosing the relationship between modern intellectuals and *philosophes*, Plumb has this to say: "They made the man of letters a moral force in society."

One may differ, and suggest, as H. Stuart Hughes[23] and George Lichtheim[24] have done, that the man of letters became a moral force long before the Enlightenment—supported by the very values of the religious structure that the *philosophes* and their revisionists discarded. The point is of course not that men of letters then became visible but that they then obtained power. They became the saints of modern intellectuals because they influenced historical conditions and freed themselves from sanctions. That does matter very much—but it seems a pity that they should be defended instead for having "escaped from the confines of ideology into a world of free comment." We all know that they did no such thing: they gave us modern ideology for better and worse, and, as far as free comment is concerned, they too were bound by the limits of their passion. If, as Plumb himself suggests, they "made a religion of the mind," then surely they must be held accountable for the authoritarian nature of that religion, as for any other.

If the modern intellectual is secular, hedonistic, and reformist that is either to be regretted or praised, depending on one's instincts. But he cannot be justified on the grounds that secularism, rationalism, and hedonism have themselves been historically validated.

The embarrassment of modern liberal intellectuals, of course, is that those they most admire in terms of quality of mind reject the Enlightenment. A hostile critic of *The Party of Humanity,*

---

23. In *An Approach to Peace* (p. 161) Hughes states, "The function of the new and the old 'clerks' in Europe always bore a *public* character. The respect these individuals enjoyed did not derive simply from the splendor of their mental operations; it reflected their position as the custodians of the higher values of society. As the Church had once enunciated the general principles that were to guide public conduct, as the clerically dominated universities had elaborated the rules of argumentation and served as the guardians of orthodoxy, so from the sixteenth century on the new class of lay intellectuals began to elaborate a richer and less confined pattern of behavior for their fellow citizens."

24. In "The Role of the Intellectuals," *Commentary* (April, 1960), p. 295, Lichtheim writes that the forerunners of the modern intellectual were "the humanists of the 15th and 16th centuries" and even the nonclerical literate of the later Middle Ages.

Geoffrey Clive, wrote that *The Legend of the Grand Inquisitor* made *Candide* seem like an entertainment by Oscar Wilde. Nietzsche's analysis of atheism made Enlightenment anti-theism look innocent; Kierkegaard's analysis of *Angst* reduced Diderot's psychology to mere mannerism; Mill and de Tocqueville simply outweighed their counterparts among the *philosophes*. There was every reason, Clive suggests, for Rousseau to have been alienated from the men of Reason—he saw the bankruptcy of the idea of man saving himself from himself through education.[25] Another critic of the same book, Jeffrey Hart, has noted that not a single great writer of our time—not Proust, Faulkner, Mann, Joyce, Pound, Eliot—has been hospitable to the movement Gay defends.[26] The intellectual, in short, has been exposed to two very different streams of thought. One of them is tragical, religious, and historical; some of its central figures are Dostoevsky, Kafka, Eliot, Kierkegaard. The other is optimistic, secular, rational and at least partly visionary; it derives from the Enlightenment. Purely in terms of this opposition a certain amount of schizophrenia among intellectuals is understandable.

It is useful to be aware that the Enlightenment bears a Platonic aspect for modern intellectuals. Karl Mannheim has reminded us that a powerful divisiveness is implied by the unqualified acceptance of possibility. Some pages of *Ideology and Utopia* are quite sobering in their analysis of the origins of liberal humanitarianism. Mannheim suggests that the "liberal idea" is accompanied by an attitude "which often hides behind a rationalist facade," and he uses the terms "ecstatic" and "chiliast" to describe it. Whether or not we accept his religious analogy we can see that this attitude does exist, that it is hostile to whatever is political and programmatic, and that it informs this decade. As Mannheim notes, it "historically and socially offers a continual, potential threat to liberalism." [27] Between those who accept futurism as a contingency and those who accept it as a first principle the conflict is irrevocable. The intellectual class, uncertain of its allegiance—whether to the

25. From "Letters," *New York Review of Books* (20 February 1964).

26. Jeffrey Hart, "Enlightenments: French and English," *The Kenyon Review* (Spring, 1964), p. 406. Used with permission.

27. Mannheim, *op. cit.*, p. 203.

Enlightenment or to the evil facts of history—will be uncertain of its allegiance to change. On this count also the liberal and the radical are at war.

If the liberal intellectual is attacked by those to the left of him for not taking the Enlightenment sense of action with sufficient seriousness, he is under fire from the conservative intellectual for taking it all too seriously. As Jeffrey Hart puts it, the belief in human progressiveness is the one premise that has united the enemies of the *philosophes:* "Surely critics of the Enlightenment like Yeats and Eliot, or the critics Gay has principally in mind—Talmon and Becker, and by implication, such writers as Bredvold, Niebuhr, Lippmann, and Butterfield—do not hold it to have been trivial or frivolous; they consider it to have been dangerous." [28] Hart's other rebuttal is worth consideration, that the major English writers of the period—Dryden, Pope, Swift, Fielding, Johnson, and Burke—were in fact ardent Christians, and highly suspicious of ideas of progress or naturalistic virtue. They were indeed the severest critics of the Enlightenment we admire. It appears then, that there were two Enlightenments. One was that of the *philosophes,* and has had its reincarnation in modern liberalism. The other was that of the men he lists, who retained the religious dimension of Humanism. It is to these men and their habits of mind that conservative intellectuals now relate.

The dual nature of the Enlightenment has not made itself clear to many intellectuals. There is a strong preference for viewing that period and the age of scientific discovery that inaugurated it as wholly secular. That this is true in part is obvious. But to view *all* of the age of science in this way is to confuse historical allegiances with facts of history. Lewis Feuer's *The Scientific Intellectual* [29] is a particularly informative example of working from present to past, and hence of establishing for the modern intellectual a base in history. It is well known that "as Robert K. Merton has persuasively argued, the Puritan ethic served as a major force to enhance the cultivation of science." [30] The scholarship that has gone

28. Hart, *op. cit.,* p. 406.
29. Lewis Feuer, *The Scientific Intellectual* (New York, 1963).
30. Quoted by Coser, *op. cit.,* p. 29.

into demonstrating the connection of science with religious belief is a major twentieth-century accomplishment, and the names of Margery Nicolson and Richard Foster Jones have become if not household at least library words.[31] The most casual reader senses the exuberance with which Milton handles the telescope and the problems offered by space, and knows that the Royal Society was committed to its work because its membership was convinced on religious grounds of the intelligibility of the universe. Newton, for example, was a highly devout man who considered his own greatest achievement to have been his religious writing. Boyle endowed the famous "Lectures" that bear his name for the specific purpose of proving the connection between science and religion. Feuer, however, brings to the study of the scientific mind the preconceptions that many intellectuals have traditionally had. He claims that the scientific intellectual offered "original merit" against "original sin"; "merriment" against "gloom"; a "hymn to pleasure" against "exaltation of pain." The terms are cloudy, but the intention is clearly to identify Protestantism with the mindless, joyless fundamentalism of some of our sects. This is not the Protestantism known either to Luther, Donne, or Bunyan.

It seems necessary for Feuer to oppose the secular and the religious; to see in the latter a metaphysics of guilt practiced by "the masochistic ascetic." A certain amount of this will follow from strained neo-Freudian convictions. Feuer's definition of religious activity is "self-punitive asceticism [which] is the outcome of an identification with or submission to the absolute superego, and this internalized self-aggression issues in self-reproach, in spiritual groveling, in humility, in torments of anxiety and guilt." One of the great moments in Feuer's book comes about in his contemplation of Newton's clock, which operated a windmill on which the scientist had placed a mouse. "How far one might see in this curious experiment a frustrated, deep-seated Oedipal longing, with the mouse and mill as male and female symbols respectively, we can only speculate. . . ." How far one might see in this habit

31. Margery Nicolson, *Science and the Imagination* (1956), and *Mountain Gloom and Mountain Glory* (1959); Richard Foster Jones, *The Seventeenth Century* (1951).

of mind a relentless secularism we can only speculate. Feuer's view of science is rather like C. P. Snow's. Like many histories, this one has a hero. It is the scientist who recreated the world in the image of reason and "cleansed" that world of its religious impurities. It is Feuer's intention to show that science delivered us from political tyranny; that, as Snow puts it, its moral energies are ingrained. But that is of course to confuse quantitative accuracy with moral honesty. Science has not cleansed the world, but may be accused by this century of serving new tyrannies quite willingly.

The conflict of "enlightened" and its opposites has taken on new form and energy. The intellectual is all too aware that faith in human nature is no longer a dogma. If he sympathizes with the *philosophes* he finds that he must revise their sense of reality. He has intense sympathy with the ends of the Enlightenment but finds it difficult to draw verification from it. I do not take seriously the alienation of intellectuals from their times, since even in the most stable and organic of cultures the intellectuals were, rightfully, alienated from the ordinary modes of life. They are, after all, supposed to be of a different order. I do take seriously their alienation from history. The liberal intellectual has willingly cut himself off from the pre-Enlightenment world. He cannot imagine a consensus of religion and authority. Modern history has cut him off from its alternatives. He lives in a vacuum, and this may be the cause of his peculiar defensiveness and irritability. He cherishes the freedom offered by the Enlightenment even while he is a disciple of Marx and Freud. On the one hand a revolutionary, and on the other a determinist; it is an awkward posture.

# The Déclassés

In *Aspects of Revolt* Max Nomad quotes the conspiritorial Auguste Blanqui on certain educated malcontents who wanted power just as badly as those below them wanted simple survival. These déclassés were, according to Blanqui, "the invisible army of progress . . . the hidden leaven which secretly raises the mass and prevents it from falling into apathy. Tomorrow they will be the reserve of the Revolution." [32] They represent what is very nearly a sub-genre of intellectuals: in Mannheim's phrase, the unattached. *Ideology and Utopia* is too rigorous in seeing the intellectuals as characteristically outside the social structure—the American experience has been quite otherwise. Yet its theory of intellectual attitudes as a function of class structure—"dynamic, elastic, in a constant state of flux"—illuminates both the history of intellectuals and their condition in the emerging cultures.

According to Mannheim the modern middle class may be divided into two groups, those with capital and those whose only capital is their education.[33] The latter are not inclined to perpetuate this condition and are polarized by the conflicts of social life. Two courses of action traditionally lie before them, to act for the whole or to affiliate with the antagonistic classes. This rather stratified approach has its limits, as I have noted, in terms of the actual American experience. Yet it is not the actual experience with which intellectuals are solely concerned. The idea of the unattached intellectual, hostile to the class of his origins, has had a powerful life of its own. During the Thirties at least, intellectuals made sustained efforts to voluntarily declass themselves.[34] That they remained essentially "bourgeois ideologists" is one of the ironies of our situation. At present we are witness to another attempt at voluntarily attaining the status of déclassés, the passionate rejection by activists of their middle-class standing. We are all aware by now that the campaigns to eradicate flaws in the social structure (in civil rights, at the universities) have with a logic of their own become directed at changing the social structure. Activist intellectuals do not want a place in the establishment; as Mills puts it, they are the group which will transcend it.[35]

We are in a sense back where we started, with the intellectuals acting, in Mills' phrase, as the "possible, immediate, radical agency

32. Max Nomad, *Aspects of Revolt* (New York, 1959), p. 158.

33. Mannheim, *op. cit.*, p. 139.

34. The best account is Daniel Aaron's *Writers on the Left* (New York, 1961).

35. C. Wright Mills, "On the New Left," *Studies on the Left*, II, i (1961), pp. 63–72. Used with permission.

of change." If we look through Crane Brinton's study of *The Jacobins* it is clear that history offers precedents. The revolutionary clubs were made up of *rentiers,* advocates, councilors, physicians, men of letters—all those to whom the theory of a proletariat could not conceivably apply.[36] Brinton writes that the leaders were men of the middle classes, and men of a significant amount of education.[37] In Lewis Coser's study of Jacobin intellectuals in power it is stated that the number of intellectuals increased as one moved up the pyramid of power.[38] In fact, Coser writes, among the twelve who ruled we find *only* intellectuals. R. R. Palmer and Brinton have made clear that a majority of the ruling twelve were lawyers. The rest were professionals. Nearly all were well off; some were moderately wealthy. All except Hérault de Sechelles were of the middle class. All except Collot d'Herbois were formally educated. Coser notes that all had undergone professional courses of study—and that all were steeped in the works of the *philosophes.* Did they revolt despite their status? Coser suggests that they did so because of it. They were educated to dominate their society but cut off from exercising the power of their talents. The importance of this historical example is that the Jacobin intellectuals in power are the models for their inheritors. The phrase Coser uses is uncomfortably close: they were all "to some extent alienated intellectuals."

In Russia particularly the déclassés were intellectuals. Here is Bertram Wolfe's summation of their status: "lawyers without a practice, graduate clerics without benefices and often without religion, chemists without laboratories, technicians, engineers, statisticians for whom industry had as yet no need, journalists without a public, educators without schools, politicians without parties, sociologists and statesmen rejected by the state and ignored by the people." [39] In the France of the Dreyfus case, according to Victor Brombert, intellectuals were assumed to be beyond the loyalties of class. According to the hostile Lagardelle they were simply dis-

36. Crane Brinton, *The Jacobins* (New York, 1961), pp. 46–72.
37. *Ibid.,* p. 64.
38. Coser, *op. cit.,* p. 146.
39. Quoted in Coser, *op. cit.,* p. 158.

satisfied, ambitious déclassés.[40] Proudhon hated these "mandarins"; Bakunin believed that they had no loyalties at all; Lagardelle accurately identified their desire for power.[41] Both left and right concurred then as now that intelligence separated from class was socially dangerous.

Brombert notes that there is a good deal of ambiguity in the status of intellectuals, and that it derives from the tortured circumstances of the Dreyfus affair in which intellectuals took a position opposed to the majority of their countrymen. They seemed to be a proletariat in terms of status, yet an elite in terms of their own self-conception. They alternated in feeling pride and social impotence. They were caught between right and left. Brombert offers one of the better biographies of intellectual traits of this decade:

> Sensibility modeled on thought; faith in the efficiency of ideas as an organizational force in the tangible world; the utilization of culture as an instrument for criticizing tradition; the unselfish, gratuitous [*sic*] pursuit of truth, but simultaneously the pursuit of a humanitarian ideal; the transmission or preaching of moral values; the sensation, now proud, now humiliating, of existing outside the social framework, and yet, on the whole, an obvious sympathy for the laboring groups of the country and a consequent attraction to Leftist political parties; a feeling of "not belonging" and of impotence; jealousy of the men of action; the cult of revolt, sometimes even of anarchy; the nearly obsessive fear of being caught on the side of injustice; nostalgia for the masses coupled with the complexes of a "*fils de bourgeois*" ashamed of belonging to the privileged classes. . . .

The description is so close in particulars as to be of value in defining the present attitude of liberal intellectuals. It is the French intellectual who is mirrored, but the American who is foreshadowed. Common to both is a kind of *arrivisme* which is both social and psychological; regardless of his real standing the intellectual tends to conceive of himself as declassed by the disparity between social circumstances and his own capacities.

40. Victor Brombert, "Toward a Portrait of the French Intellectual," *Partisan Review* (Summer, 1960), p. 488.
41. *Ibid.*, p. 490.

In an essay in *Commentary* J. G. Weightman suggested that the historical situation of the déclassés had in fact taken contemporary form.[42] Modern French intellectuals, like their antecedents, have much less faith in the workings of the social structure than in the idea of influencing some source of power such as the benevolent despot or the Party. The fact that they are themselves middle class (in fact the governing class of France) leads to a certain complication: Since there is no objective force to struggle against, they must attack their own status. Hence, Weightman writes, their feelings of guilt and sentimentality, and their willingness to go outside of their condition and internationalize their aims. According to Hugh Seton-Watson (in *Neither War Nor Peace*) the separation of the intelligentsia from other social groups is of particular consequence in the present—the first stage of this process was European but the second is in the underdeveloped countries.[43] This is particularly meaningful because, although radical politics are Western European in origin, they take on new and unrestricted form in Africa and the East. And, in turn, the new forms have come to influence Europe and America—Patrice Lumumba, Kwame Nkrumah, and Fidel Castro have become part of the modern intellectual tradition.

One of the legacies of post-war optimism was the hope that the African and Asian nations would become democratic. They became no such thing, as we well know. In fact, according to Seton-Watson, a new ideology was incarnated, based on the repudiation of traditional values and on the acceptance of Western materialism as a new cultus. In short, an exaggeration of our own condition. This of itself is meaningful, but it is coupled with a dangerous frustration. These emerging cultures cannot realize the new ideology because of economic impotence. As a consequence, resentment of some magnitude is generated, and aimed at those who furnish the models but seemingly deny the resources for transformation. The accusation of colonialism exists on a level neither material nor historical; our very slight involvement in African

42. J. G. Weightman, "The Mandarin Left," *Commentary* (March, 1965), pp. 96–98.

43. Hugh Seton-Watson, *Neither War Nor Peace* (New York, 1960), p. 164.

politics, for example, is not really related to the view that we are a colonial people. The matter exists on another plane—our colonialism has been psychological. We have evolved certain ideologies and, in a sense, appropriated them. In the twentieth century the idea of progress through industrial, democratic civilization has had very wide acceptance but very narrow exemplification. It is only the West (or those nations under the hegemony of the United States) that offers such exemplification of the idea. Inevitably we must be seen as the sole possessors of things that should be universal. Inevitably this must seem intentional. Seton-Watson's summation is worth thought, for it clarifies the disjunction between the intellectuals conscious of a tradition and those contemptuous of reliance on the past. He writes that Asian and African intellectuals, like the *philosophes*, are readily inclined to reject the traditions of their countries because they identify these with a hated social order. That order has been suspiciously close to its former rulers, and seems in any case incapable of modernization. The intellectuals are Westernizers in the sense that they wish to have immediately the material amenities of our culture. At the same time they hate the West as an oppressive force and blame it for their own failures. The notions of historical progress and constitutional reform seem to them irrelevant.[44]

Hans Morgenthau seems to have been in substantial agreement with this in a recent symposium in *Commentary*.[45] He assumed that the values of the West were quite dispensable—it was its *standing* that appealed to the thinkers of the new nations. Perhaps the most relevant work to the present discussion is that of Theodore Draper, who has consistently argued that the Cuban revolution is in the line of déclassé intellectual revolutions. In an exploratory *New Leader* article in 1960 Draper outlined the middle-class background of the Castro government, and stated that the revolution was not undertaken by workers and peasants. It was a revolution "by the sons and daughters of the middle class in the name of the workers and peasants. In its present stage, the peasants are benefit-

---

44. *Ibid.*, p. 182.
45. "America and the World Revolution," *Commentary* (October, 1963), pp. 278–296.

ting from it the most, the workers very little or not at all, and the middle class as a whole has been marked for destruction." [46] The irony of this situation is that the revolution was brought about by those with educations which their society was too stagnant to utilize, and that by repression and through emigration their own class has dissolved.

Draper's major study of the intellectual problems involved is "The *Déclassé* Revolution" in *Castroism: Theory and Practice* (1965). In this book he points out that the greatest challenge to understanding Castroism rests on understanding the situation of the middle-class intellectual. The revolution was led by a lawyer without clients and a doctor without patients. It was financed by middle-class supporters, backed by urban middle-class sympathizers. But it was particularly a revolution of the disenfranchised middle class, "the sons and daughters of the bourgeoisie." Both Draper and Lino Novás Calvo [47] believe that the crux of the matter lies in the experience of generations—the fathers were entrepreneurs and the children were in the liberal professions and bureaucracy. The vehicle which turned generational differences and professional disappointments into revolution was education. Given an economy with limits imposed on it by industrial capacity; given the stupidity and barbarism of government; given a society with a sudden rise in technicians whose wealth is intellectual and hence only potential; given a university system in which politics was the real *élan vital*, and, Draper argues, we have a paradigm of modern intellectual rebellion. That it was by no means unique is borne out by the experience of Czeslaw Milosz. *The Captive Mind* has this to say of the experience of Eastern European intellectuals:

> We were all in revolt against our environment. None of us was of the proletariat. We derived from the intelligentsia, which in that part of Europe was a synonym for the impoverished nobility or the

46. Theodore Draper, "Cuba and the Revolution of Our Time," *New Leader* (July 4 & 11, 1960), pp. 3–4. Used with permission.

47. Lino Novás Calvo, "La Tragedia de la Clase Media Cubana," *Bohemia Libre* (New York, 1 January 1961). Quoted in Draper, pp. 112–113.

lower middle class. Gamma's father was, as I said, a retired officer; George, a poet, was the son of a provincial lawyer; Theodore, a poet, (later shot by the Polish underground as a Party propagandist), bore an aristocratic name although his mother was an employee in a bank; Henryk, an orator, writer and politician (later shot by the Germans), was the son of a railroad engineer. . . . my family belonged to the Lithuanian nobility, but my father had migrated from the country to the city to become an engineer. The revolt against one's environment is usually *shame* of one's environment. The social status of all of us was undefined. Our problems were those of the twentieth century, but the traditions of our families bound us to concepts and customs we thought ridiculous and reactionary. We were suspended in a void. . . .[48]

It is clear that in the last two decades a good deal of thought has gone into the matter of the déclassé intellectuals. From very different viewpoints very similar conclusions have been reached: Max Nomad wrote that the owners of an invisible hence useless capital would become revolutionaries; Whittaker Chambers, that the forces of revolution in the West were now an "intellectual proletariat." [49] They were in revolt, Chambers said, not only because of their status, but because they had lost faith in the validity of their ideas. Those who have concerned themselves with American intellectuals take another stand, but it is a position which I believe must be modified by our knowledge of the world-wide condition of the déclassés. Lipset's *Political Man* acknowledges the divergence between the real condition of the American intellectual and his own sense of that condition. Lipset believes that the American intellectual's sense of himself seems to be one source of his leftism.[50] No matter how much intellectuals in this country are influenced by our equalitarianism, and no matter what their actual status, they feel themselves to be underprivileged and lament the perquisites of their European counterparts. Significantly, income and prestige

48. Czeslaw Milosz, *The Captive Mind* (New York, 1953), pp. 142–143. Used by permission of the publisher, Alfred A. Knopf.

49. Nomad, *op. cit.*, p. 151; Whittaker Chambers, *Cold Friday* (New York, 1964), pp. 67–88.

50. Lipset, *op. cit.*, p. 326.

are not the only issues; they are low on the ladder of *power*.[51] Lipset makes a connection between this and the support by American intellectuals of the déclassés abroad. The former identify with and support those parties which criticize the existing structure of privilege.

Richard Hofstadter sees the cult of alienation as a phenomenon of the déclassé order. The Beats, he writes, have withdrawn from serious argument with the bourgeois world.[52] His conclusion to *Anti-Intellectualism in American Life* is valuable for its sense of hip and Beat writers who strive to preserve peace, democracy, culture, and individuality in such a way as to betray an attitude fundamentally inhumane. They have passed the boundary between reform and rejection, and are in this sense in the déclassé tradition. Since Hofstadter wrote, the new radicalism has occurred, which is a more important manifestation. I suggest something to be taken up later in this book—the new déclassés, like their counterparts in history, are quite conscious of their role. The recent bill of particulars drawn up by Irving Howe captures a sense of what is representative in activism:

> The "new leftist" appears, at times, as a figure embodying a style of speech, dress, work and culture. Often, especially if white, the son of the middle class—and sometimes the son of middle-class parents nursing radical memories—he asserts his rebellion against the deceit and hollowness of American society. Very good; there is plenty to rebel against. But in the course of his rebellion he tends to reject not merely the middle class ethos but a good many other things he too hastily associates with it; the intellectual heritage of the West, the tradition of liberalism at its most serious, the commitment to democracy as an indispensable part of civilized life.[53]

To take this seriously is to admit that C. Wright Mills had some logic on his side when he proposed the intellectuals as the immediate and radical agency of change. It need not be reiterated that our cultural task is to make that kind of change unnecessary.

51. *Ibid.*, p. 322.

52. Richard Hofstadter, *Anti-Intellectualism in American Life* (New York, 1963), p. 420.

53. Irving Howe, "New Styles in Leftism," *Dissent* (Summer, 1965), p. 307. Used with permission.

# Intellectuals
# and Policy

Since *The Republic* it has been assumed that intellectuals have a distinctive role to play in public policy. Their part in the revolutions of France and Russia seemed to establish that role as a right, or at least to imply that such action was prescriptive of their condition. In the Sixties their relationship to policy has become the subject of what may be called the literature of disappointment. In relation to no other matter except, perhaps, mass culture, has there been so much pessimism over the function of those who think.

Those who use reason have characteristically expected social problems to yield to it. If the intellectual could not administrate he was expected to advise; the relationship between mind and policy was accepted as that of cause and contingency. Henry Adams was the first modern to see that this no longer obtained; the world of policy had become too large, too corrupt, and too much subject to process for intellectuals to affect. His "education" was intentionally ironic—a use of the term involving precisely those qualities which our idea of learning has been reluctant to recognize. Education after Henry Adams could no longer be viewed as *paideia*, which was the training of the mind to participate in the *polis*, but as a psychological readjustment, a kind of ironic and resentful awareness that learning no longer had any reference to public life.

Outside the West *Diamat* has convinced intellectuals that ideas do not originate policy but are in themselves part of a deterministic process. The anger of Milosz, of Djilas, and of the new generation of revisionists in Poland and Russia relates, if only in part, to this awareness. Inside the West the role of intellect has increasingly been seen as peripheral, and our native anti-intellectualism has been reinforced by the failure of intellect qua intellect as an element of public life. One of the circumstances of the presidency of John F. Kennedy was, in fact, the seeming discrediting of intellect in politics. It had been expected by many liberal intellectuals that President Kennedy would rectify our traditional imbalance of intellect and power, that he would bring to office those qualities of rationality which would cut through and eventually dissolve the enigmas of politics. When, as in the Cuban confrontation, he ignored the *values* of many of his liberal supporters, and took the position that *politics* seemed to call for, it was widely felt that he had betrayed the imperatives of "reason" in favor of *raisons d'état*.

In his review of the history of intellectuals vis à vis power Lewis Coser remarks that certain modalities rule the relationship of ideas and action.[54] The Jacobins and the Bolsheviks exerted power; the Fabians directed power; the Brain Trusters adapted it. The Drey-fusards criticized power, and brought it to an awareness of the claims of morality. But the theoreticians have given way; in the East it has been discovered that critical intellect can be a liability. In the West the antagonism of power and intellect has become a theme of public life. This is taken up by Robert Merton in an acute essay on bureaucracy.[55] The intellectual in public office is generally in the process of being converted to a technician. He acts within an area of inquiry which is specifically delimited; his function is generally that of implementing fixed alternatives. In some important cases the bureaucratic intellectual is constrained by the nature of policy itself; Merton uses the example of bureaucratic versus unattached intellectuals dealing with racial segregation. The latter will tend to work at eliminating racial prejudice, but the former will be constrained to work within a program recognizing it. For example, the bureaucratic intellectual may be forced to "make segregation tolerable if not palatable to the Negro worker." And he may be forced to make a schizoid division between his own values and those of the institution. The major part of Merton's conclusion deals with the frustration of intellectuals in power. Their research may be exploited for political reasons; action may be based on expediency rather than on evidence; policy makers have a certain contempt for them; the bureaucratic structure itself inhibits the operation of thought.

This may be viewed simply as an adaptation of a well-known comment by Walter Lippmann: "it is impossible to mix the pur-

54. Coser, *op. cit.*, pp. 135–144.
55. Merton, *op. cit.*, pp. 167–178.

suit of knowledge and the exercise of political power and those who have tried it turn out to be very bad politicians or they cease to be scholars." It is of course Lippmann himself whose career is most deeply symbolic of the intellectual in politics. Arthur Schlesinger's essay on Lippmann in *The Politics of Hope* [56] seems to me to alternate between two themes. The first is that of the intellectual as hero—but the second is that of the intellectual as tragic figure. The operatic nature of the conception is not altogether wrong. Lippman began by invoking the Platonic connection between mind and politics; assuming that the statesman and the intellectual could act in concert. The essay of Schlesinger is concerned with the transformation of this position into one of modern disillusionment. Schlesinger seems to be ambivalent. He uses Lippmann as the paradigm of the public-minded intellectual to whom both he and John F. Kennedy evidently owed something of their own self-conceptions, and he uses him also as a representative figure for the failure of intellect. Indeed, the essay is concerned with the debacles in the career of Lippmann—the failure of science as a political discipline, the failure of politicians like the two Roosevelts to accept criticism, the failure of intellectuals to divorce themselves from the will to power, the failure eventually of the intellectual to extract from diversity the nature of universality. It is these themes from the life and writings of Lippmann that are selected, and it is important to see them as representative. After Theodore Roosevelt was attacked in the *New Republic* over his response to Wilson's Mexican policy he quite naturally gave up his friendship with Croly and Lippmann; the politician valued loyalty not rectitude. He "never forgave us. . . . After that we never had any close personal association with any public man." The man who in 1920 called for a body of experts motivated by selfless equanimity was to write some fifteen years later of intellectuals in politics that "nothing they say can be relied upon as disinterested." And it was his fate to argue that "there are certain obligations binding on all men who are committed to a free society, and that only the willfully subversive can reject them" even as intellectuals entered the age of ideology.

---

56. Arthur Schlesinger, Jr., "Walter Lippmann: The Intellectual *vs.* Politics," *The Politics of Hope* (Boston, 1963), pp. 126–154.

A strain of idealism persists in defining the relationship of intellectual to policy, even when it seems to take on the guise of pragmatism as in George Lichtheim's study of "The Role of the Intellectuals." [57] Lichtheim is tough-minded in his discussion of the end of the "liberal century" (1830–1930). He sees both nineteenth-century liberalism and conservatism as bankrupt, and subscribes to the current thesis that "the fascist crisis signifies . . . liberal society, at any rate in Europe, is on the point of giving up the ghost, its dominant class having lost the will and the capacity to rule." The demise of liberal culture has been hastened by the end of bourgeois social structure; the new hierarchies are managerial, impersonal, dependent on new and abstract loyalties. The old forms of intellectual protest are no longer adequate, and such movements as socialism become conscious of their impotence. Daniel Bell has written in *The End of Ideology* of socialism's awareness that it is oriented toward dispersion rather than production of wealth. Lichtheim adds to this the ethical disappointment of socialism—the sense of its intellectuals that communal existence can no longer be brought "into conformity with the human essence." Socialist intellectuals are convinced that they cannot exert public power, and become "stoical and gloomy."

As Lichtheim sees it, liberalism itself is no longer relevant to the industrial age. The crisis of liberal civilization consists in its having become aware of its own limits. In these new circumstances, in which ideologies have become homogenized and radical convictions have evanesced, the role of the intellectual has quite naturally been changed. My own conviction is that the relative powerlessness of the intellectual should be recognized; Lichtheim prefers to express what I think is unrealistic faith. What he calls a new rationalism is supposedly to be the product of our social evolution. The increasing centralization of our society, and its increasing susceptibility to quantification, seem to him hospitable to the development of a new stratum ranging from "the managerial and technocratic to the genuinely intellectual." It is these who will form a new, rational intelligentsia, and who will control the

---

57. George Lichtheim, "The Role of the Intellectuals," *Commentary* (April, 1960), pp. 295–307.

workings of the body politic. Lichtheim's analysis of the past is much more convincing than his view of the future in which he sees decision-making as the province of science. He sees a Wellsian social order free of the inanities of politics and the passions of ideologists. On the grounds of probability alone I am suspicious of this, but, supposing for the moment that a new union of science and politics should come about, I suspect that it will do so in other terms. And these terms will be antithetical to the intellectual. The point is that the managerial and technocratic do *not* progress to the genuinely intellectual. If we want some evidence of this I would adduce what I think is one of the most meaningful statements made in recent years. The following is from the writings of one of our most successful liberal technocrats. What it reveals is that the hope of intellectuals to objectify their ideas in a new, scientific order is based only on myth. Here is Clark Kerr on the role of thinkers in social institutions:

> The intellectuals (including the university students) are a particularly volatile element. . . . capable of extreme reactions to objective situations—more extreme than any other group in society. They are by nature irresponsible, in the sense that they have no continuing commitment to any single institution or philosophical outlook and they are not fully answerable for consequences. They are, as a result, never fully trusted by anybody, including themselves.[58]

The response of policy-maker to thinker is here, I suggest, quintessential.

* * *

It is in fact the separation of the intellectual from policy that is the theme of some significant writing of this decade. The Sixties began with a certain measure of assurance. The new President was himself literate, hospitable to the use of reason, surrounded by men who seemed to have transcended the distinction between

58. Clark Kerr, *Industrialism and Industrial Man* (Cambridge, Mass., 1960), pp. 70–72. Used with permission of the publisher, Harvard University Press.

professors and politics; a transcendence which, in the terms of Lippmann, was flatly impossible. The failure of the invasion of Cuba led to a re-examination of the advisory process in government, as in a notable essay by Hans J. Morgenthau which appeared in the *New Leader* in 1961.[59]

Morgenthau outlined the conflict of talent (if not of interest) between the men of facts and the men of ideas. He sided with the former because he believed that ideas in the world of the intellectual do not really have consequences. In the political world, however, ideas become policy, and take on material form. The intellectual inhabits a rather small world in which all things seem possible to the informed mind. He has no sense of limits and is dazzled by "that innocuous and frequently irrelevant pastime which we call pretentiously the academic dialogue." There is enough truth involved to elicit assent, and enough bias to temper it. When Morgenthau speaks to certain issues he notes that vis à vis Cuba, disarmament, and the national purpose the President "said hardly anything of substance, but he said it in beautiful prose." His central point is that all the apparatus of intellectual dialogue was present in a situation which could as well have been bungled by customary methods. The Cuban invasion was mismanaged because the administration, incredibly, failed to understand that totalitarianism is based on popular support. The advisors to President Kennedy entered the dialogue with the idea that a democratic revolt was inevitable. The Cuban fiasco demonstrated that the Castroite social order was a much more meaningful part of Cuban experience than a conflict of ideologies. As for the issues of disarmament and national purpose, Morgenthau notes that the President and his advisors developed no concrete modes or vehicles of policy but rested on concepts and rhetoric.

In the academy it is fairly common to meet the opinion that the power of intellectuals to affect policy has decreased, is decreasing, and ought to be strengthened. But the reaction of specialists in political science has been otherwise, as we see in Morgenthau. H. Stuart Hughes addressed himself in 1962 to the failure of in-

---

59. Hans J. Morgenthau, "Failure and Challenge," *New Leader* (3 July 1961), pp. 3–5. Used with permission.

tellectuals in public life.[60] He accepted the fact that matters of public policy were by nature resistant to the intellectual process, and blamed intellectuals for not being aware of this. In addition, he stated that it was unrealistic to explain the failure of intellect in government as due to either anti-intellectualism or McCarthyism. As to the first, he believes that intellectuals have exaggerated the hostility of government: "When American intellectuals voice their grievances . . . they had better omit the charge of ingratitude on the part of their government . . . they chose of their own free will to serve the state, and in so doing they took inevitable risks. They stuck their heads into the lion's den and it was only to be expected that now and then the lion would bite." As to the second cause, McCarthyism was only transient. The real constraints on freedom of thought are "official and semi-official procedures"—the apparatus of restraints which both major parties submit to in order to give the executive more power and the constituency less freedom. With unexpected harshness Hughes attacked intellectuals who either served or criticized the state. The first became technicians and lost the power of honesty. The second, prey to "the confusion, lack of poise, and self-abasement of the American intellectual," were neutralized by their reformist passions and ideologies. Such are the unexpected reverberations of the invasion of Cuba, which bids fair to be our own Dreyfus case.

Henry Kissinger was more cautious in *The Necessity For Choice* [61] but still inclined to doubt the value of intellectuals in matters of policy. He identified the characteristic sin of the policy-oriented intellectual as dogmatism, and stated that if the activist engaged in a cult of success the intellectual suffered from a cult of rejection. While Kissinger remained strongly opposed to the Commissar whose world was defined in other-directed terms, he was equally opposed to the man of analysis, who failed to relate thought to action. As he put it, the quest for certainty may be paralyzing when pushed to extremes. The search for universality, one of our Faustian intellectual habits, imposes dogmatism upon national affairs. It is worth noting that Kissinger, Hughes, Morgenthau

60. Hughes, *op. cit.*, pp. 164–175.

61. Henry Kissinger, "The Policymaker and the Intellectual," *The Necessity For Choice* (New York, 1961), pp. 340–358.

and other critics seem motivated neither by anti-intellectualism nor conservative politics. Yet they are profoundly sensitive to the criticism of the right directed at liberal intellectuals. The position they take must of necessity be critical of liberal practice, because the very pattern of intellectual involvement in policy originated under the New Deal and New Frontier. Certainly the disappointment of radicals in programmatic politics has a basis in fact—especially when we consider that the argument of these men refers evidently to an attitude they detect in *liberal* political scientists. That is to say, in liberal theory as in the practice of Bundy and Schlesinger over Cuba, the rights of intellect and certainly those of ideology have been subservient to those of policy. The hostility of radical intellectuals to liberal men of policy may be summed up in the remark of Irving Horowitz in a recent issue of *The Nation:* "we've been betrayed by Walter Lippmann and James Reston." [62] This refers to the Dominican intervention, but betrayal has in fact been the fate of most intellectuals who undertake programmatic rather than ideological action. Today the leading candidates for the role of Judas are Bayard Rustin and Michael Harrington. A year ago this would have seemed inconceivable, but the relationship of idea and policy makes it seem in fact natural.

Perhaps the two most powerful attacks on liberal intellectuals involved in policy are those of Robert Nisbet and Henry Fairlie. The former, writing in *The Yale Review*, theorized that certain dogmas obstruct useful comment on public policy.[63] One is "the chiliastic vision of the transforming moment" which, as Mannheim foresaw, is part of radical motivation. The other is the attitude of the left toward private power—such power appears to be intolerable. The diversity of private power, its independence, its actual popularity in the culture at large seems to the left to be subversive of true order. Public power is endowed by the liberal-rationalist with natural superiority and with a kind of immaculateness that has theistic reverberations. As for its opposite, that carries much the same odium that aristocracy carried for the *philosophes*. The attitude of liberal intellectuals toward power is polarized by this

62. "New Forum For Reason," *The Nation* (31 May 1965), p. 577.

63. Robert Nisbet, "Power and the Intellectual," *The Yale Review* (March, 1964), pp. 321–340.

habit. Nisbet notes that the nineteenth century liberals, including Mill, saw in private power a valuable check on the power of the state and the masses. Modern liberals are committed to "unitary political rationalization," hence they favor public over private power, and presidential authority over congressional initiative or delay. Since so much of the realization of power is precisely in areas of doubt, compromise and divided authority, it follows that intellectuals of the liberal persuasion will have difficulty in dealing with it.

Henry Fairlie's scathing piece on "Johnson and the Intellectuals" appeared in *Commentary* [64] a short time after the President assumed human status, which was, in turn, shortly before the Vice-President did the same. He dealt with one of the specific aspects of policy that I have mentioned, the relationship of intellect to presidential power. Fairlie observed the widespread revulsion among intellectuals over Johnson's style or lack of it, and he found that it had its basis in a rather immoral experience, what he called the raping of the intellectuals by President Kennedy:

> At all times, and no matter who exercises it, power is ugly and brutalizing: President Kennedy was allowed to make it appear attractive and redeeming. Power is shoddy: President Kennedy was allowed to glamorize it. Power is for the aged: President Kennedy was allowed to cast over it the magic of youth. Power is un-intellectual: President Kennedy was allowed to give it intellectual excitement. Power is safe only if it is exercised without enchantment, without claim to reason, and without pretense to virtue: President Kennedy was allowed to endow it with all three. Power is, no doubt, necessary: President Kennedy was allowed to make it seem desirable.

The President, in short, became a symbolic figure in the dialectic of intellect and power, although, I should think, his attitude toward that dialectic was quite close to that of Franklin Roosevelt.

Lyndon Johnson, on the other hand, reassuringly made a mess of things when he pretended that political decision arises from the encounter of intellectually upright alternatives. Yet for that reason

---

64. Henry Fairlie, "Johnson and the Intellectuals," *Commentary* (October, 1965), pp. 49–55. Used by permission of the author.

he was dumped by the intelligentsia. His weapons are after all "the proper political arts of flattering, cajoling, bartering, bribing, purchasing, intimidating, and (if necessary) trampling." These are if not repugnant to the intellectual usually unavailable to him. Fairlie concludes with what is certainly a sobering point:

> America is today paying the political price for voting as if the choice were between right and wrong, between good and evil. No one assisted in presenting the choice [between Johnson and Goldwater] in these terms more effectively than the intellectuals. When they should have been skulking in their lairs, using the quiet but insistent voice of the intellectuals to warn that a stampede to one leader or one party is always democracy's dearest mistake, they instead helped to whip up the stampede. It was the intellectuals, as much as anyone, who created the Colossus; they, as much as anyone, who worked for the annihilation of one of the great parties of the state; they, as much as anyone, who provided the reasons why a democracy should elect a dictator.

In political terms they argue at a disadvantage. Johnson's strength depends on support for his domestic program. The only way of bargaining with him is by *obstructing* his domestic program. It is of course impossible to allow him a consensus at home and deny it to him abroad. Politics is, Fairlie concludes, in this sense, one. The outlines of what I called the literature of disappointment are fairly evident. The response of the activist left is in this recent tradition, whether it takes the form of honest anger or simple resentment, of demonstrations or "inner emigration."[65] It deserves its own chapter.

---

65. The term was used by David Riesman and Michael Maccoby in "The American Crisis," *Commentary* (June, 1960), p. 461 ff.

# 3.

# *RELIGION AND*
# *THE INTELLECTUALS*

## *The Intellectual*
## *and Ethical Judaism*

The condition of the Jewish intellectual has generally been thought
of in terms of dynamic oppositions. There is the historical situation of the Jew in America: involved, as Will Herberg has written, in the triparite meeting of Sephardic, German, and East
European cultures.[1] There is the dialectic of generations, that of
the ghetto, the twice-born sons of the Thirties, the assimilated

---

1. Will Herberg, *Protestant-Catholic-Jew* (New York, 1955), pp.
186–226.

grandsons of the Sixties. There is the class dynamic, from a generation of workers to a generation of professionals. There was the
alternative (it no longer really obtains) between Zionist and
nativist. There is still the distinction between the organizational
and the unattached: between those who vote for the Democratic
party and those who finance it; between those who operate the
AJC and those who are members only of the AAUP. There are
those who love the middle class and those who loath it; those who
are alienated, psychoanalyzed, and intermarried, and those who yet
cultivate their gardens. The diversity is appalling, and would be
impossible even to consider unless the Jewish intellectual had the
unifying conception of his sense of self.

It was that sense of self which was most clearly displayed in the
*Commentary* symposium of 1961, "Jewishness and the Younger
Intellectuals." [2] The symposium began under circumstances that
were to some extent determined by recent history. It followed the
symposium of 1944 in which the notable generation of Lionel
Trilling, Alfred Kazin, and Delmore Schwartz had defined the
separation of the Jewish intellectual not only from the culture at
large but from his own origins. Lionel Trilling then made the
statement that "as the Jewish community now exists, it can give no
sustenance to the American artist or intellectual who is born a
Jew." Norman Podhoretz, who edited the second symposium, concluded that it had turned out very much like the first. He remarked on the distance of the later contributors from their class
and family, their criticism of Jewish tradition, and on the "atmosphere of idealism" in the whole discussion. By this he meant that
the specific issue of Jewishness had for these intellectuals been
transcended, i.e., they conceived that "the essence of Judaism is
the struggle for universal justice and human brotherhood." It
should be noted with no particular irony that this is not the historical meaning of Judaism—the symposium was intentionally limited to those intellectuals not committed to the doctrines of
religion. This omission, so lamentable from the point of view of
Jewish conservatives, is invaluable from that of the onlooker.

2. "Jewishness and the Younger Intellectuals," *Commentary* (March,
1961), pp. 306–359. Copyright © 1961, by *Commentary;* used by permission of *Commentary* and the authors.

Those who in the course of discussion addressed themselves to the meaning of Judaism established polarities of a predictable kind. For Joseph Kraft the touchstone of Jewishness was what he called community. Like many Jews he was raised with no religious training; his experience was environmental. The common values of his upbringing were "work, books, education, settlement houses, art, and the New Deal." Most of the contributors acknowledged this kind of cultural force, and scrupulously avoided the subjects of chicken soup and Yiddish jokes. The dialogue was, suspiciously, on a higher plane—as in the terms of Philip Green who understood Jewish tradition as "concern for humaneness and social justice throughout its existence." The ethical sense was so often invoked as to appear to be a standard. Robert Lifton wrote that the essential character of Jewish culture was its "special concern for basic human emotions" and he singled out the Jewish writer, analyst, and comedian as therapists and benefactors of humanity; Enoch Gordis wrote enthusiastically about Judaism's inherent "ethical insights" which led it to strive for tolerance, idealism, and "universal peace." Other participants found the value of Judaism to consist in its understanding for minorities, respect for books, and concern for moral issues. There was, in short, a significant group —indeed a majority—who valued Judaism as a mode. One may accept this as characteristic of modern religious thought, and view it as Daniel Bell did in an essay which also appeared in *Commentary*.[3]

Bell began by noting that the acceptance of ethics usually meant the rejection of ritual; the consequence was not only a loss in sensibility but a deprivation of the quality of mind. The attitude of ethics is not sufficiently irrational to comprehend the real. As far as identity and reality are concerned:

> Theologically, there is no more justification for a special Jewish ethic than for a Unitarian one, or for Ethical Culture, or for any nonritualistic creed. The creed dissolves the parochial, and takes away from individuals that need for the particular identification

---

3. Daniel Bell, "Reflections on Jewish Identity," *Commentary* (June, 1961), pp. 471–478. Copyright © 1961, by *Commentary;* used by permission of *Commentary* and the author.

which singles them out and shapes their community in distinctive terms. . . . In ethical Judaism, a simplistic idea of human nature has led to the belief that there are few human ills which reason cannot remedy. But beyond that, the view of life represented by ethical Judaism is one of simple good and evil, unaware that a tragic component of choice is the fact that it must always involve some evil.

This seems to forecast with some accuracy the ethical subjectivism of Gordis: "I can accept no theology. . . . Ethical insights, in my view, are in principle derivable from many sources, so the Jewish religion and others are dispensable in this regard." As for "reverence" Gordis suggested that it proves valuable to fill the "gap in the emotional resources of many modern children," and should be cultivated without a specific object. The religious attitude displayed is private and should be immune, but the intellectual attitude seems to invite response. In purely descriptive terms it is a-historical and relativist. It fails to make a connection—one that is a commonplace of sociology—between the particular ethic and its particular source. It has a rather odd sense of the values of emotion. Finally, it clarifies both assimilation and the loss of personal identity, both of which evidently require a surrender of the sense of validity.

If the majority of respondents were content to argue from grounds like these some were much more intransigent. Irving Feldman rejected "this Jewish ethical appetite [which] now devours itself in endless self-inquisitions, in self-accusation and self-pity." Barbara Probst Solomon argued feelingly that "the great thing about the Jews is precisely their religion. . . . They died for their God—and not for some bastardized 'culture'." But these were in the minority, and most of the writers seemed to agree with Raziel Abelson, who said that the rejection by the Jewish intellectual of his past was both voluntary and valuable. He found himself unable to identify any values that have been preserved continuously in Jewish history and suggested that the experience of most value to Judaism was the Enlightenment. Abelson's conclusion was that "ritualism" and religious "fantasy" were passing phases of which Judaism was well rid; the real metier of the intellectual Jew was "rational social change." His summation of the meaningful figures in Jewish history is important as a representative statement. "It is this aspect of Jewish history, whose heroic figures are Spinoza, Marx, Freud, and Einstein, to which I feel most directly linked." This revaluation is recurrent: Werner Cohn's list of great models includes Jesus, Freud, Marx, Einstein, and Trotsky; Michael Maccoby writes about the supreme tradition of nineteenth-century scientific optimism; Marcus Raskin writes of Marx, Freud, and Einstein as modern prophets; Podhoretz finds that the heroes of 1961, like those of 1944, were "the great post-Emancipation figures who rushed out of the ghetto to devour and then recreate the culture of the West: Marx, Freud, Einstein."

The de-Judaized intellectual is satisfied to the extent that ethical Jewishness has been culturally productive. There seems to be some point to this position—it is after all difficult to argue with Marx and Freud. Difficult, that is, if they represent a characteristic accomplishment. The point of course is that they do not. The accomplishments of modern secular Judaism, no matter what emotion attaches to them, are in fact a diminution. Broadly speaking, they fall into these categories: socialism and the labor movement, the politics of the Thirties, the liberalism of the present. If ethical Judaism is deficient, in the terms of Bell, because of its tenuous grasp on reality, then other critics have argued that it is deficient in the accomplishments upon which it rests. Bell has stated in *The End of Ideology* that socialism is itself finished; and the labor movement has been discredited in the eyes of intellectuals at least. It began with the heroic sacrifices of the sweatshops and seems to have culminated in David Dubinsky. It would be a major work simply to classify and cite the attacks on labor by the intellectuals during the last decade; the example of the clash between ILGWU and NAACP is probably sufficient. Herbert Hill testified before Congress about the union's discrimination against Negroes and Puerto Ricans, and then published a very critical article in *New Politics* stating the NAACP position.[4] The public image of the ILGWU was indeed moral, for it seemed that the union stood for reforms central to the rights of labor. In fact the union was a rigid bureaucracy in which nonwhites had no chance at equal wages, status, or representation on the executive council. The antipathy between Negroes and Jews was not directly mentioned but it

---

4. Herbert Hill, "The ILGWU Today—The Decay of a Labor Union," *New Politics* I, 4 (1962), pp. 6–17.

would seem idealistic to doubt its presence. Hill's article was answered by Gus Tyler of the ILGWU in the succeeding issue.[5] Tyler's rebuttal was no more fascinating than his conclusion, which hinted darkly at the "McCarthyism" of the NAACP. The matter or mess was unresolved—as Paul Jacobs wrote in *Dissent* it would seem to have been part of the larger disenchantment of the NAACP with the AFL–CIO.[6] And it was part, I think, of the disenchantment with organized labor itself. As Nat Hentoff put it in his contribution to the symposium, the tradition of the Jewish socialist in labor has died of respectability.

Jewish involvement in the Thirties has been revalued by the present generation and found wanting. Activists reject it with a certain contempt. Others, like Robert Brustein, find it "simpleminded." [7] In *The Immediate Experience* Robert Warshow wrote of "the disastrous vulgarization of intellectual life" for all who were involved.[8] It was, he said, a time in which nothing in the realm of intellect was allowed to exist on its own terms but was forced into some larger consideration which perverted its meaning. Those who look back at the Thirties with nostalgia have been brought up sharply by a new generation of critics. There is no better example of this than the *Judaism* symposium of 1964, in which Melvin Tumin reminiscently praised the values of "the last thirty years." [9] He was attacked by Michael Wyschogrod:

> The last thirty years, I take it, refers to the Jewish radical tradition starting in the 30s. But if that is taken by Prof. Tumin as more or less identical with the capital investment of the last two thousand years, then Prof. Tumin is mistaken. Judaism has never been radical in the economic or political sense of that word. It has been a religion

---

5. Gus Tyler, "The Truth About the ILGWU," *New Politics* I, 5 (1962), pp. 6–17.

6. Paul Jacobs, "No More Cousin Toms," *Dissent* (Winter, 1963), pp. 6–12.

7. Robert Brustein, "Arthur Miller's *Mea Culpa*," *The New Republic* (8 February 1964), pp. 26–30.

8. Robert Warshow, "The Legacy of the 30's," *The Immediate Experience* (New York, 1962), pp. 33–48.

9. "Conservative Trends in American Jewish Life," *Judaism* (Spring, 1964), pp. 131–155.

of law against anarchy, of reverence for the past and love for its traditions and heritage. It has always had a very realistic appraisal of what lurks in man and the necessity for social and political bounds within which responsible freedom is exercised. . . . It is the radicalism of the last century that has been the aberration in Jewish history.

I, for one, do not lament the Jewish break with this radicalism.

This has the merit of historical precision. But there is another point to be made for the position of Brustein, Warshow, and Wyschogrod: The performance of Jewish intellectuals in the Thirties was simply trivial. Let us for the moment dispense with the emotionalism and the sense of guilt, and ask what important ideas or works were generated. I can think of none. The neutral observer of the movements of the Thirties can only conclude that they were taken in by Stalinism and by themselves. Their ideology has, rightfully, been abandoned and dissipated. As for their experience—what they discovered does not make them unique in history. As for the writing, surely no other time was as sterile. Who now reads the fiction of the Thirties or pauses over its essays? Who can see Miller's *After the Fall* without a sense of embarrassment for those who participated in the Thirties and are now weak enough to recall it? It was an undistinguished decade which has been romanticized out of all reality. It needs a Mencken to describe the curious, Byronic pride of the men who now admit to having lived through those glories which have been magnified by time, and to having sinned greatly.

The last of the accomplishments of secular Judaism is the liberalism of the present. In the *Commentary* symposium there is a good deal of ambivalence about this subject. One of the targets of the respondents is the rote liberalism of temples and organizations which expresses itself in self-congratulation and attendance at lectures by Max Lerner on alienation. As Nat Hentoff put it, Jewish liberalism is now a cliché—too much has been achieved to risk real change. Perhaps the best summation of Jewish liberalism is that by Nathan Glazer and Daniel Moynihan: "Jewish liberalism, it is true, supports the NAACP, CORE, the reform Democrats, freedom riders in the South, and a variety of liberal Democratic candidates who come to New York to refresh their campaigns with

Jewish money. But what now supports Jewish liberalism?" [10] The tone of Jewish liberalism, the authors add, is self-congratulatory while its accomplishments now are empty. It is the successes of the past which engage it; but the tradition of social engineering has come to a halt. As Glazer and Moynihan see it, the Jewish community (they refer specifically to New York) is unable to *do* anything with its liberalism. It is paralyzed in the face of the proletarianization of the city and can only react by sharing the movement of other moneyed groups to the outskirts or the gilded ghetto. It is hostile to reform in labor, urban design, and *de facto* school segregation. Its interests are no longer liberal. Yet it faces the problems of the present with the tattered slogans of the past. The authors predict that a loss of identity will ensue—but surely it will follow a crisis of identity, in which those who live ideologically as liberals but habitually as conservatives will discover this paradox.

**\* \* \***

The *Commentary* symposium allowed ethical Judaism to speak for itself and to reveal itself in its intellectual nakedness. There have been other intellectual positions. In 1948 Irving Kristol showed the extent of reaction to ethical Judaism.[11] He argued that Jewish religion had been perverted into philanthropy and that Messianism had dwindled into humanitarianism. He took, in short, the same position vis à vis Judaism that Reinhold Niebuhr took in relation to Protestantism in *Pious and Secular America*. It was Milton Steinberg's *Basic Judaism* which activated Kristol's remarks: "Rabbi Steinberg's Judaism is reduced to an earnestly moral socio-political liberalism, with divine sanction to boot. What are we to make of a rabbi who claims for the Mishnah and the Talmud that they guarantee the right to strike—thereby providing

---

10. Nathan Glazer and Daniel Patrick Moynihan, *Beyond the Melting Pot* (Cambridge, Mass., 1963), p. 176. Used by permission of The MIT Press.

11. Irving Kristol, "How Basic is 'Basic Judaism'?", *Commentary* (January, 1948), pp. 27–34. Used by permission of *Commentary* and the author.

Holy Writ with the satisfaction of having paved the way for the
National Labor Relations Act!" It was not one of the merits of
Judaism, Kristol observes, that it permitted its believers to read
*The New Republic* with untroubled souls. What I think is the core
of Kristol's argument is his statement on the Good as social action:
"The horror that breathes into our faces is the realization that evil
may come by doing good—not merely *intending* to do good, but
*doing* it. That is the trap of social action that the movements of
progress and enlightenment of the 19th and 20th centuries fell into;
and we . . . haven't the faintest inkling how to get out." The gulf
between man and righteousness has widened not narrowed—and,
Kristol concluded, those social and psychoanalytic idiocies found
even in the pulpits were simply failures to encounter the real. It
is this line of reasoning which has developed in the Sixties and
which self-evidently strikes at the Enlightenment and its heirs.

Kristol's attack has been followed up. One of the most acute of
the critics of ethical Judaism has been Emil Fackenheim, who
makes this clear choice:

> The liberal Jew of today is in a dilemma. His Jewish conscience
> urges him to look for an authority which might guide and direct his
> Jewish life. But his liberal conscience frowns on that desire, as a
> temptation to be resisted. As a Jew he fears that, unless individuals
> such as himself accept an authority, there will soon be an end to
> Judaism. But as a liberal he fears that, should they in fact accept it,
> there will soon be an end to liberalism.[12]

The two poles of the argument are freedom and authority, and it
is the intention of Fackenheim to force the realization that freedom
is enlarged by historical experience and diminished by secular
dogmas. There is a point at which autonomy becomes subjectivism;
when the liberal conscience rules out the authority of the past
completely it rules out also the authority of learning itself. The
consequence is either atomism or a meaningless religion of mankind. The latter seems to be a reasonable term for the Platonic
Idea of the *Commentary* symposium.

There was of course one element of Fackenheim's argument

---

12. Emil Fackenheim, "The Dilemma of Liberal Judaism," *Commentary* (October, 1960), pp. 301–310.

which forced the rest to cohere—the premise that Judaism is not in fact secular. One tends to agree. Others like Michael Wyschogrod, Eugene Borowitz, and Norman Frimer have proceeded on this assumption. Perhaps the most pointed as it is the most darkly amusing of examples is Jakob Petuchowski's "The Limits of Liberal Judaism." [13] In this essay it is noted that a Reform rabbi in Michigan proclaimed himself an atheist—and declared that there was no visible machinery within Reform Judaism to revoke his ordination or even discipline him. It is finely remarked that atheism and agnosticism have been with Jews for a long time, but until recently Jewish unbelievers have had a certain sense of the fitness of things and knew that they did not belong in the pulpit. Petuchowski opposes "limitless Liberalism" to Revelation and Law:

> Liberalism can have no limits. It cannot be bound by any fealty to dogma or authority. It cannot move along the grooves of preconceived notions, nor can it be held back by the fetters of tradition. . . . Part of today's confusion may be traced back to the fact that not a few rabbis, and a not insignificant number of laymen, owe their allegiance to Liberalism. Liberalism is their philosophy, and Liberalism is their religion. . . . Such Liberalism may even go hand in hand with a proud affirmation of Jewishness. But it is a Jewishness of the ethnic and cultural variety.

The community, he ends wryly, must learn that the term *rabbi* is now no guarantee that the holder really has specific religious views.

The terms to which Petuchowski appeals are *revelation, law, tradition, god.* The terms he opposes to these are *liberalism* and *reason.* The usages of others in this dialogue are as resolvedly anti-Enlightenment. Frimer notes that Jewish novelists habitually take for their subject the hopelessness of mere ethical or moral values and suggests that these values are simply a by-product of religious conviction.[14] Borowitz defends the nature of authority and proposes that the saving remnant be extracted from the secular cul-

---

13. Jakob Petuchowski, "The Limits of Liberal Judaism," *Judaism* (Spring, 1965), pp. 146–158. Used by permission of *Judaism.*

14. Norman Frimer, "The A-Theological Judaism of the American Community," *Judaism* (Spring, 1962), pp. 144–155.

ture and the others left to the rationalist vagaries of their lives.[15] The most intelligent of the attacks on Enlightenment ethics is that of Michael Wyschogrod:

> *We are living in the post-Enlightenment period, and Jewish philosophy can therefore return to its own sources instead of validating itself by criteria foreign to it.* The Enlightenment came to an end irrevocably in the work of Søren Kierkegaard who . . . brought down the two basic pillars of the Enlightenment: the notion that what the Biblical world saw dimly and mythologically can be seen clearly and definitively by philosophy; and the notion of progress which is implicit in this view. Jewish philosophy, strangely enough, has been least affected by this revolution. Jewish liberalism flowered in the second half of the 19th century, and this momentum has carried it almost up to the present. While in Protestant and Catholic circles liberalism has been on the wane for at least forty years . . . in the non-Orthodox Jewish world progressive liberalism has shown marked tenacity, almost to the point of anachronism.[16]

The Jewish intellectual, when he does not simply give up on his Jewishness, has two choices. He can identify Judaism with "liberalism," "humanism," and "ethics," and enlarge it to a universal religion. Should his inclinations lie that way the chances are that the Enlightenment is his version of the prelapsarian state. His sympathies will be most strongly engaged vis à vis radicalism, the memory of the Thirties, and virtues of a "progressive" kind. His other choice lies with theology and authority, and with, it is now generally acknowledged, open hostility to the first alternative. He may, as Emil Fackenheim has written, find that tolerance and relativism are simply passivity writ large.[17] He will most certainly oppose the current values of Jewish liberals with the weapons of history. He will hold the belief that the Enlightenment was a mistake and that modern Jewish emulation of it was intellectually

---

15. Eugene Borowitz, "Crisis Theology and the Jewish Community," *Commentary* (July, 1961), pp. 36–42; and "The Jewish Need for Theology," *Commentary* (August, 1962), pp. 138–144.

16. Michael Wyschogrod, "Agenda for Jewish Philosophy," *Judaism* (Summer, 1962), pp. 195–199. Used by permission of *Judaism*.

17. Emil Fackenheim, "Apologia for a Confirmation Text," *Commentary* (May, 1961), pp. 401–410.

frivolous. In this he will demonstrate that the Sixties is a divisive decade. But it will prove, I think, a creative one. The single tradition of liberalism of which Lionel Trilling once wrote is being dissolved, and it may come as a shock after the intransigence of liberals in the Thirties, and their sentimentality after the war, to find that the new Jewish radicalism is conservative.

# Christian
# and Post-Christian

### BACKGROUND: MAX EASTMAN AND THE RELIGION OF POLITICS

When Protestantism became, in the terms of Karl Barth, Culture-Protestantism, it dispensed with fall, incarnation, judgment, and resurrection. The human enterprise became the end of religion and the churches accommodated themselves to this life rather than the life to come.[18] One consequence was the capitulation of religious doctrine to a whole range of secular movements, Social Darwinism, Humanism, Socialism. Andrew Carnegie was able to preach the Gospel of Wealth; Henry Ward Beecher preached the value of prosperity; William Henry Channing preached "reverence for man." As Protestantism subsided the way was made clear for the real religions of this century, ritualistic National Socialism and messianic Communism. The attitude of intellectuals toward religion has been molded by this transference. The two principal modes of religious recognition, conversion and confession, released in secular experience those feelings which, before modernity, were possible only for the mind engaged in a struggle for salvation. Conversion and confession became political acts.

William James began his chapter on conversion in *The Varieties of Religious Experience* by remarking that it is the process by which a self divided becomes unified. The insight is true, although we may feel that there is too large a philosophical distance between the reasonableness of his argument and the experience it tries to define. We tend to distrust his rationality not only because of the

---

18. See H. Richard Niebuhr, "The Christ of Culture," *Christ and Culture* (New York, 1951), pp. 83–115.

nature of the modern experience but simply because conversion is not so exotic in our world as it was in his. It is not a cautionary tale of the pre-Reformation but something we recognize as typical and inescapable. If for him it expressed the unlikely nature of religion for us it must express the necessary nature of politics. There is a further difference. We have found that beyond conversion lies recantation.

This is the subject of political confession, a document which goes some way toward explaining the vulnerability of intellectuals to ideas. The confession has now become a genre, if not an avocation. For that reason we should not demand the wrong things of it. A genre is a habit as well as a form, and it is as good to know about one as the other. Yet I think many reviewers of Max Eastman's autobiography have done to the author what Macauley did to Boswell, that is, they have confused the man, who is not important, with the life, which is. The friendly observers saw in Eastman a brand plucked from the burning, and instead of criticizing they only celebrated his work. The hostile reviewers found in Eastman's life the same difficulties as that of Dos Passos; they concentrated on his fallibility and on the bad taste of his current political opinions. There was not much sense of Eastman's centrality to our experience. He would have mattered if the only thing he had done was survive in the world of ideas from 1900 until now, but he has done much more than that. Edmund Wilson once compared him to the winter-log which saves the pool within which it floats by taking on itself the pressure of contracting ice. He served, in other words, as our representative in accepting and living out certain ideas. It would be ungenerous to complain in life of what we seek out and praise in characters of fiction.

The first religion through which Eastman lived was Christianity. His grandfather was a frontier evangelical of heroic proportions. His parents were liberal ministers of various Eastern chapels. *Enjoyment of Living* describes three generations: the first addressed itself to God; the second to ethics; the third to dialectical materialism. The progression, Reinhold Niebuhr thought, was inexorable:

---

A dissipated evangelicalism relied on "love," while the Enlightenment relied on "reason" to achieve utopia on earth. But both the secular and the religious version of utopianism denied the real problems of human existence and expected dreams to turn into reality cheaply. That is why the religious revival in America is only partly a reaction to disappointed secular hopes and is partly a religious expression of those same hopes.[19]

The sects changed only their name—how far is it from Channing's dynamic liberalism (the "reverence for man") to the visions of Eugene Debs? One wrote about a new social Christianity which would "revolutionize society and create relations among men not dreamed of at the present day" while the other "fired vast meetings throughout the country" with "the glow of certainty that the future was in hand." [20] A synthesis was evidently ready for completion; Channing using the metaphor of revolution and Debs raising the chiliastic hopes of evangelicalism.

The time that Debs looked to was at hand, the *annus mirabilis* of 1912. In that year the Socialists polled almost a million votes for President and held over 1000 political offices. There were Socialist dailies in every conceivable language; there were schools and encampments, lecturers and intellectuals of the new social gospel. The arts themselves changed so that poems, short stories, novels and essays now reflected the message of the new kingdom. It was the year *The Masses* was started, whose first editor was Max Eastman.

Before the new movement split into sects, there was a great community of those who had faith in the kingdom and in the revolution which would establish it. There was a right wing, which was principally for reform—but it was the revolutionary left, from Debs to Big Bill Haywood, from Max Eastman to John Reed, which wanted to rebuild the temple from bottom to top. They had enough to work with. The mining strike in West Virginia and the Ludlow massacre were only symptoms of the Big Change. America was equipped for the nineteenth century when it was our turn to enter the twentieth. That was to happen between 1912, when the vision of revolutionary change was abroad, and

19. Reinhold Niebuhr, *Pious and Secular America* (New York, 1958), pp. 9-10. Used by permission of the publisher, Charles Scribner's Sons.

20. Irving Howe and Lewis Coser, *The American Communist Party* (New York, 1962), p. 4.

1917, when it suddenly appeared that it might become material. American radicalism left its old origins in the multitudinous sects and began its internationalist career. The energies that had ranged from anarchist to Wobbly were more and more tightly confined under Communist centralization, a change, perhaps, from a Protestant to a Catholic phase.

Eastman's *Love and Revolution* is a document of the change from religious to political sect, from the old American dream of infinite liberty to the new internationalist dream of infinite order. Without being heavy-handed I would like to maintain the religious metaphor—Eastman himself begins by talking about "a conversion, a dedication, a profound emotional experience such as Upton Sinclair and other socialists have described." He is of course describing Marxism in terms that are by now thoroughly familiar and even orthodox. Yet the conversion is no more meaningful than the recantation; in James we read that four out of every five who convert are backsliders. The recantation occurs because men are pluralistic while ideas are monistic. In Eastman's case the rebellion came from the flesh quite literally; among all the other confessions of political sorrows only that by Chambers has a like human dimension. The mind of Eastman was repelled eventually by the scientism of Marxism, but the book is about his body as well. It kept his mind off dialectical materialism.

Eastman was too bohemian to be a good Communist. The story of the old *Masses* shares space with the erotic life of Greenwich Village, a life which meant as much for this century as the intellectual ambiance in which it occurred. In a sense Eastman's love affairs were dynamic liberalism carried to its logical conclusion—but some allies of radicalism could not accept the implications of what they urged. There is a record in *Love and Revolution* of a very funny correspondence between Eastman and George Bernard Shaw, who was outraged by the "carnal" element in *The Masses*. What happened was that the old style of radicalism overflowed into Eastman's life; it took the form of free love and broke up his marriage; it took the form of free thought and kept *The Masses* honest. The difference between the old *Masses* and the new, parasitic form was that between the party line and romanticized Christian love.

Bertrand Russell made the first of the great modern recantations upon his return from Russia in 1920. "The rest of us followed," Eastman wrote, "some sooner and some later, but all stepping rather precisely in his tracks." The first phase was scientism. Eastman wrote in *Reflections on the Failure of Socialism* of his admiration for the "practicality" and "factualness" of Lenin's "experimental" mind. He refers to Lenin's "The Soviets at Work," an essay which overpowered Whittaker Chambers as well. "I gave my heart to Lenin," Eastman says, "in every line he seemed to realize my ideal of a scientific revolutionist." [21] This has the evangelical tone, but seems to indicate a Christian Science phase—not only in the man but in Communism itself.

Yet Eastman was slow to convert, and he never reached the spiritual unity that James saw as the end of conversion. Instead, he moved from Hegelianism back to his peculiarly American pluralism, leaving behind "the mystic priest-begetting over-allness of the Marxian theory" and those of his allies who could not understand the heresies of independence. They had become integrated by conversion—some ending like Lincoln Steffens, paralyzed by good intentions, others, like Mike Gold, with the faith to move mountains and forget purges. The importance of Eastman depends on multiplicity; love is as important for him as revolution. That he is painfully pious about sexuality is obvious, but the meaning lies not so much in tone and taste as in the viability of a sectarian habit of mind: "to me lust is sacred, sexual embraces nearer to a Holy Communion than a profane indulgence—a partaking, so to speak, of the blood and body of Nature." It is American evangelicalism speaking; the only difference—and as Niebuhr suggests, not a major one—is that the erotic has taken the place of the social forms of love. It is a statement inconceivable to a European, unless we except Lawrence. We ought to recall, as Hannah Arendt wrote of Marx, that he opposed "sensuous, perishable life against permanent, unchanging, suprasensuous truth." That is why Marxism attracted so many Americans, and why Leninism repelled them. This is not

---

21. Max Eastman, *Reflections on the Failure of Socialism* (New York, 1962), pp. 10–11. Used by permission of the publisher, The Devin-Adair Co.

to overvalue our evangelical lusts—but, after all, de Tocqueville remarked the peculiar resistance our enthusiasms offer to dogma.

Around 1920, Eastman began his "recoil against the churchlike features of the American Communist Party." The Party was then entering its age of heresies and synods—Theodore Draper calls it the time of "the great schism." Independence was the issue. Was Communism to become autonomous or centralized? In his essay "The Revolution Devours Its Children," Draper makes it clear which alternative was taken and why. The first indication of the papal role to be played by the Comintern was the defeat of John Reed in 1920. The primary issue was whether the IWW was to be abandoned, and Reed had too much respect for it to acquiesce. But the issue resolved itself into another form, and the last of Reed's battles was against the dogmatic authority established by Lenin, Zinoviev, and Radek. Like Eastman, Reed had the unfortunate capacity for experience which dilutes the single-minded power of fanaticism. He loved the IWW and he hated Zinoviev; his was an admirable failure of objectivity. He died, Eastman believes, on the edge of revolt.

Eastman's own trip to Russia was a notable comic experience. The story is something like combining More's *Utopia* with the memoirs of Casanova. He was fascinated by Lenin and Trotsky, but his deepest feelings seem to have been engaged by the "Garden-of-Eden-like freedom" of the body. His language is sentimentally lyrical, and he uses every available cliché to express his beatific sense of beach and sky, body and earth. While the carnivorous struggle for power went on in Moscow, Eastman was making love in the Crimea and working toward that total integration of self which is the pride of the converted. For a while it seemed as if Russian free love would be more effective than the class struggle. It led him to a sense of "living in the truth" which betrays by its phrasing the origins of his vision. Luckily, such raptures have their period, and Eastman, when free of this erotic piety, could engage in that other sectarian habit marked by Niebuhr, the admiration of reason.

Between the freedom of the body and the habits of his mind, Eastman was lost to Hegelianism. He worshiped man, which is on the whole a more attractive heresy than the worship of ideas. His books are about heroes, from his grandfather, Morgan Lewis, who sought in Christian love "a tidal wave of sweet and tranquil joy" to Big Bill Haywood, a "natural wonder in those days that one would travel miles to see." When the heroes were disgraced or destroyed, he could not help but lose faith. One of his best observations on the heroic and the dogmatic is about Haywood and William Z. Foster. The discarded Haywood was living in Moscow on dreams of "a free society of workingmen, in which politicians, even of the democratic socialist stripe, would not exist." Foster, however, knew better than to prefer the spiritual to the temporal church:

> I have spoken of the contrast between these two men; in Moscow it acquired a tragic significance. Haywood had a vision of the future . . . but he was no student and had no quickness of mind—not even enough to be "taken in" by the fast-talking highbrows of Bolshevism when he got to Moscow. They merely dazed and overwhelmed him, and left him inarticulate and sad. Foster was keen-witted, versed in the revolutionary lingo. Although he had started off with what Lenin called anarcho-syndicalist opinions, and indeed worked as an agitator for the IWW, he was flexible and practical-minded enough to catch on to the importance of the party.

Haywood died and Foster, at a certain cost, became one with the Spirit. Reed and Haywood were among the last of the radicals; Foster was our first Leninist. The last of Eastman's heroes was Trotsky, and when he went down covered with the sins of "factionalism," "anti-Bolshevism," "antiproletarianism," and "petty-bourgeois deviation" Eastman got a passport out of paradise. It remained only for Trotsky to reject Eastman's defense of him, and for Stalin to identify Eastman as a heretic. From that time on Eastman lost his influence, and gained the ironic perspective of recantation. He became a representative figure of the intellectual who has experienced ideology.

From his return until the Purge of 1936 and the Pact of 1939 he was, as he wrote to Trotsky, the "Left Opposition" embodied in one man. It was a lonely eminence. Daniel Aaron puts it this way: "Eastman's views, though not unique, alienated orthodox Communists and hardly satisfied the chronic Red-haters who despised both pro- and anti-Stalinist radicals." His position, however, enabled him to write of the underside of a very undistinguished decade. One is more interested in the Thirties as they were than as they have been rehabilitated; in the incredible laxity of mind which took a Mike Gold—"Hail! red youthful giant, as you go marching and singing out of the tragic present into the glorious future!"—for either a poet or a thinker. One is interested in the character of that other representative man, Lincoln Steffens, who told Eastman that to reveal the truth about Stalin's betrayal of Trotsky was to indulge in liberalism. It was wrong to be right—as bad, Steffens said, as the terror, "*which we have begun to understand.*" It is a privilege to be present at the birth of a habit of mind. Perhaps the harsh value of *Love and Revolution* is that it shows men plainly wrong, and viciously wrong, and wrong beyond the saving grace of their intentions. It is something to have rejected that. Its final utility is that it shows the inherent difficulty of transforming religion into politics. That kind of alchemy was to haunt the intellectuals of the next two generations.

FOREGROUND: RELIGION AND CULTURE AFTER THE SECOND WORLD WAR

The *Partisan Review* symposium of 1950, "Religion and the Intellectuals," attempted to explain the postwar religious revival.[22] That it failed to do so is itself a conclusion. One of the problems of the symposium was that those who participated were largely former radicals who admitted the difficulty of accepting a non-naturalistic view of life and the special obstacle of submission to the authority of dogma. Most of the argument was conducted outside of theology except for contributions by Paul Tillich, Sidney Hook, and W. H. Auden. As a result there was very little sense of movements like neo-orthodoxy, and there was rather too much concern for issues like the conversion of Evelyn Waugh. As Hook noted, rational theology did not really interest modern intellectuals who preferred "the tormented inner experience of Augustine, Pascal, Kierkegaard." Indeed much of the argument (due partly

22. "Religion and the Intellectuals," *Partisan Review* (February, 1950), pp. 103–142; (March, 1950), pp. 215-256; (April, 1950), pp. 313–339; (May–June, 1950), pp. 456–483. Used by permission.

to the questions set by *PR*) was loosely tied to religion in literature and suffered considerably from the connection to "myth" which was for the time being in vogue. Within its limits the symposium mattered; it articulated a special awareness that the values of intellectuals could not really assume objective form.

The particular issue was that this discussion was taking place after one kind of God had failed. John Dewey's phrase for it was the loss of intellectual nerve—the shock caused by the failure of the idea of progress. Sidney Hook wrote of the decay of socialist belief; Philip Rahv stated that the unpleasant historical verities of the twentieth century had seriously undermined secular radicalism's claim to interpret the nature of both men and system; James T. Farrell wrote that secular thinking had degenerated because of its attachment to social movements which put it to the test of action—the liberal intelligentsia had discovered that there was a political form of manipulated theology. Not all concurred. Meyer Schapiro argued that the emancipation of the last three hundred years had been discredited not because of any intrinsic faults but only because it required a time "when men are intellectually free and masters of their own lives." Schapiro's defense of radical values gives a fairly accurate sense of what most of the respondents had given up: "It is largely in the radical movements that most of the higher values which religious people think are necessary for social life and obtainable through religion alone, have operated during the last hundred and fifty years. Ideals of justice, brotherliness, cooperation, self-sacrifice have been strongest in the radical groups and among isolated fearless individuals of radical intellectual temper." He offered socialism as an alternative to religion, and of this not much more need be said than that it was at least one generation behind the movement of history.

The intellectuals were impaled between past and future. Schapiro's hope for a Platonic intellectual freedom was complemented by Irving Howe's own form of traditionalism: "I remain loyal, not to one or another doctrine, but to the underlying values of the 1930s." That these values had failed and could not be alternatives to anything was evident to most of the others. Politically, Dwight MacDonald said, these values were either parodied by American liberalism or distorted by Stalinism. Culturally, progressivism had simply become assimilated into the *vordringen* of the middle class. Scientifically, that confidence in rational thought so characteristic of radicalism was eroded by the demonstration that science was only method, and could with equal success be employed for humane or homicidal purposes. James Agee made what was perhaps the most conclusive statement on the failure of this particular God. Some, he wrote, have outgrown the delusion that science is God. Others, pathetically, have outlived the millenial hope that "ultimately, indeed pretty soon, Science would settle all the imponderables and solve all the problems of living." The postscript written to this in the next decade by Lionel Trilling's unsentimental resolution of the Leavis-Snow imbroglio left no doubt as to the essential correctness of Agee, A. J. Ayer, and Alfred Kazin, who all tempered very considerably the modern admiration for deified scientific man.

In the realm of values then, the intellectuals were at an impasse. The radical movements which were the major source of values for a generation and more had failed, and the theological foundation of values was not acceptable. Agee's amusing question—"How can anyone who has swallowed the doctrines relating to penis-envy or the withering away of the State, strain at the doctrine of Transubstantiation?"—could not be resolved in precisely the terms he put it. The most acute of those who addressed themselves to the foundation of values were Newton Arvin and Hannah Arendt; both concluded that ontologically and metaphysically there could be no rational commitment to religion. As Hannah Arendt said, one really cannot escape the question of truth. Either God exists, and is a more important fact than all the pseudo-problems of culture, or he does not exist. The dilemma of culture is that it cannot simply act as if he existed: "I must confess that the notion that one can or ought to organize religion as an institution only because one likes to have a culture, has always appeared to me as rather funny. The idea of somebody making up his mind to believe in God, follow His Commandments, praying to Him and going regularly to Church, so that poets again may have some inspiration and culture be 'integrated,' is simply exhilarating." Yet this was the position in which many intellectuals found themselves. To their credit they were conscious of the absurdity, and attempted to find their way out of the dilemma by assuming that their individual lives were a process in which the assumption of religious truth might become validated, or at least exorcised.

That there was a need of resolution was plain: Agee wrote that insofar as reality itself was concerned secularism was incomplete and evasive. Even the nonreligious were aware that evil was distinct from ignorance, error, selfishness, aberration, egotism, or simply the flaws of upbringing. Yet it was only the religious who seemed to be equipped to act on this premise. As for responsibility, Agee believed that it was rare for the nonreligious mind to confront adequately the problem of guilt. It became "the relentless daily obligation to stay aware of, hep to, worked-up over, guilty towards, active about" the sufferings of people in relation to whom one had no meaningful connection.

The position of intellectuals was summed up by MacDonald, who has more than once been taken for a representative figure. While his sympathies were for "Enlightenment," "socialist," and "bourgeois-democratic" values his sense of reality was shaped by those outside the world of naturalism: Tolstoy, Gandhi, Simone Weil, Albert Schweitzer. As William Philips remarked, the *Zeitgeist* is never wrong. The religious revival had the same tone and exhausted the same possibilities as any other modern movement. It seemed to Philips not in itself religious but a kind of attitude about religion. That would seem to have been forcibly demonstrated by Robert Gorham Davis, who wrote that the Nicene Creed "opens the door to the totem feast, the rites of Attis and Dionysius and the sacrifice of the saviour-hero, born of the union of earth and sky." He praised the ability of religion to connect legends with "man's widest ritualistic satisfactions and deepest mythic needs"—an example perhaps not of dispensing with religion but absorbing it. A myth is not much of an improvement over a legend; as an imperative it is strikingly less so. As a truth which demands the response of action it has no existence.

The unresolved questions of the Fifties became the inheritance of the succeeding decade. The terms, however, were to undergo a significant change. The de-mythologizing of the Gospel was once again to focus the attention of intellectuals on the rational authentication of values as opposed to their dogmatic acceptance; the political events of the Fifties were to stimulate a sociology hostile to the institutions of Protestantism; the new values of neo-Freudianism were to establish themselves as alternatives. In fact, the religious revival of the Fifties was, according to Gabriel Vahanian, the explicit cause of the post-Christian advent.[23] It replaced secularity, which is simply the awareness that life is temporal and cultural, with secularism, "for which the present and the immanent are invested with the attributes of the eternal and the transcendent." There were three indications of the ascendency of secularism: Faith no longer required an actual theological object; Christianity no longer gave culture any special tone; syncretism made Christianity superfluous. That the case for this was not purely cultural has been argued by Vahanian and others. Eric Mascall has stated in *The Secularisation of Christianity* that the fault lies with modern theology itself—particularly with Bultmann, Barth, van Buren, Robinson, and their followers.[24]

As Mascall sees it the primary error of this kind of theology is that it forces the Gospel to adjust to secular logic. A first step, as in the thought of Bultmann, is to separate those things which are historical from those which are mythological. What remains when myth is removed is *kerygma*, that which is credible and necessary far salvation. What is removed, unfortunately, is not simply in the realm of myth. One of the central problems of the Gospel is that miraculous events are testified to on a historical basis by witnesses who were presumably competent. And, the ethical meaning of Gospel is not independent of the supernatural condition of Christ, but in fact a function of that condition. There is a further problem. What Bultmann removes and what he accepts depend on a subjective idea of history and myth. Although the idea of a three-story universe is given up (Heaven, Earth, Hell), as well as the idea of the intervention of spirits, Bultmann accepts both the historicity of Christ and the crucifixion, *as well as its meaning*. An existential

---

23. Gabriel Vahanian, *The Death of God* (New York, 1961), p. 203.
24. Eric Mascall, *The Secularisation of Christianity* (London, 1965); Rudolf Bultmann, *Kerygma and Myth* (New York, 1961); Karl Barth, *Church Dogmatics* (Edinburgh, 1949); Paul van Buren, *The Secular Meaning of the Gospel* (New York, 1963); J. A. T. Robinson, *Honest to God* (London, 1963).

act of faith has been substituted for a religious one—Bultmann insists that it is the act of preaching which is the *real* equivalent of the crucifixion and the resurrection. That is, participation in the sermon is the actual experience which the suffering of Christ represents. That the conservatives should attack Bultmann is understandable—but he has been attacked by the theological left as well. In the view of the latter he is inconsistent; having removed the miraculous from Gospel he is obliged to remove the unlikely dependence on the historical Christ.

Van Buren and Robinson take their origins from a famous passage by Dietrich Bonhoeffer, "Honesty demands that we recognise that we must live in the world as if there were no God . . . God himself drives us to this realization.—God makes us know that we must live as men who can get along without him. . . . We stand continually in the presence of the God who makes us live in the world without the God-hypothesis." The premise is noble, but one objection (as Hannah Arendt pointed out) is that a certain duplicity is involved: We are either autonomous or theocentric. If the general sense of this position is existential the particular argument is linguistic. Van Buren proposes that the incarnation is actually a "response" very like that of the prophets. That is, Jesus was simply a man who, as it were, took the decision for God. Like Bultmann, van Buren demythologizes and reconstitutes, conceiving that the language of the Gospel is simply metaphorical and tautological. If the incarnation is only a metaphor for the decision of Christ to interest himself in religion the resurrection and Easter-experience are only metaphors for that same decision on the part of the disciples: "Easter was the turning point in the way the disciples *looked at and spoke* of Jesus; from that time, *they saw him and spoke of him* in a new way." [25] An intellectual experience, in other words, required that the figure of Jesus be set into the myth of incarnation-crucifixion in order to supply appropriate imagery. Yet, as Mascall observes, the facts about Jesus that van Buren accepts, as well as those he dismisses, come from the same sources, introducing a logical problem of very considerable proportions.

---

25. Mascall, *op. cit.*, p. 73. I have relied on this useful book.

The Easter-experience was then a psychological event of great intensity—as van Buren puts it a "discernment-situation" in which the disciples saw both Jesus and themselves in a new way. What prevents the whole matter from being resolved into a question of ethics framed in the language of metaphor is the resistance of Gospel concept. When Jesus states "He who has seen me has seen the Father," the argument seems to be literal rather than figurative. To substitute for this statement, "take me as the key to your understanding and living of life," evades the issue of biblical literalness. Robinson carries the issue somewhat further when he suggests that mysteries and dogmas are poetic ways of presenting concepts. For example, following the lead of van Buren, he suggests that the Virgin Birth is a myth which "is a profound way of expressing an inner truth about Jesus." [26] The heart of religious belief is our response to the world: "*Anything* that achieves this or assists towards it is Christian worship." With ponderous toleration Robinson asks whether the supranaturalistic element of Christianity may not survive as part of the "magic" of Christmas: "Yes, indeed it can survive—as myth. For myth has its perfectly legitimate, and indeed profoundly important, place. The myth is there to indicate the significance of the events. . . . We must be able to read the nativity story without assuming that its truth depends on there being a literal interpretation of the natural." This serves at least to place the Bishop of Woolwich—somewhere, one guesses, between Leslie Fiedler and Robert Gorham Davis. "Myth" and "magic" bridge many a position, excepting that of truth. The corner into which modern Protestantism has painted itself is fairly evident. In attempting to make the circumstances surrounding the origin of values credible it has made them relative; once literalism becomes allegory the number of interpretations possible becomes infinite.

When one considers the fact of religiosity, the diversity of the Protestant establishment, and the neutralizing effect of modern Protestant dogma, it appears that the problem of authority is fairly desperate. William Bartley has written of Protestant liberalism that its refusal to take up a dogmatic position credible to the masses

---

26. *Ibid.*, p. 147.

placed it in danger of committing suicide.[27] It gave up authority and seemed to objectify the remark of Santayana in "Modernism and Christianity": "What would make the preaching of the gospel utterly impossible would be the admission that it had no authority to proclaim what has happened or what is going to happen, either in this world or in another." Yet it is Bartley himself who, in arguing against Protestant authority, is representative of a new and important secular attack. He believes that "authoritarian and even totalitarian attitudes" are the real danger for Protestantism, since they are the only means left to compel orthodoxy. The observer of the contemporary religious scene may differ, and believe that authority is not the same as authoritarianism. But this is by no means to dismiss Bartley, who argues intelligently from a rationalist viewpoint; the issue, of course, is that his "spiritual unity offered by the open and critical exchange of beliefs" is not by any definition a church.

What Bartley stands for is a religion of intellectuals. The attempts of Tillich and others to teach belief first and defer analysis seems to Bartley typical of the Grand Inquisitor mentality. The rather innocent proposal of John Courtney Murray to teach Christian humanities in the universities is seen as a conspiratorial prohibition of the power to reflect; the remark by Sir Walter Moberly that there has been a certain "disintegration" of tradition among academic people leads to outrage at the invasion of the rights of reason. In short, his attitude toward Protestantism is highly suitable for the administration of a university. Yet it is an attitude immeasurably more thoughtful than, for example, the ditherings of Harvey Cox. If Bartley would temper belief with rationality, Cox would abandon belief in favor of action—a much older position than the novelty of *The Secular City* would seem to indicate, and one that, with the passing of each generation, is yet more wearily approved.

Cox's hideously modish essay on "The Church as God's Avant-Garde" begins with the statement that churchmen "have tended

---

27. William Warren Bartley III, *The Retreat to Commitment* (New York, 1962), p. 57.

to be inordinately obsessed with various aspects of the doctrine of the church." [28] In view of the dilemma I have tried to outline, this is neither surprising nor willful. But, the solution to the attempt to find an authority for values is much easier for Cox than for others because values do not in his view require substantiation; the "crucial" function of the church is social change, particularly in civil rights. The hidden premises in Cox's argument are political. Since the shape of the future is urban the church is committed to specifically social programs. The "stubborn residue of tribal and town ideology" (for this read "all those Republicans who live outside of New York") is simply a historical anomaly. The attitudes it fosters—"bourgeois and small town . . . enshrined in suburb, county seat, and Congress"—are out of date and irrational. These attitudes are not really identified, but the goal of "centralization of authority" as opposed to "divided" and "semiautonomous" local power gives some concrete evidence as to what they may be.

Authority and values take on not new but rather familiar form in *The Secular City*. If men like Bartley are anxious about the voluntary nature of authority in the church, Cox is simply oblivious to its coercive nature in the state. What he calls "fragmentation of power" is the real evil, and can be remedied only by concentrating power in the state. The present condition is termed anarchy while the future hope is, in a phrase oppressively familiar to our times, "long-range planning." The context, which would seem appropriate only for a state of martial law, is simply our present difficulty in making the cities useful. Cox's strategy which underlies these tactics makes plain in what sense he views the problem of values; only "structural changes in the larger society" will solve our problems. This is the myth of the state with a vengeance, the solutions proposed by the Berkeley activists and applied to Protestantism. That the myth failed for religion in the Twenties and for radicalism in the Thirties seems of no consequence. What matters is that the transference of authority from church to state is viewed as a solution. Marx said that history repeats itself as farce. What is most ironic is that the values of Cox are self-defining. Without in any

28. Harvey Cox, *The Secular City* (New York, 1966), pp. 125–148.

way wishing to intimate that the problem of minorities, particularly those of Negroes, are without meaning and do not deserve our passionate respect and action, I yet would like to suggest that the solution of these problems is not in itself a value. Yet this is precisely what Cox believes. Throughout *The Secular City* the author's prophetic outrage and messianic hope are reserved for civil rights. There is nothing to which this is subservient.[29] In fact, it dictates that our entire economic, religious, and moral structure be changed to accommodate it. The question arises, when, in the course of the next century, the problem of civil rights diminishes due to racial assimilation and, one hopes, enlightenment, what happens to the value system that it stands for? What happens when a value that is a problem faces its own solution? What happens when, as a movement, it attaches itself to other movements like student demonstrations or those pro- or con- foreign policy? It would appear that religious authority is best concentrated on the formation of circumstances that make programs possible. Logic suggests a distressing example, although not, to the reader of Kahn or Morgenstern, an unlikely one: Should the bombs begin to drop and, quite intentionally, wipe out the urban culture we have erected after dispensing with "tribal," "bourgeois," and "local" values, what would be the predicament of the secularized, urbanized church? Every problem to which it had been directed (and hence every value) would be extraneous. The example is only extreme, not illogical—the best evidence for this is that most of the world lives in precisely those circumstances today, i.e., in conflict with nature rather than with the highly temporary issues of urban life.

The movement of this century has been from Liberal Protestantism to what I would call Activist Protestantism. It is instructive to listen to Paul Goodman on this subject: "But actions like the *Golden Rule* or the recent beautiful resistance to the spurious Civil

---

29. Cox's solutions are questionable but it is generally agreed that Protestantism has failed to provide alternatives. Reinhold Niebuhr wrote that "the role of the church in the desegregation crisis has not been impressive . . . we have the ironic fact that the sports field, the trade unions, theaters, and music halls of the nation have been more creative than the churches in establishing community between the races." (*Reinhold Niebuhr on Politics*, New York, 1960, p. 234).

Defense in New York are, indeed, even simpler. They are what used to be called Bearing Witness." [30] The sense of transference is acute and intentional—it is a phrase as useful to the historian as Max Eastman's "living in the truth" of Soviet socialism. It is sufficient to conclude that the central problem of establishing a basis for values in religion has not for this decade been resolved. In fact, the consecration of activist politics has matched the deconsecration of Gospel.

30. Paul Goodman, "On Wise Action," *Columbia University Forum* (Summer, 1960), p. 41.

# 4.

# THE NEGRO

## Civil Rights:
## Internal and Strategic Problems

The Supreme Court decision of 1954 began a decade of relative optimism. It seemed as if demonstrations, political action, and the mobilized sympathies of the white liberal community would combine to grant full citizenship to the Negro. The Civil Rights Bill of 1964 seemed to confirm that end. The outlook is now different and the participants, both black and white, are much less certain. Demonstrations worked until Albany, when it became clear that the police compound was an adequate answer to the march of protest. They worked in the North until overtaken by natural inertia, as in the failure of Bayard Rustin's protest over school segregation, and until they were dissipated by the strategy of the combatants, as in the CORE sit-ins on the East River Drive and at the World's Fair. Political action had its legislative victories, but it was soon discovered that putting them into execution in the South was another matter. Senator Eastland's hundred-year time-table of change now begins to look accurate. In the North, it has been discovered that political action has reached its limits—in spite of the apparatus of laws governing housing, employment, and personal rights, the ghetto gets worse. If the great event of the Fifties was the decision of the Supreme Court the great event of the Sixties was, I think, the publication of the Moynihan Report (*The Negro Family*).[1] The former defined the external, political limits of the problem—the latter defined its inherent character. The Report qualified the idea of progress and implicitly criticized the ideology surrounding civil rights.

The sociology of civil rights, unlike its politics, argues that the realities of change are not solely matters of law; it argues that the limiting factors of change are not solely those of the white com-munity. *The Negro Family*, with its description of social pathology, was particularly demoralizing to those who gave their faith to po-litical action. Yet it did not initiate a new sense of the Negro con-dition. It was only a sad but intelligent summation. Long before it was published there had been the disillusioned insights of novel-ists, essayists, and biographers. Ralph Ellison, James Baldwin, and Claude Brown, to take only a few, have registered the damage done to Negroes by the condition of their lives. It was not the kind of damage visited on other minorities, the effect was to prevent the Negro from entering into the American competition and to in-capacitate him as a social being. The novelists were more honest than the politicians—they were in fact alone among Negro pro-fessionals (except for the rare intellectual like E. Franklin Frazier) in their insistence that the quality of Negro life was tragic. I mean by this that the Negro writers refused to indulge in meliorism. They wrote with great honesty of a community of the lost. It was an irremediable community—Claude Brown's *Manchild in the Promised Land*, like the *Autobiography of Malcolm X*, is about a life that is, finally, separate and invincible to our pieties. Their

---

1. *The Negro Family*, Department of Labor (March, 1965).

sense of the Negro community was that it has nothing to which the individual can appeal; it is in fact the Negro community which is most dangerous to the Negro intellectual. As to its "primitive" virtues—James Baldwin's contempt for the banalities of Kerouac and Mailer speaks for itself. Baldwin's phrase—the "gates of paranoia"—offers a more realistic sense of the Negro intellectual, a sense of living among those who have no solutions.[2]

*The Negro Family* was preceded by Moynihan's and Nathan Glazer's *Beyond the Melting Pot,* whose point was that the Negro community was itself resistant to improvement.[3] The problems have been formulated by slavery, depression, and segregation. The result is a condition of social inertia; and no matter what the causes there seems to be a terrible impasse between the desires of the Negro community and its own responsibilities. As far as employment goes, the Negro has failed (in spite of a half-century of urging from men as various as Booker T. Washington and W. E. DuBois) to create his own commercial environment. As the authors state, "the small businessman creates jobs." This kind of enterprise (the Chinese restaurant, the Jewish grocery) is run on an ethnic basis and is a natural source of minority patronage and employment. Granted the difficulties of competition, the authors still believe that the Negro community has failed to take advantage of commercial opportunities. It has let some traditional forms of Negro business lapse, and has not branched out into new fields. As compared to West Indian Negroes who have come to Harlem the native Americans came off badly. They did not save, they did not, when they had money, think to invest it in Negro enterprise; they had no program for changing unskilled to skilled labor. The criticism of this thesis has been that commercial enterprise was impossible for the poor—Michael Harrington replies that the Negro has been too degraded by poverty to think of long-range improvement.[4] Glazer and Moynihan believe otherwise. They point out

2. James Baldwin, "Fifth Avenue, Uptown," *Nobody Knows My Name* (New York, 1961), p. 60.

3. Nathan Glazer and Daniel Patrick Moynihan, *Beyond the Melting Pot* (Cambridge, Mass., 1964), pp. 24–85.

4. Michael Harrington, "The Decadence of the Poor," *The Accidental Century* (New York, 1965), pp. 111–143.

that not only the West Indian but the native professional class has risen out of degradation. It might be added that the Black Muslims, regardless of their other qualities, are notable examples of economic self-help.[5] It is not often realized how central for them is the idea of self-employment.

Economic weakness is a consequence of "the relative weakness of clan and extended family feeling." Perhaps the subject most objectionable to the liberal readers of *Beyond the Melting Pot* was the inadequacy of the Negro family. Glazer and Moynihan began their essay on "The Family and Other Problems" by noting some familiar statistics: one-quarter of Negro families in New York are headed by women; the rate of Negro illegitimacy is fourteen or fifteen times that among whites. There are, in short, more broken than unbroken homes among Negroes, and the typical experience of a Negro child is that of residence in a number of domiciles and institutions rather than within a stable family.[6] But the conclusion is that "prejudice, low income, poor education explain only so much." The disorganization of the Negro community has its origins in the Negro family, a unit with little economic authority and close to no moral authority. The Negro middle class has done little to remedy this "in money, organization, or involvement." A massive self-help effort is not likely. The social problems of segregation will remain; the Negro middle class will continue to

---

5. E. U. Essien-Udom, "Economic Nationalism and Organization," *Black Nationalism* (Chicago, 1962), pp. 163–171. The author quotes Marcus Garvey's admonition, "support the resident or racial merchant"; and Elijah Muhammad's "Economic Blue Print for the Black Man" states:

1. Recognize the necessity for unity and group operation (activities).
2. Pool your resources; physically as well as financially.
3. Stop wanton criticisms of everything that is black-owned and black operated.
4. Keep in Mind—*Jealousy Destroys From Within.*
5. Observe the operations of the White Man. He is successful. He makes no excuses for his failure: He works hard—in a collective manner. You do the same. . . .

6. See Charles Silberman, *Crisis in Black and White* (New York, 1964), pp. 226–228.

pursue its own limited goals of adaptation; the lower class, in the absence of its own resources of responsibility, will continue in its course.

*The Negro Family* is both more specific and disheartening. It begins by noting that the formal machinery for equal rights has been guaranteed even as the Negro condition is worsening. The single most important social fact in our country today, according to the report, is that the Negro drive for equality of results is fore-doomed; the cause is the deterioration of Negro society. The Negro community is being broken down into two classes, a (relatively) stable, self-seeking middle class and a pathological lower class. In the latter there is nearly total disorganization. The statistics which reveal that one-quarter of urban Negro marriages are dissolved, that one-third of Negro homes are broken, and that one-quarter of Negro births are illegitimate seem to speak for themselves. They unfortunately need interpretation. It is pointed out that they "do not measure the experience of individuals over time." That is, the experiences represented by these statistics are not confined to one-quarter or one-third of the population. During the normal life span a *majority* of the Negro lower class is subject to this pathology. I know of no better illustration of this then Claude Brown's *Manchild in the Promised Land*, which is a cultural biography as well as the story of a man. One of the most significant things in this book is the depiction of Negro family life over a period of years. The family that in one given period is "normal" will in the next period be suddenly immersed in the urban syndrome of adultery, drugs, crime, unemployment, hopelessness. Social pathology, in other words, is endemic, and in the ghetto there is no immunity.

Unemployment has become not an economic but a social problem. It has long been a cliché that Negro families are matriarchal, but the meaning of this is arresting when translated into specific terms. There can be no male leadership when the husband is unemployed and when custom holds out for him only the alternatives of welfare, subsidence into a state of dependency, alcoholism and drugs, and finally disappearance. These become more rather than less probable because of the nature of urban employment today. There is an increasing market for women and for the skilled, and much less of a market for manual labor and the untrained. In normative terms this means that a woman can work as a domestic, or collect welfare checks with a proportionate loss of pride. In pathological terms this means that the Negro woman who is "in the life" of prostitution serves the same function for her man.

Within the family a pattern of failure begins to operate. Thus the female head of the household is liberated from male authority when that authority depends on financial power. An acute essay by Lee Rainwater in *Daedalus* goes over the dissolution of family sanctions after the Negro male loses his job.[7] He is relegated to a secondary status and is not expected to retain his authority; eventually he will be ignored, left unfed, rejected, and encouraged to leave the household. Infidelity is a kind of *lex talionis* in the lower-class family—or simply one of the modes of marital retribution. Rainwater notes that in terms of experience the household is centered on women—the rite of passage from adolescence to maturity is pregnancy. After one or two pregnancies marriage may come about—but it is viewed with ambivalence because of the nonsexual problems it poses. Hence the "boy friend" of those mature women who are not bound in stable marriage—a man or series of men who live outside the complications of family, but who are sexually useful and who provide a certain social standing. There is a great deal of displaced rage because of this, particularly when a stable household becomes, due to the exigencies of unemployment, a functioning, castrating matriarchate.

The middle class is free of economic pressures but subject to others. In *Nobody Knows My Name* James Baldwin writes mordantly of the successful southern Negro who has discovered the price to be paid by black bourgeoisie. It means being an intermediary between the mass of Negroes and white governing interests—and being a cultural cipher. If the middle class is useful to the white world it may mean little to the black. It may withdraw, like Ralph Ellison's memorable Dr. Bledsoe, to its own world of satisfactions. Nat Hentoff's *The New Equality* has a chapter on the self-imposed segregation of the northern middle class, which has

7. Lee Rainwater, "Crucible of Identity: The Negro Lower-Class Family," *Daedalus* (Winter, 1966), pp. 172 ff.

abandoned whatever connections to the Negro culture it could.[8]
There is an interesting quote from a Los Angeles Negro who described the migration of lower-class Negroes to that city: "The
majority of those people are not like us. . . . we are a little, maybe,
embarrassed by the fact that here we are going to have a mass element come in that is going to create a tremendous social problem
. . . to which we find a great deal of difficulty in relating." Jewish anti-Semitism has long been joked over, but it seems time for it
to move over. Perhaps the most acute of essays on the Negro middle class are those by Bayard Rustin and Whitney Young. The
former notes that protest over Jim Crow was in effect centered on
anachronisms—those segregated facilities in hotels, libraries, ter-
minals which impeded the mobility of the middle class. In other
words, the Negro middle class mobilized to fight for middle-class
rights. Young believes that the middle class is already alienated; in
escaping from the ghetto it has separated from the people in it.[9]
After taking on the values of the outer world the middle-class
Negro tends toward symbolic goals to which other Negroes are
completely indifferent, i.e., the opening of a rest-room in a Southern airport couldn't mean less to the lower class Negro. "Each
class," Young adds, "may at times be working toward different
goals. This is evidenced in support by working or lower-class
Negroes for certain schools and public-housing projects near or
in their ghetto districts, and a resultant clash with middle-class
Negroes who may oppose erection of such buildings because they
regard them as strengthening segregation instead of weakening it."
Young is pessimistic; he believes that the new Negro middle class,
like the old one, will be indifferent to the lower class; that it will
prefer withdrawal and cynicism to political action. And he believes that, should this occur, it will disappear as a class, since the
Negro professional draws his livelihood from the Negro community.

These inherent problems are beyond the palliatives of ideology.

8. Nat Hentoff, "Closing in on the Negro Middle Class," *The New
Equality* (New York, 1964), pp. 85–93.

9. Whitney M. Young, Jr., "Middle-Class Negroes and the Negro
Masses," *Freedom Now!*, A Westin, ed. (New York, 1964), pp. 315–319.
Used by permission of Basic Books, Inc., Publishers.

All this is to say nothing of other social issues like those of delinquency and education. It leaves out the inferno of sexual complications described by Calvin Hernton in *Sex and Racism in America*. It says nothing of the devastating problem of identity outlined by Charles Silberman in *Crisis in Black and White*. It ignores what Kenneth Clark, in *Dark Ghetto*, called the "chronic debasement" of the Negro mind. It ought to be fairly plain that the characterization of Rufus in *Another Country*—the one honest part of the book—translates much of this into psychology. His inarticulate rage is what is most expressive of his condition.

* * *

The inherent problems are accompanied by those of strategy. As Murray Kempton put it, "the great demonstrations have shrunken down to public failures like the march for Democratic Schools, or they have fragmented into isolated gestures like the World's Fair 'stall-in.' A chapter is over; all the energy, the imagination, the courage and the hope which wrote that chapter could hardly not, before long, be revived again. But whatever chapter comes will be something new." [10] The first step in the change, as Kempton notes, was the dwindling of demonstrations. The second was the apparent replacement of the demonstration by the riot. The demonstration was white-led, or at least white-supported. It was conspicuously middle class, and a good deal of resentment was aroused by the brutalities suffered by Northern students, ministers, housewives. The riots in Harlem and Watts were spontaneous, hence they gave the impression of being more of a true indication of Negro feeling than the demonstration. (The idea that they were planned by Muslims or malcontents or anarchists is a red herring. Neither the report of the McCone Commission nor the infinite number of analyses on the New York riots showed that such riots were *strategic*.) The Watts riot in particular, because of

---

10. Murray Kempton, "No More Parades?", *The New Republic* (30 May 1964), pp. 5–7. Reprinted by permission of *The New Republic*, copyright 1964, Harrison-Blaine of New Jersey, Inc.

its close resemblance to the facts and experience of war, was a particularly important event in the history of Negro hostility. It made plain that *The Fire Next Time* was unreasonable, and at least partly true.

The third step in the change was from class to race. It was a radicalization intensely surprising and disappointing to the original white supporters of civil rights. The movement from legalism to direct action had two important consequences; it replaced white moderates with Negro activists and white radicals with Negro radicals. Many moderates were gradualists; others were Democrats who worried increasingly about the effect of Negro agitation on the Kennedy administration; still others (like some leaders of labor) were more interested in fair words than in the dangerous politics of equality. August Meier wrote in 1963 of the then-new attack by Negroes on white liberals: "some white liberals, no longer regarded as authorities on strategy by Negro integrationists, amazed at some of the demands that Negroes are now making—such as bringing white children into Negro areas for school so as to create racially balanced educational facilities, and giving Negroes preferential treatment on jobs until employment equality is achieved—must feel rather like the Girondists did when overtaken by the Jacobins." [11] As for the white radicals who originally flocked to the movement— Socialists, Trotskyites, Communists, aesthetes, hipsters, and existentialists—they found that theory and political posture were handicaps in the new stage of the process. In 1962, Meier wrote, "Attending the SNCC meeting . . . was like going to a Popular Front affair in the 1930s." After that it was farewell to the white liberal. An important article by Meier and Tom Kahn, "Recent Trends in the Civil Rights Movement," [12] chronicled this departure. As the authors state in this 1964 essay, "the term 'white liberal' is used indiscriminately by most Negro militants. It refers in a general way to white supporters of the civil rights movement; used pejoratively, it implies an underlying hypocrisy." Those to the left of liberals submerged for a time in the civil rights movement, but were not

11. August Meier, "New Currents in the Civil Rights Movement," *New Politics* (Summer, 1963), pp. 7–32. Used by permission.

12. Tom Kahn and August Meier, "Recent Trends in the Civil Rights Movement," *New Politics* (Spring, 1964), pp. 34–53.

able to influence policy. A mélange of Progressive Labor Movement Maoists, Trotskyites, and just plain Communists tried to attach themselves to the movement, and were successful principally among the militants. But, as the authors delicately put it, their high visibility and crude sectarianism dissipated their intentions. The old radicals have not been nearly as successful as the new ones, whose activities on the campus, in SNCC and CORE are important.[13]

The fourth and at this time most recent step in the development of civil rights strategy concerns the structure of the larger society. It is probably the most important as it is the most political of the phases. Its aims are best stated by Bayard Rustin in a speech which, significantly, was given at Berkeley in support of the FSM: "I believe that the Negro's struggle for equality in America is essentially revolutionary. While most Negroes—in their hearts—unquestionably seek only to enjoy the fruits of American society as it now exists, their quest cannot *objectively* be satisfied within the framework of existing political and economic relations." [14]

There seem to be three principal modes involved in this stage: moral suasion, political action, and a new, intensified form of Negro dogmatics. I think we can dismiss the first—certainly it is now dismissed by Negro leaders themselves. For one thing, in order to keep in advance of the wave they have been forced to become increasingly militant. And they perhaps feel some deserved contempt for a mode so little likely to produce immediate effects. The other responses are figured in Rustin's "From Protest to Politics." Rustin was much influenced by the development of the Birmingham protest which replaced the idea of individual rights with that of

13. However, there certainly is some connection. Walker Percy describes SNCC this way: ". . . [it] has no use not only for Southern whites but for the Negro middle class, Martin Luther King, the NAACP, and the FBI—and a certain reticence about Communism and the presence of Communists in the Movement. Bob Moses . . . will not discuss Communism: 'It's divisive and [according to Moses and Sally Belfrage] it's not a negotiable issue with us'." In the *New York Review of Books* (1 July 1965), p. 4.

14. Bayard Rustin, "From Protest to Politics," *Commentary* (February, 1965), 25–31. Used by permission of the author.

collective struggle. It was not the anachronisms which interested him—the right to drink at a white water-fountain or sit at a white lunch-counter—but the more substantial matters of social life. Public accommodation was, he recognized, not so important to the Negro as getting the money and status to enjoy it. There can be little argument with this, but a great deal of argument may be expected about Rustin's conclusion: "the minute the movement faced this question, it was compelled to expand its vision beyond race relations to economic relations, including the role of education in modern society. And what also became clear is that all these inter-related problems, by their very nature, are not soluble by private, voluntary efforts but require government action."

The argument for special consideration for Negroes *as a group* has polarized intellectuals of both colors and all beliefs. Conservatives like Ernest Van Den Haag and Jeffrey Hart have argued that this leads to a new definition (and corruption) of liberty. Van Den Haag states that there is a difference between employment and the "irrelevantly selective" matters of eating, housing, and schooling. Discrimination in the latter can be corrected without compelling congregation and impairing freedom of social selection. The only justification for involuntary association might be to correct material disadvantages—as in employment—to any group or person.[15] Relevance, it might be suggested, is rarely that objective. My own sense of the idea is that it must operate uniformly throughout the social group. In other words, the power to assume that a thing is or is not relevant must reside in alternatives available to all persons. In purely pragmatic terms, you cannot block a man from full social participation and expect him to be *satisfied* that this blockage reflects truths of social organization. Jeffrey Hart's tack is more convincing; he states that conservatives regard freedom of property to *be* a human right. It is banal, he urges, to object that some property owners use their freedom in unideal ways; freedom, by definition, opens up precisely that possibility. It is better to retain freedom undiminished than to compromise it in a good cause. The force of law, he suggests, should neither compel segre-

---

15. Ernest Van Den Haag, "Negroes and Whites: Claims, Rights, and Prospects," *Modern Age* (Fall, 1965), pp. 358.

gation nor integration. It should treat people as individuals and not groups, as it traditionally has done in America.[16]

Liberals like Nathan Glazer have argued that, at the least, color-consciousness changes the order we know as pluralism:

> The white community into which the Negro now demands full entrance is not actually a single community—it is a series of communities. And all of them feel threatened by the implications of the new Negro demand for full equality. They did not previously realize how much store they set by their power to control the character of the social setting in which they lived. . . . The new Negro demands challenge the right to maintain these sub-communities far more radically than the demands of any other group in American history. . . . If we do move in this direction, we will have to create communities very different from the kinds in which most of us who have already arrived—Protestants, Catholics, Jews—now live.[17]

Finally, extremists like James Baldwin have carried the argument somewhat further by stating that the present social structure is so decadent as to make the matter of civil rights contingent to a cultural revolution.[18]

Rustin's argument then, proceeds from the necessity of collective action and takes the form of pressure politics. In the course of moving from his premises to their ends some fairly meaningful positions are taken. The idea of self-help proposed by Glazer and Moynihan is summarily rejected. Equality of opportunity is rejected for "the fact of *equality*." White moderates, symbolized by *The New York Times,* are perceived as the real antagonists, because they are unwilling to take the radical step of remaking the social structure. The only satisfactory response, according to Rustin, is a transcendence of tokenism. This involves the "reallocation of national resources," and it impinges upon foreign policy. Like Martin Luther King, Rustin finds himself forced to enter this

16. Jeffrey Hart, *The American Dissent* (New York, 1966), pp. 114–115.

17. Nathan Glazer, "Negroes and Jews: The New Challenge to Pluralism," *Commentary* (December, 1964), pp. 29–35. Used by permission.

18. James Baldwin, *The Fire Next Time* (New York, 1963). Used by permission of the publisher, The Dial Press, Inc.

area of discussion. For one thing, he is led to oppose the Vietnam war in order to solidify a coalition between Negroes, pacifists, and anti-war liberals. And he is convinced (his argument here appears to derive from Michael Harrington) that if the Vietnam war were abandoned the funds it exhausts could be used for that reallocation.

The position taken by Rustin indicates that strategy and dogma may be very much at variance. Successful pressure politics are based on interests not on ideology. The history of Jewish and Catholic urban politics, to take some familiar examples, shows clearly that pressure politics are local. They can work when broadly based in a given community which is politically organized. They must, in brief, have aims that are specific, finite, and material. They must frequently surrender (as in the case of the egregious Dawson machine in Chicago) ideological purity for political power. Finally, they must have aims that the electorate approves and understands. Very little of this is plain to Rustin and the spokesmen for equality of results—although it must be acknowledged that Rustin seems positively judicial when compared to someone like Stokely Carmichael. The attempt of the new Negro dogmatism to coalesce with activists has had short-run success, but has had to go to certain lengths to please them. Such a passage as the following, with an error or untruth in each of its conclusions, shows how far activist ideology may penetrate into strategy and compromise it: "The revolutionary character of the Negro's struggle is manifest in the fact that this struggle may have done more to democratize life for whites than for Negroes. Clearly, it was the sit-in movement of young Southern Negroes which, as it galvanized white students, banished the ugliest features of McCarthyism from the American campus and resurrected political debate." Cromwell's corpse was never so handled as the ineffectual bones of Joseph McCarthy. We have seen him resurrected in Barry Goldwater, in Richard Nixon, and, it seems, Rustin wishes us now to see him resurrected in Clark Kerr. I have enough trouble believing in Lazarus.

The idea of coalition politics which this essay has made famous has another form—union not with the activist left but with the institutions of moderate liberalism. This seems eminently practical

—although the divided nature of the Democrats repels leaders of civil rights, and the do-nothing stance of organized labor has thoroughly angered them. It is self-evidently the road to power, and even in Mississippi this mode is leading to the gradual erosion of the Freedom party and its SNCC affiliates. The dilemma involved here is that the purer activists resent coalitionism bitterly, and recognize that a union of civil rights with the moderates means the end of their own influence. One of the most familiar of present polemics is the accusation that coalitionists like Rustin are traitors, and the famous attack on him by Staughton Lynd, with its communoid vocabulary of betrayal, is a sufficient example.[19] The new Negro dogma is about to choose its targets: whether to continue the attack on moderate liberal "hypocrites" or to seek less visible but more significant objects. It is about to decide whether or not activism is a kind of protest really acceptable to the body politic. It is about to decide whether the mélange of positions it demands on free speech, free sex, the right to use drugs, pacifism, and even simple *ressentiment* is worth the adoption. There are bound to be lost leaders—the attempt of Martin Luther King to bridge the gap between Vietnam and the rights of Negroes has asserted both sensibility and ideology, while it has shown a fatal indifference to the nature of politics. It would appear that purely as a strategy attacks on the "power structure" are too negative to take hold. The attempts of Negro leaders in the last two years to express sympathies with activism seem to have been exploratory. One guesses that the white moderate will soon be re-examined, and found to be financially and politically a better bet. The dual thrust of Rustin's argument will resolve itself into one, dropping the "power structure" thesis and turning to the politics of coalition and local pressure so familiar on the American scene. At this time, however, it is the discovery of differences between the white liberals and Negroes that has center stage.

---

19. Coalitionism may enrage those whose purity is compromised. Staughton Lynd's rabid attack on Rustin in *Liberation* (June–July 1965, pp. 18–21) is a pretty fair example. In this essay Rustin's attempt to gain moderate support earned him epithets like "labor lieutenant of capitalism . . . campism . . . élitism . . . hypocrisy."

# Negro and Liberal

That the alliance of Negroes and white liberals is shaky is by now a commonplace. A whole library of reappraisal pieces has been issued: "The Push Beyond Liberalism," "White Anxiety and the Negro Revolt," "The Black Man's Burden: The White Liberal," "The White Liberal's Retreat." [20] The last of these, by Murray Friedman, made something of an impression on the liberal community when it delineated the conflicts of interest between classes and races. The civil rights revolution has been easy to encourage and hard to live with, particularly for those who must send their children to integrated schools which are physically dangerous and culturally second-rate, and who must themselves work with and live among Negroes. The culpability of the white liberal has been measured out more or less in ratio to one's political and racial position. SNCC has no use for whites, or even for liberal Negroes. Some whites in the movement have no use for themselves —they are well described by Norman Podhoretz:

> There are the broken-down white boys like Vivaldo Moore in Baldwin's *Another Country* who go to Harlem in search of sex or simply to brush up against something that looks like primitive vitality. . . . There are the writers and intellectuals and artists who romanticize Negroes and pander to them, assuming a guilt that is not properly theirs. And there are all the white liberals who permit Negroes to blackmail them into adopting a double standard of moral judgment.[21]

20. Sam Bottone, "The Push Beyond Liberalism," *New Politics* (Summer, 1964), pp. 35–45; Michael Parenti, "White Anxiety and the Negro Revolt," *New Politics* (Winter, 1964), pp. 35–39; Charles B. Turner, Jr., "The Black Man's Burden: The White Liberal," *Dissent* (Summer, 1963), pp. 215–219; Murray Friedman, "The White Liberal's Retreat," *Freedom Now!*, pp. 320–328.

21. Norman Podhoretz, "My Negro Problem—And Ours," *Commentary* (February, 1963), pp. 93–101. Used by permission. This might be compared to Kahn and Meier: "To be accurate, it should be said that there is a substantial group of white activists who are not alienated by criticism of whites within the movement, but actually appear to relish it and even engage in the practice themselves. Some of these people seem to be guilt-ridden masochists who openly applaud denunciations

Those whose activities embrace more than civil rights, who attack what C. Wright Mills called the power-structure, blame the white liberal for his hidden conservatism: as Sam Bottone put it in *New Politics*, "Liberalism's basic commitment to the status quo stood exposed to view" when civil rights came North.[22] In short, liberalism is for this persuasion an appendage of the Democratic Party whose interest in Negro rights is ulterior.

Many reasons have been proposed for the new hostility to liberalism. Bottone believes Liberals are in fact conservatives in disguise—which is far from being a wild assumption. The daily lives of most people are in fact dominated by the conservatism of habit and interest. Podhoretz claims that the difficulties are caused by a residue of irrational intolerance, and somewhat weepily postpones eventual settlement until we are all intermarried.[23] Michael Parenti disposes that "way down inside himself the white liberal wants the Negro to feel indebted to him, and appreciative of him, perhaps to absolve his own sense of guilt for enjoying the advantages of being white in a racist society. . . . White liberals always have indulged in self-flagellation." [24] Daniel Bell, J. C. Rich, and Paul Jacobs have written about the conflicts in liberal labor unions, in which the principle of seniority and the practice of family, clan, and ethnic restrictions delimit aspiring Negro membership.[25] Alexander Bickel, in an essay much criticized by the activist left, declared that demonstrations had a purpose and, more to the point, a limit.[26] He

---

of white activists. Related to these are the white 'Uncle Toms' who, possibly out of a mixture of guilt and condescension, consider it bad form to criticize the actions of anyone who happens to be a Negro."

22. Bottone, *op. cit.*, p. 35.

23. James Baldwin is possibly more reserved: "Actually I don't want to marry your sister, I just want to get you off my back."

24. Parenti, *op. cit.*, p. 36.

25. Daniel Bell, "Reflections on the Negro and Labor," *The New Leader* (21 January 1963), pp. 18–20, and "The Negro and Labor Unions," *Freedom Now!* (pp. 290–295); J. C. Rich, "The NAACP vs. Labor," *The New Leader* (26 November 1962), pp. 20–21; Paul Jacobs, "No More Cousin Toms," *Dissent* (Winter, 1963), pp. 6–12.

26. Alexander M. Bickel, "After a Civil Rights Act," *The New Republic* (9 May 1964), 11–15.

expressed a prevalent middle-class view in urging that Negroes aim solely at those ends which were likely to be accomplished. His rhetorical question—"What good is it to anyone to force white children to accept inferior schooling? Such white children as are at all able to do so would flee the public school system, which would, in turn, be simply destroyed"— suffered from the disability of being ideologically unthinkable.

Negro responses to white liberalism have of course been most critical. The range of Negro reaction to liberalism is best expressed by the following pair of quotations:

> I must confess that over the last few years I have been gravely disappointed with the white moderate. I have almost reached the regrettable conclusion that the Negroes' great stumbling block in the stride toward freedom is not the White Citizens' "Councilor" or the Ku Klux Klanner, but the white moderate who is more devoted to "order" than to justice; who prefers a negative peace which is the absence of tension to a positive peace which is the presence of justice . . . who lives by the myth of time and constantly advises the Negro to wait until a "more convenient season." [27]

> It is just this group of amateur social theorists, American Liberals, who have done most . . . to insure the success of tokenism . . . liberals, are people with extremely heavy consciences and almost nonexistent courage. Too little is always enough. And it is always the *symbol* that appeals to them most. The single futile housing project in the jungle of slums and disease eases the liberals' conscience, so they are loudest in praising it—even though it might not solve any problems at all. The single black student in the Southern university, the promoted porter in Marietta, Georgia—all ease the liberals' conscience like a benevolent but highly addictive drug. And, for them, "moderation" is a kind of religious catch phrase. . . .[28]

---

27. Martin Luther King, "Letter From Birmingham Jail," *Freedom Now!* (New York, 1964) pp. 10–21. Used by permission of Basic Books, Inc., Publishers.

28. LeRoi Jones, "tokenism: 300 years for five cents," *Home* (New York, 1966), pp. 68–86. Copyright © 1961, 1962, 1963, 1964, 1965, 1966 by LeRoi Jones; used by permission of author and William Morrow and Company, Inc., Publisher.

It would seem that there is no range at all between these two, since they are substantially the same. The range is in the sources: The second quotation comes from LeRoi Jones, the first from Martin Luther King's *Letter From Birmingham Jail*. That in itself is of some meaning.

A good deal has been said about the white liberal and most of it, unfortunately, has been murky and abstract. The white liberal's commitment to order is rarely connected to the special status of property in our culture, and to the rights surrounding it. His commitment to law has been made to seem unreal when compared to the vigorous *vita activa* of the demonstration. His reluctance to share housing with Negroes has been made to seem an arbitrary act of cowardice, although class and ethnic background would seem to operate here as in any cultural situation. Far too little has been said about the white liberal mind.

A good beginning might concern itself with defining the white liberal from the Negro viewpoint. One attempt has been that of Nathan Glazer: The white liberal who is attacked as a hypocrite "is generally (even if this is not spelled out) the white *Jewish* liberal—and it could hardly be otherwise, in view of the predominance of Jews among liberals." [29] Glazer's thesis has become well-known, that is, that the aims of Jewish liberalism are not compatible with those of Negro equality, although they had been compatible with Negro advancement. Nor were Jews as a minority *naturally* disposed to a covenant with Negroes, and vice versa. There are the complications of Negro anti-semitism, which flourished when the Negro was directly exploited by Jewish merchants and landlords; when the Negro occupied neighborhoods in the process of being vacated by Jewish families; when Negro professionals perceived themselves as being in competition with Jewish doctors and lawyers. There was simple antagonism between races and classes—whose power and permanency has been clarified by the events of this decade. There is the strange *odi et amo* relationship revealed by this dialogue from *Manchild in the Promised Land*:

I said, "I don't know exactly what it is, Judy, but there seems to be a strong attraction between Jewish people and Negroes. Most of

29. Glazer, *Commentary* (December, 1964), pp. 29–35.

the white girls who you see around here going with colored fellows will be Jewish. And most of the white guys you see going with colored girls will be Jewish guys."

"Oh, I didn't know that. I don't know of anybody who has done anything like that. I thought it was a very unusual thing."

"It is, but when it does happen, it's with Jewish people."

"Oh, I thought it was something that rarely happened with Jewish families, because Jewish people have strong family ties. I have a cousin who married this Puerto Rican fellow. Her family just doesn't have anything to do with her any more. . . . my aunt and my uncle say that she isn't their child any more." [30]

There is the loud silence of Southern Jewish communities on the issue of segregation. And there is the new antagonism of equality. On the one hand, the Jewish community has found its interests to conflict with those of Negroes; on the other, Negroes have experienced the disappointment of those who recognize the weakness of allies.

The old conflicts of Jew and Negro were social—that between tenant and landlord, merchant and customer, supervisor and worker.[31] The new conflict is ideological. The Jews have been that group in America which most emphatically put its trust in individual achievement, whether in business warfare or in the ferocity of university examinations. The Jewish sub-culture is based on the ethic of competition. Nothing is so profoundly Jewish as the contempt for failure—a contempt which has never been absent from Jewish thought about Negroes. Nowhere has the system of merit been more conspicuously approved by Jews than in education and bureaucracy. It is precisely these fields which Negroes wish to remove from the operation of competition and standards. "When they challenge the use of grades as the sole criterion for entry into special high schools and free colleges, they challenge

30. Claude Brown, *Manchild in the Promised Land* (New York, 1965), p. 345. Copyright © Claude Brown, 1965; used by permission of the publisher, The Macmillan Company.

31. See the review of Negro anti-semitism by B. Z. Sobel and M. L. Sobel, "Negroes and Jews: American Minority Groups in Conflict," *Judaism* (Winter, 1966), pp. 3-22.

the system which has enabled Jews to dominate these institutions for decades." [32] Perhaps of equal significance is another system, one based on family and clan. Jewish enterprise is pretty much endogamous.

Another point of Glazer's concerns the rediscovery of pluralism. Our system of law recognizes only individuals, but our social system recognizes only groups—as Will Herberg has written, there are only three possibilities of being a person in our culture, Protestant, Catholic, and Jew. We demand that pluralism take on the material form of identity. The relationship among these three divisions has been conceived of ideally as one of assimilation, but in social terms it has taken on the form of differentiation. Glazer notes that most Jews want to remain members of a distinctive group. No matter how critical they are of exclusiveness they implicitly accept social divisions. From their own point of view such divisions are not only conditions of fact but in themselves highly legitimate. The Jewish intellectual, it is clear, sees his own identity in separateness.

The new equality challenges the rights of pluralism. It makes demands that American society outside of its political structure cannot fulfill. Fashionable theorizing on the need to change the American "power structure" seems frivolous when measured by this social fact. And this theorizing is based on an embarrassing contradiction, that is, the rights of white groups to exist as groups is challenged even as the demand is made that color-blindness be changed by fiat to color-consciousness.

There are other complications, and these are of a peculiar and

---

32. Milton Himmelfarb's "How We Are," *Commentary* (January, 1965), reviews the battle over the City University of New York. Urban Negroes have allied with upstate conservatives in order to introduce tuition fees and lower "artificially inflated"—i.e., traditionally high—entrance requirements. The effect of this and of proportionate representation from the high schools would be to increase the number of Negroes at City University and decrease the number of Jews. Since most Negroes would be exempt from tuition fees because of financial inability, their scholarship support would in effect be supplied by their Jewish rivals. There has been a notable uproar on the part of Jewish Democrats.

indeed psychic order. This has nowhere been so intelligently expressed as in a statement by Arnold Wolf, rabbi of Congregation Solel, in Highland Park, Illinois.[33] In a long letter to *Judaism* Rabbi Wolf identified himself as a man involved in civil-rights, and the list of his involvements shows how far into the secular world it is now appropriate for a cleric to proceed to demonstrate his faith. The letter is divided into two parts: the first, like the essay by Norman Podhoretz, gives an ashamed account of some unvarnished truths: "No—I do not really wish to work with you! I do not wish to swim with you! I do not wish to go to jail with you! I do not wish . . . to be one of you!" He made clear that he was both Jewish and middle-class, and subject to the compulsions of being both. If this seems discomforting there is rather more to be said. It is precisely in the forbidden area of religion that the Jew and the Negro are incompatible.

All matters are eventually religious matters. For Rabbi Wolf the fulcrum of this debate is the nature of Liberal Judaism. Having dispensed with God this faith has not found a reasonable (or, even more to be wished, an unreasoning) substitute in man. The point about social justice is that it goes only so far as is convenient: "our theological convictions have come home to roost. A God Who is my own best nature is not God enough. My own best nature does not care much about the Negro or the poor." If Judaism becomes the enactment of Democratic Party platforms, it will be bound to precisely their limitations. It has lost two important things that are at the core of the Negro revolution: the sense of charisma and a literal, evangelical faith in God. It is these things which energize the revolution, and which separate the believing Negro from the secular Jew.

The terrible fact about the Jewish liberal who is a Liberal Jew is that he is free. He lives in a secular world, and that world is singularly loose in its imperatives. The Negro revolution is essentially a Christian revolution. Its imperatives are not so rational as those of Marx and Freud, but they are much more overpowering. Their totality is bad from a strategic point of view, but essential to

33. Arnold Wolf, "The Negro Revolution and Jewish Theology," *Judaism* (Fall, 1964), pp. 478–493. Used by permission.

what may be called the heart of the matter. There is, finally, a difference between us:

> What we fear from Martin Luther King, what I feared to find in St. Augustine, [he means the city; but it is a useful ambiguity] is not only a hard job but a hard Taskmaster. My liberal theology had protected me against surprise or rebuke. The God of my father and my grandfather had learned to be polite. Chastened, He did not ask for much nor, to be sure, promise more. He was decorative and decent. He was a True Liberal.

It is unpleasant, but someone eventually had to say it: The Negro is animated by religion and the Jew is animated by something else. The great figures of the Negro movement are charismatic. They are preachers, whether of religion or not. They are fundamentalist Christians who believe as Jews do not in the final value of what they are doing. They are not good men trying to be better—only men trying to fulfill a will less unswerving than their own. The Jewish Liberal's fear of human opposition has no correspondence to their sense of infinite possibility. The white liberal's politics have no correspondence to their prayer. It is perhaps needless to insist that the Negroes' Christianity is the source of their distance from and ambivalence to the Jews. There is really no difference quite as emphatic as that between the justified and the irresolute.

In sum, it may be argued that the community of Liberals—like the community of Conservatives—believes essentially in rights which resist the demands of equality and which are in fact not "human" as that term is now being interpreted. Liberals both Jewish and Christian have an immense respect for property. That is why demonstrations and riots lost a good deal of support, and why the bill to insure integrated housing in California was beaten. Liberals are united by a respect for the rights of merit. So egregious an example as Max Lerner may be cited, who illustrates the elitest strain in liberalism. If liberals have rejected a historical and traditional elite they have only transferred their allegiance to an elite of intellectual and social achievement. It is not easy to be elitist and equalitarian at the same time. The Jewish liberal especially will not translate sympathy into equality. There is an immense, indeed an unbelievable, difference between the Jewish liberal who works through ponderous organizations dedicated to meliorism, and the

Jewish activist who works through mercuric coalitions dedicated to cultural revolution. Perhaps those most fanatically committed to the ideal of American competition are Jewish professionals. I submit that the bourgeois Jewish Liberal is liberal only in the political sense. He may be ruinously so, but there are limits to his political life. He works well under capitalism and deeply resents proposals to change it. To "socialize" is rather a dirty word among Jewish physicians. And in many ways the Jewish physician is the central figure in his subculture. The Jewish liberal has a certain amount of clan consciousness—not so much as before, but still a disproportionate amount when compared to that of the culture at large. His bitterest opposition is reserved for those who impede the education of his children and their road to cultural and economic exclusiveness. He honors achievement (the means do not really matter) and has a certain distaste for gesture. A specific case may be put: The death of Schwerner and Goodman may be thought of as martyrdom, but in the New York Jewish community it looks simply like failure.

The complexity of the Jewish liberal's response to the Negro cause is considerable: from the guilt so cloyingly represented by novelists, to the search for primitive authenticity, to the ideology of toleration. But there is no doubt in my mind that only Jewish activism exceeds self-imposed limits. By far the majority of Jewish liberals—those who finance the NAACP and the freedom rides—wish to maintain their exclusiveness. They resent the Christianity of Negroes, or pity it, or misunderstand it. They are inflamed by Negro anti-semitism. They resent the idea of equality; after all, they do not have that themselves. Their attitude toward Negroes is tolerant, even patriarchal. But there is the contempt of the literate for the undisciplined, and that of the success for the failure. It is perhaps needless to insist that the religious tradition of Judaism is not one of social protest. There are in fact almost no *Jewish* religious sanctions that may be invoked vis à vis civil rights.

## Beyond Moderation

The modes of the civil rights movement have been legalism and extremism. The first operates through the politics of accommodation; it involves the Negro middle class and, however cautiously, the white liberal. Its aims are limited and its passions are contained. It works with the Democratic Party and the Christian churches. Its great symbolic action was the March on Washington. The mode of extremism involves the Negro (urban) lower class and those intellectuals with a deep, articulate contempt for the American system. It is not dominated by organizations, although disparate groups like SNCC and the Black Muslims give it a certain amount of form. The spokesmen for extremism have been Robert Williams, James Baldwin, LeRoi Jones, Malcolm X, among other Negro (and white) figures. Its aims are not limited, and its strategy is not to discipline feeling but to express it with as much moral damage as possible. It has an intense hostility to whatever public action is programmatic. Its great symbolic actions are the manifesto and the riot.

It is advisable to repeat that riots seldom have ideological causes. But they do serve ideological purposes. One of the most important consequences of the Watts riot of 1965 was the general sense that riot had become revolution. As civil disorder, the Watts riot appeared to be a matter of felonies directed against life and property. As a cultural event it has taken on other status. Some have welcomed the chance to prove the existence of a world-wide conflict between black and white; others, less extravagantly, see it as at least an intelligible event. William McCord's essay in *The New Leader* is an example of the latter.[34] McCord was one of the few white men voluntarily in Watts during the riots. These riots made sense to him, and he in turn makes a case for their intentions. He is in fact more lucid than the McCone Report, which is hedged by pieties.[35] The big point of his essay is that Watts was not a race riot. Violence was selective, "directed against the white merchants who controlled the business of the area and against white policemen." Individual whites were not the special object of violence—there are accounts in his piece of the lengths to which Negroes went in order to protect him, and to explain themselves to him. Personal violence was casual; the real passions were those directed

34. William M. McCord, "Burn, Baby, Burn!", *The New Leader* (30 August 1965), pp. 3–5.

35. See the review of the McCone Report, *Violence in the City* by Elizabeth Hardwick in the *New York Review of Books* (31 March 1966).

against property. As McCord puts it, the riots "were neither an expression of pure lawlessness nor the product of civil rights demonstrations." They were actually rather complicated; roving gangs of delinquents indulged themselves in destruction; a certain number of have-nots used the occasion to become property owners; Muslims found an opportunity to exercise their leadership. Police brutality was not really an issue—what was an issue was the indignity of police tactics, which were based on the premise that only preventive police action would work in the ghetto.[36] The essential point is that the riots began with the circumstance of poverty among those outside the sanctions of law, a circumstance aggravated by the recent failure of Proposition 14, which had given notice that the ghetto was there to stay. And, it must be added, they were animated by racial hatred.

A number of analyses from the activist left took a rather different view. Some were tendentious but valuable. They made it clear that it was only the Negro middle class which rejected the riots; the fact was that many other Negroes saw the riots as a rough form of justice. A member of the Non-Violent Action Committee(!) wrote that there was an enormous amount of *joy* in Watts among the celebrants of the riot. Even those who did not participate felt in some way confirmed. If the matter is put in a somewhat literary way it still carries conviction: "A lot of the people are saying with all of the looting and the burning and the rock throwing, 'Dammit, I exist.' 'Here I am.' And that's soemthing [*sic*], because that whole ghetto has been invisible in the sense of Ralph Ellison's *Invisible Man*." [37] Other activists were

---

36. The most familiar kind of police action is direct action, a response to a felony. The Los Angeles Police Department works under preventive action, which aims at the conditions producing felonies. Although preventive action keeps down the crime rate it is a constant irritant, since the police must continuously stop drivers, check pedestrians, and so on, in an attempt to identify *potential* felons. In the Negro district preventive action is more fully used—and hence more a reminder of the Negro condition—than in other areas of the city. Preventive action "started" the riot when the car of a drunken driver was impounded in order to prevent its illegal and possibly dangerous use.

37. Jerry Farber, *The Campus Core-Lator* (Fall, 1965), p. 8.

attracted to the expression the riots offered to their own beliefs. It was caused, some said, because of revolutionary awareness in Watts, and it was connected by them to such disparate things as the war in Vietnam and the betrayal of Negroes by *menshevik* liberals. One of the most acute of these essays argued that true riots are aimless but that the Watts rebellion was highly specific. The author, Michael Parker, a graduate student at Berkeley,[38] suggested that a certain amount of social consciousness was generated. As Parker noted, a good deal of *pride* was produced by the violence. He quotes one Negro observer, ". . . they feel morally right about what they have done. They look upon it as a revolt rather than a riot and therefore subject to a different value system. They see their insurrection as an opportunity to achieve dignity and self respect."

If the rioters are eased of guilt those who did not riot are pretty well hung up to dry. Not surprisingly, it is the white liberal whom Parker attacks. Indeed, one of the consequences of the riot was to give the activist left a position from which to attack the moderate left. In Parker's opinion the orthodox liberal explanation denies the facts and refuses to admit the separation between social classes. He observes that no middle-class Negro, including Martin Luther King, had the slightest influence. In fact, King's suggestion that the police were necessary negated his moral influence. As to the apologetic claim made by some liberals that only a small part of the Negro community was involved, Parker counters with this conclusion: "The overwhelming majority of ghetto Negroes participated in or identified with what happened." It is his sense that liberals have tried to write off the riots as caused by hot weather and momentary aberration, but that "what took place was the product of the failure of liberalism to deal with the problems and conditions of life in the ghetto." He is of course unfair; there are many other reasons. Among them is the guilt and neglect of conservatives as well as liberals. There is the failure of city and state government to go beyond welfare, which was of relative indifference to Watts. And there was of course the failure of the Negro community itself.

---

38. *Ibid.*, pp. 11–19.

I think these are the facts about the Watts riot: The failure of Negro leadership was total because it was not dealing with the middle class; the malaise of the ghetto could only be redeemed by the most primitive masculine acts; the distance between those who were propertied and those who had no visible stake in society was too great for comprehension. One doubts whether the rioters read James Baldwin. One is well aware that their impulses found an appropriate vacuum in the social structure—there are no riots in Levittown. There were two shocks involved in Watts. The first of these was exaggerated by middlebrow journalism. It was the assumption that Negroes are hidden racists who would butcher all Whites if they could. Since this is a lie, no matter how eloquently it is proposed by the carnivorous Mr. Jones, it has gradually sunk back into the intellectual limbo where all such things reside. It was, after all, Malcolm X who said, "the *brotherhood!* The people of all races, colors, from all over the world coming together as one! It has proved to me the power of the One God." [39] Not a very original declaration, but one which held for him the difference between death and life. The second shock is only now dawning. It shows the operation of a system of life not conceived of in middle-class America. The very poor are not like us.

One would have thought that the awareness of this fact might prepare us for its meaning, but such has not been the case. By late 1967 the misconceptions of both races had their natural consequence. The riots in Newark and Detroit virtually destroyed the *anima* of the Liberal-Negro alliance. On the side of some whites, there was a relieved severance of moral ties with the Negro community. On the side of the Negroes, there was a total rejection not only of middle-class leadership but of the concept of social integration itself. Negroes split into a small minority of respectables and a large majority of insurrectionaries. It should be noted that this involved a sudden shifting away from the Protestant values that had for a long time energized Negro protest. The new heroes were entirely removed from both religious piety and middle-class ideals. They were, to use a phrase of LeRoi Jones, the *fellaheeen*

---

39. *The Autobiography of Malcolm X* (New York, 1965), p. 343. Used by permission of the publisher, Grove Press.

of modernity, the dispossessed. The new leaders were young, without property, and with no commitment to the kind of social progress which satisfied their predecessors. Their renewed interest in the idiom of revolution—we think of Stokely Carmichael's pilgrimage to Havana immediately after the Newark riots—made it plain that new motives had entered racial conflict. Those who have been brutalized do not wish justice, they hunger for revenge. They are poor judges of depraved leadership.

To some extent, official liberalism is responsible. The grand tactics of its politics are simply donatives carried to an extreme. For example, the millions of dollars distributed in Watts lined the pockets of administrators; the new bureaucracies had very little bearing on the daily life of unemployed men. As for Detroit and Newark, they were distinguished by welfare programs much in advance of many of their sister cities. Very little has been done to translate liberal ideology into fact—the reconsiderations of moderates have in fact alienated Negroes. The widespread acceptance of segregated education in the North is now reflexively liberal. The new generation of Negroes views this with suspicion, and in any case they view the ideas of liberalism as mere subterfuge. Whether they judge the effects of social progress or the philosophy which creates those effects they are dissatisfied. Some notable ironies have been generated: The horror with which the southern lynch mob was once received has been transferred to the northern riot mob. Mass cult psychology, ever ready to explain the phenomenal world, has accounted for the one in terms as easily applied to the other. But the fact is that there is a tremendous difference between the agitator and the looter, between the sniper and the opportunist. Even a riot has its social—and ideological—structure. There will be more of them, and our sociology had better be ready to comprehend this.

The blame for the Negro riots of 1967 has been apportioned already, but I do not think it has been done quite accurately. Let us start with Negroes. They were no longer willing to endure a life of savage inequality. They were neither literate nor articulate, and could respond to the material world only in material ways. It is of interest that a society infatuated with fake rebelliousness in individuals professed to be horrified at the operation of the real thing in groups. Let us go on to the liberals. With a collective sigh of gratitude they disavowed Negro "extremists" and put their faith in the doctors, lawyers, and functionaries whom they could understand. Which is to say that they detached themselves from 80 percent of the colored people in America. The Negro extremist, so admired in drama and literature, proved to be uncomfortable at close quarters. The blunt truth is that liberalism does not any longer have a vocabulary of ethics that includes the extremist—he can only be viewed as a case of atavism from the viewpoint of our reigning system of thought. Let us go on to conservatives. They were free of the sins of commitment because they suffocated in their own rectitude. They were those who did not act, and America will not easily forget those who made the great refusal. I am not speaking of their attitude toward the limits of legislation, which is entirely defensible. I am speaking purely of conservatives as individuals and social groups who were distinguished by the most absolute inertia in dealing, as partners in the social enterprise, with Negroes. As for the rest, there is a gradation from those morons in uniform who shot everything in sight to the rest of us who simply did as the Indians used to, destroying cattle by leaving them to die unmilked.

* * *

The kind of opinion about Negro extremism that floats through our culture is unsatisfactory. Far too much is made of racism, and far too little has to do with, for example, the religious motives of Malcolm X; the obscurantist effect of the search for identity on James Baldwin; the mixture of racism and commercialism in LeRoi Jones. In the long run, riots like those of Watts and Harlem will not have the effect of ideas. It is the ideas that I would like to outline now, especially those of the three men I have cited. In so doing I will stress that extremism is less monolithic than appears. It is no more free of intellectual foliation than any other system. In the case of Malcolm X this is of particular importance, for it was his life which most pointedly showed that, in America, ideas still have consequences.

There is a kind of experience in America (it is as much a part of mass culture as of literature) which involves the discovery of things as they are. The vein has been played out because there is a limit to what may be found in social life. Unmasking has now become ritual, and, given the nature of those who practice it, lacks moral force in any case. The importance of Malcolm X was that he exempted himself from this last qualification. He was the young man from the provinces with that great demand on life about which Lionel Trilling has so finely written. That he was Negro was an enabling factor. He saw more that way. The first important thing about his life was that he had the alternatives of existence or consciousness. The *Autobiography of Malcolm X* is a record of many things, but primarily of an increasing awareness of and respect for the process of thought.

I think the importance of his life can be roughly drawn this way: the discovery of Harlem; the discovery of Black Nationalism; the discovery of his powers of mind as opposed to those of rhetoric. There are few accounts of Harlem which are more level than his, and which give more of a sense of how the city can incarnate a man. Before his arrival Malcolm X was a petty criminal in Roxbury; afterwards he was in some sense a person. I do not mean by this that his life of crime in Harlem supplied the "experience" we all need to mature into more genital personalities. But it did become the subject of his reflections, and it became incorporated into his view of himself. The point of this particular part of his life is that it was viewed as an intelligible process. Drugs, crime, and prison exhausted its possibilities. The dogmas of Black Muslimism made Malcolm X conscious of this and, in going through the typically modern experience of conversion, Malcolm X found an ideology available to him.

Black Muslimism is fairly complicated. As a religion it adheres to the position that Christianity is a form of white propaganda, and it seeks the purer form of Africanism. As a society it takes the position that the Negro must stay segregated until he is granted that area west of the Mississippi and south of Colorado. As a mythology it holds that the white man is a kind of android invention of the devil. And as a racket it shares the characteristics of a number of other sects. The increasing rationality of Malcolm X led to a certain embarrassment about the myth. More important, his late and invaluable discovery of his own morality made it impossible for him to continue living on purely ideological terms; it is ironic that both Right and Left overlook this in their concentration on the earlier positions he took and on his demonic energy.[40]

Malcolm X was first impressed by the ritual content of the movement and its social forms—the white-gowned women, the harmony between members, and the austerity of their lives. Nothing is so pronounced in his autobiography as the religious sense he brought to experience. He was in fact a religious enthusiast, and it was this which led first to his development and later to his death. The point I think is this: Black Muslimism is far from being an extremist organization and is in fact endangered by the kind of extremism that operates in the mind of individuals. The movement flourishes within the *status quo*. It can hardly wish for the ghetto to be emptied since that is the principal source of its strength. It is authoritarian, and by definition against cultural or personal change. The error made by those who have gone over the life of Malcolm X has been to confuse his ideas with those of the sect. Tom Kahn and Bayard Rustin dismissed him as merely another evangelist.[41] They wrote, in "The Ambiguous Legacy of Malcolm X," that he was socially impotent because he was a "conservative" committed to a kind of improvement outside of politics. As to his being an evangelist they were quite right; one wonders, however, if their own political premises enable them to understand that individualism is a fairly legitimate position in itself. In the sense that I use the term it is religious. Because he had no plans for transforming the "power structure" seems a singularly poor reason to misunderstand his real concern, the development of moral awareness.

One thing characteristic of all Malcolm's speeches was his at-

40. "One of the major troubles that I was having in building the organization that I wanted—an all-black organization whose ultimate objective was to help create a society in which there could exist honest white-black brotherhood—was that my earlier public image, my old so-called 'Black Muslim' image, kept blocking me. I was trying to gradually reshape that image." *Ibid.*, p. 381.

41. Tom Kahn and Bayard Rustin, "The Ambiguous Legacy of Malcolm X," *Dissent* (Spring, 1965), 185–192.

tempt to cause pain. He was the best accuser of the white man of this decade—and perhaps of the Negro as well. Not that everything he said was true, far from it. But what he said was calculated to do moral damage. The single point he made repeatedly was that what had been done was too much to forgive. He made plain the *impasse* between our intentions and our actions. Since he talked about guilt in an unaccustomed way—it was not the kind of thing that membership in the Democratic Party could assuage—he was unpopular among those who put their faith in politics. The pain he felt in being black and the hatred he had for those who had injured him were forms of honesty. On the whole it was good to have them expressed. The one thing he accomplished was to lift the matter of civil rights out of politics. Like most evangelists he tried to bring it down to guilt or innocence. And like most evangelists his real intention was to wound his hearers into consciousness.

In the year before his death Malcolm X came to religious conclusions which would have made it impossible for the Muslims to survive in their habitual form. The Muslims are violent rhetorically, but have no intention of putting their position into action. Part of this is necessarily strategic—but part of it concerns the difference in nature between the Church Temporal and the Church Eternal. The Muslims, as Malcolm X found to his considerable anger, were very much a temporal organization. The danger he posed was that he seemed on the point of linking Muslimism to the international Moslem movement. Briefly, he was forcing religious orthodoxy on a sect. On the national level, it appeared that he would break Muslim authoritarianism by infiltrating the movement with the dangerously independent middle class. He stood for orthodoxy, for reform, and for the heresy of inquiry. Finally, he offered the Black Muslims all the dangers of a program.

Nothing is more ridiculous than to elevate Malcolm X to the status of a Lumumba or martyr of his race. For one thing, comparison to the Congolese paranoiac would do him no honor. I think the following passage brings to bear what is meaningful in his life. He wrote this shortly before his assassination:

> Throughout my travels in the Muslim world, I have met, talked to, and even eaten with people who in America would have been considered "white"—but the "white" attitude was removed from their

minds by the religion of Islam. I have never before seen *sincere* and *true* brotherhood practiced by all colors together, irrespective of their color.

You may be shocked by these words coming from me. But on this pilgrimage, what I have seen, and experienced, has forced me to *re-arrange* much of my thought-patterns previously held, and to *toss aside* some of my previous conclusions. This was not too difficult for me. Despite my firm convictions, I have been always a man who tries to face facts, and to accept the reality of life as new experience and new knowledge unfolds it.[42]

The myth of Negro extremism is not served by this habit of mind. If so complicated a thing as a human life may be summarized it may be said that Malcolm X modified extremism itself. It is embarrassing to compare certain passages of *The Fire Next Time* with this, for Baldwin moves so easily with the current. Just at the time that some Negro intellectuals were attracted by the energies of racism, and others fantasied about changing the "power structure," Malcolm X returned to a simple but dangerous examination of the connection between extremism and the individual mind. We know that it was more than a gesture.

The extremism of James Baldwin and LeRoi Jones is integrated with their style and dependent on certain concepts now in vogue. It becomes very nearly a matter of literary criticism. Baldwin's use of the current "post-Christian" strategy was pretty well explored in a review of *The Fire Next Time* by Garry Wills.[43] The color issue became another issue entirely—as Wills noted, the idea was "that Christianity had done nothing for the Negro." Baldwin's point was not that Negroes were mistreated by whites but that white civilization was unfit to survive. Among other *obiter dicta* were deliverances on "the wave of history, the courage to change, the need to export our revolution." Our cultural guilt was to be measured by our passivity in regard to Spain and our activity in regard to Cuba. In short, the essay was informed by a kind of politics and guilt which were yoked somewhat forcibly to the issue at hand. Another review, by F. W. Dupee, was formidable on

---

42. *Autobiography of Malcolm X*, p. 45.

43. Garry Wills, "What Color is God?" *National Review* (May 21, 1963), pp. 408–417.

Baldwin's use of his own personification, "the Negro *in extremis,* a virtuoso of ethnic suffering, defiance and aspiration. His role is that of the man whose complexion constitutes his fate, and not only in a society poisoned by prejudice but, it sometimes seems, in general. For he appears to have received a heavy dose of existentialism; he is at least half-inclined to see the Negro question in the light of the Human Condition." [44] These attacks from both Right and Left seem accurate, and leave Baldwin little ideological space to defend. But there are other matters that may be taken up. *The Fire Next Time* is partly a neo-Reichian tract. The cause of Negroes is tied to that of sexuality; the evident ideal is not simply emancipation but genitality.

There is a certain equivocation on the subject, much as in *Another Country.* Baldwin proceeds in *The Fire Next Time* from a biographical sketch of his childhood involvement in the Baptist Church; the intention is to show that the problem of love is insoluble in Christian terms. A transfer is quickly made from Christian to American and from one kind of love to another. There is a powerful indeed admirable description of his religious anguish, but it is suddenly broken by this passage: "Yes, it does indeed mean something—something unspeakable—to be born, in a white country, an Anglo-Teutonic, antisexual country, black. You very soon, without knowing it, give up all hope of communion." [45] The burden seems intelligible, and the reader of Gabriel Marcel will agree with at least part of this. But the cant phrase "antisexual country"—could that be "another country"?—disturbs and distorts the tenor. The meaning is soon developed.

"One dare not speculate," writes Baldwin, "on the temperature of the deep freeze from which issue their brave and sexless little voices." This refers to the difficulty of jazz for the white man, but, in a characteristic expansion, it attaches to the quality of white life itself: "White Americans . . . suspect that the force is sensual, and they are terrified of sensuality and do not any longer understand it." These remarks are located somewhere between the

44. F. W. Dupee, "James Baldwin and the 'Man'," *New York Review of Books* (Special Issue, volume I, 1963), pp. 1–2.

45. *The Fire Next Time*, p. 44.

existential and the aesthetic. They are part of an argument—one did not think to see a Negro intellectual address himself to it—that Negroes are more highly sensual than whites. The fact that Baldwin dresses up this argument with shreds and patches of "communion" and "the force of life" does not really alter the case. What he is saying is that jazz is a more highly developed form than its white alternatives because it has roots in sexual feeling. It is therefore more "real"—and, because it is the art form of an oppressed minority, has more social value. The argument is familiar, as we see in Kerouac, Mailer, and Seymour Krim. LeRoi Jones writes in *Blues People* that Beat sensibility is connected to jazz, and Kerouac and Ginsberg in particular seem to link their capacities for feeling with the blues.[46] But the ability to love can reach a comic reduction—it was Krim who wrote that "my love of jazz and raging enslavement to sex came together and focused burningly on the colored girl." That discovery preceded another, which was that jazz could be rather intellectual, and Negro sexuality one of the few enterprises available for survival.[47]

The general position of Baldwin may be clarified by a passage in *Blues People*, ". . . the feeling of rapport between the jazz of the forties, fifties, and sixties with the rest of contemporary American art is not confined merely to social areas. There are aesthetic analogies, persistent similarities of stance that also create identifiable relationships." [48] The similarities of stance are certainly there in Baldwin. He has taken up a position first tentatively explored by the Beats, developed by Mailer, dogmatized by neo-Reichians both white and black. It is in essence a contempt for consciousness. The matter of racial character is a vehicle for Baldwin—what he is trying to assert in this essay, as in *Another Country*, is that sexuality is the supreme human mode. He is claiming for it not the power of pleasure but of civilization itself.

As Baldwin sees it, jazz is the vehicle of negritude—a performance which asserts the superiority of feeling and indeed of human capacity. That is why, in an essay devoted to racial injustice, it

46. LeRoi Jones, *Blues People* (New York, 1963), p. 233 ff.
. 47. Seymour Krim, "Ask for a White Cadillac," *Views of a Nearsighted Cannoneer* (New York, 1961), p. 45.
48. Jones, p. 233.

occupies such a defining position. Jones is quite right in seeing that jazz has "analogies . . . similarities . . . relationships" with other aspects of our creative culture It is one of the literary myths of this decade that the higher life of unconsciousness is incarnated by sex and explained by music. I suggest that this is Platonism in reverse.

Throughout *The Fire Next Time* this kind of reasoning appears and submerges. Again and again we are exposed to the idea that white civilization is *sexually* pathological. The whole relationship of Negroes and whites is reduced to one misconception, that the essential problem of the white is his inability to come to terms with himself sexually. This difficulty leads him to destroy the Negro, whom he perceives as having the sexual beauty and confidence lacking in himself. Of this several things may be said. It is first of all a reflection of Baldwin's own famous sexual dilemma. It refracts some of the more visible literary strategies of the decade, those which Leslie Fiedler and Norman Mailer connect to "the music of the orgasm." In short, the Negro of *The Fire Next Time* is not a social but a mythological figure. He does not think but only suffers. He has the enormous capacity to love which fascinates those who practice fiction. The weakness of this book is that it creates a figure instead of a person.

Jones has himself written on the subject with a good deal of rage. The central episode of *Dutchman*, the murder of a Negro by a white woman, is oriented around jazz and sex. The point is that the white understands neither, and kills the Negro who is an incarnation of both. It is a Reichian allegory. Perhaps the only thing that differentiates the hero from the villain in Jones' *The Slave* is that one is a potent Negro and the other—a university professor. The confusion is intentionally developed in Jones' essays. There are two fundamental purposes sex serves for him, an act of revenge by black upon white, and a kind of racial education. The first has been subject to such fakery by mass-cult psychology as to be simply unusable as a concept. This is part of the commercialism of Jones, his easy assimilation of conventions for the stage. The second purpose takes on the same shape for Jones as for Baldwin: "The white man has never reunderstood the sex act since the dissociation of childbirth was made. . . . The white man must fear things that are alive. . . Life and creation (of Life) are equally terrifying to him." [49] Jones is aware of the direction of his own analogies:

> But in the white man's sexual life is found the exact replica of his conscious, unconscious, social life. Reich has written about the repression of sexuality in the white man, and how this blocking of natural emission and other violent energies causes cancer and madness or white Americans. And this sexual energy is a dirtiness, an ecstasy, which always threatens the "order," i.e., "rationalism," the ahumane asexual social order the white man seeks with all his energies to uphold. [50]

The extension and trivialization of Jones' racial position is fairly clear. George Dennison's *Commentary* article, "The Demagogy of LeRoi Jones," observes that Jones does not speak for change, but for effect. [51] He is a perfect inversion of liberalism who addresses his rhetoric to a system of values traditionally open to his kind of totalitarian attack. On every issue, whether it is that of sexual restraint or racial injustice, he addresses himself to the guilt of liberalism—a guilt which exists because liberalism refuses to make the leap between what it is and what, given its doctrine, it might become.

Jones, then, exists only in relation to something else. What he calls The Theater of Destruction is, I think, the central metaphor for his work. His essays are enactments or perhaps the term should be autopsies. We are all aware that social issues have more than one form, the political-historical and what may be called the subjective form. Has it struck anyone how much Jones hates those who see things in terms of the first? What he says about Martin Luther King, James Baldwin, or Peter Abraham is pretty much the same as what he says about Whitey. One of his rhetorical questions is enlightening. He refers to the statements of Abraham and Baldwin on the racial barrier, and likens the latter to "the innocent white liberal made fierce by homosexuality. Again the

---

49. LeRoi Jones, "american sexual reference: black male," *Home*, pp. 227–232.

50. *Ibid.*, p. 233.

51. George Dennison, "The Demagogy of LeRoi Jones," *Commentary* (February, 1965), pp. 67–70.

*cry*, the spavined whine and plea of these Baldwins and Abrahams is sickening past belief. Why should anyone think of these men as individuals?" My own answer is, why not? But that is the kind of thing which would have the effect of translating ideology into reasoning. It would have the disadvantage of having to grant, say, to Baldwin, that what he says is worth listening to. It is interesting to see that the real things Jones dislikes are words like "sensitivity," "reason," "respectability." They are in his context all synonyms for thought. I suggested earlier in this chapter that racial extremism was not monolithic, and I meant by this that it could be broken down into components of religion in Malcolm X, Reichianism in James Baldwin, anti-liberalism in LeRoi Jones. As a structure of ideas it is almost incredibly complex. But it really is monolithic as an attitude. In the case of Jones, although compromised by the need to sell, it is a kind of universal negation. It is certainly not too much to say that he hates Negroes as much as whites. But the position requires a Satanic firmness which is not in his reach. It is a truism that destruction can only match what it acts on. Jones has chosen targets which are only of secondary importance—and he does not have the intellectual power to discover the big ones. He represents the ontological failure of extremism.

# LIBERALISM: ATTACK FROM THE LEFT

## The Totalitarian Liberal State

On the new left there are three interpretations of liberalism: corporate liberalism, conservative liberalism, and fascist liberalism. The further left one proceeds the more choric these interpretations appear. The last, with its attendant vocabulary, is of particular interest. Those who subscribe to it view liberalism as a conspiracy imposed by the old left and its former enemies. They are therefore hostile to the idea of political dialectic, and have little use for activists like Bayard Rustin and Michael Harrington who are willing to make their radicalism programmatic. It is customary for them to begin—and terminate—argument with the declaration that current American history is a recapitulation of the history of the

Third Reich. At the same time they are themselves passionately attached to totalitarian democracy of the "direct" or "*de facto*" kind, especially as it operates in such iconic cases as that of Cuba. Perhaps a brief review of the concept of fascist liberalism will be useful, if only for the sense it may generate of new left historicism. The subject is of course qualified by the irony that liberalism, in its crusade against the ogres of the right, furnished the semantic of fascism to those who now attack it.

There is some orchestration to the use of the fascist liberalism concept. It is sometimes put in the form of a metaphor and sometimes in that of elaborated argument. Yet it is at all times an expressive attitude and belongs to the realm of feeling. Here are some indications of the shaping of a new political vocabulary:

> The most hated government in the world today is the government of our country. In the remotest corner of the earth, the initials U.S.A., which once stood for hope, have replaced the crooked cross of Nazi Germany as the symbol of tyranny and death.[1]

> Vietnam is the Guernica, the Rotterdam, and the Lidice of the 1960s. Johnson to most of the world recalls Hitler, invoking "national honor" and anti-Communism to rationalize mass murder.[2]

> It is doubtful if the non-Jewish people of Germany were as well informed of the Nazi cruelties as the American people are of these obscenities in Vietnam. But like the Germans, whom we have been condemning for twenty-five years, we prefer not to dwell too long on such unpleasantnesses—nor to face up to the pattern they form when joined to American actions in Latin America and the Congo. The worst crimes of the Nazis took place under a crude fascist government and in the midst of the dislocations of a losing war. . . . Ours are being carried out against a background of domestic security.[3]

---

1. From the Constitution of the Progressive Labor Party. Quoted in *The New Radicals*, by Paul Jacobs and Saul Landau (New York, 1966), p. 188.

2. "A Statement From Leaders of the Vietnam Day Committee," Norman Mailer, *et al.*, *We Accuse* (Berkeley, 1965), p. 158. Used by permission of the publisher, Diablo Press.

3. "Liberalism in the Pursuit of Extremism," *Liberation* (February, 1965), 3. Used by permission.

There is a certain casualness about accuracy, but surely the important thing is the symbolic function of language as opposed to its historical use. When Norman Mailer implies that "Adolf Hitler's motives" are ours [4] and when M. S. Arnoni likens "intellectuals from the State Department" to "Eichmann's cold efficiency" [5] a new political habit is evidently in gestation.

Those who practice this historicism are or would be intellectuals. They are students, professors, writers, and bureaucrats of activism. Since they are men of a certain knowledgeability the question of their intentions seems to frame itself in strategic terms. One tends to reject the merely polemical—some theoretical purpose seems to be served by current insistence that liberalism is a form of fascism. One rejects also purely unself-conscious belief, which is not likely given the intellectual equipment of, say, Staughton Lynd. An example may be helpful. In *Studies on the Left* Warren Susman of Rutgers wrote of liberalism as economic fascism—although, to be sure, it was ready to assume political character:

> Let us face what now exists: A corporate state in serious economic trouble. Politically, it is clearly and simply a dictatorship, generally benevolent although afraid it might lose its power if it becomes too benevolent (cf., civil rights)—but a dictatorship clearly and distinctly. . . . This is as complete a dictatorship as ever existed in history. Hitler had no more power than John F. Kennedy—in fact he had less. So John F. Kennedy takes the Sudetenland (Cuba)—what will he want next? [6]

Ernst Nolte, in his history of fascism, has written of opinions like these that they form a category outside of mere history of ideas.[7] They are metaphors and intuitions: "A lie which the intellect sees for what it is but which is at one with the deeper motivations of life." Nolte refers to the famous article of Maurras on the suicide of Colonel Henry, an article which cannot be said so much to have resisted fact as to have transcended it. By the time Maurras had

---

4. *We Accuse*, p. 10.
5. *Ibid.*, p. 63.
6. Warren Susman, "The Radicalism of Exposure," *Studies on the Left*, III (1962–1963), pp. 72–73. Used by permission.
7. Ernst Nolte, *Three Faces of Fascism* (New York, 1966), pp. 57–58.

done, Henry was seen to have been executed by the Dreyfusards. This kind of lie is not strictly speaking propaganda: Like the legend of the stab in the back of the German army, it signifies what is really an intuitive agreement among those who subscribe to it. It is so resistant to demonstration as to have its improbability assert the limits of faith.

It is in fact an article of faith at present that the liberalism of the Sixties is a form of fascism. When the matter was brought to consciousness, as in the imbroglio over the statements of the Vietnam Day Committee, the result was to *satisfy* the true believers of the superiority of metaphor. The VDC movement, like other elements of the left, has been engaged in the discovery of its own ideology. In the course of this it has hesitated between the alternatives of metaphorical and literal belief—in the case of fascist liberalism between the kind of habit of mind displayed by Susman and a more intelligent if less honorable equivocation. The latter may be seen in this defense of the VDC: "Yes, one can compare Hitler and Johnson—or Stalin and Johnson. The comparisons are unfair— comparisons always are. We make them partly because language fails us." [8]

In outline, this is the way the matter developed, the VDC published a conclusion to the ceremonies at Berkeley whose purpose was to prove that "Liberalism can not solve our problems." The mode of this conclusion was analogical, which is a fact of some importance. There were "connections" established between Vietnam and Mississippi, Vietnam and the Watts riots, Vietnam and the FSM movement. There were analogies suggested between Johnson and Hitler, between the crimes before the Nuremburg tribunal, and those of liberal America. Some liberals objected, among them a group of Berkeley faculty who had previously supported the FSM. They stated that the "series of comparisons . . . of President Johnson with Hitler, or the present-day United States with Germany under the Nazis . . . constitutes a travesty of evident historical truth." [9] They argued analytically, and quite seriously demonstrated that the United States was not at all like

---

8. "Comment by David McReynolds," *Liberation* (November, 1965), p. 29. Used by permission.

9. *Liberation* (November, 1965), p. 20.

the Third Reich. In this they made themselves ridiculous and were superbly put-on by the response ("We Demand An Apology" [10]) of the VDC. The point was of course that the concept of fascist liberalism was not responsive to analysis since it was an intuitive metaphor.

This response, and the comments of Paul Goodman and David McReynolds,[11] were in the nature of those "higher considerations" of the old left written of so contemptuously by Robert Warshow. The VDC claimed that the unity of the left transcended matters of analysis; Goodman wrote that the sinking condition of America excused the vagaries of rhetoric; McReynolds, most interesting of all, wrote that the metaphor of fascism was *or could be* literal:

> I would pursue one point. The VDC bothered you because, in your view it was out of place to compare Hitler with Johnson, or Germany with the United States. Hitler came to power in the mid-thirties. It was not until several years had passed that he launched a war or began a persecution of the Jews. . . . How many hundreds of thousands of Jews or Poles had Hitler killed in the first several years of his regime? No, no of course one cannot compare Hitler with Johnson—Hitler moved more slowly toward murder.

On the new left this posture enjoys a certain respectability. Imbecile as it is, even the theoreticians support it. Staughton Lynd can argue that the assassination of President Kennedy proved that "the perspective for the coming period is fascism" [12] and James Weinstein, also a para-intellectual, can argue that "there are, indeed, many similarities between American society today and that of Germany in the years before and during Nazi rule." [13] It is notable that for Weinstein as for many on the left, Adolf Eichmann has assumed the status of a proto-liberal; the only part of Hannah Arendt's book that has been absorbed by the new left has been the enabling idea of cultural guilt. It allows the left to pursue analogy

---

10. *Ibid.*, pp. 22–25.

11. *Ibid.*, p. 25 ff.

12. Staughton Lynd, "Waiting for Righty: The Lessons of the Oswald Case," *Studies on the Left*, IV (1964), pp. 135–141. Used by permission.

13. James Weinstein, "Nach Goldwasser Uns?", *Studies on the Left*, IV (1964), pp. 59–64. Used by permission.

in a self-interested way: "Like so many American bureaucrats and military men, Eichmann emerges from Miss Arendt's account as a man of very limited ideological commitment. . . ." [14] There would appear to be some truth in the argument that the new left is anti-historical. Its famous dismissal of historical for moral ideology has had certain advantages, particularly in civil rights. But, applied to the realm of history itself, moral ideology has had a supremely anti-intellectual effect. In any case the function of the fascist liberalism metaphor is not intended to be analytical. It is a mode of manipulating history and making it manageable. History is for the new left not differentiated from other elements of life. It is perceived simply as offering the same opportunities as, say, university politics. Its attitude toward history can best be summed up by a remark on the Castro dictatorship—what matters is not "form" but "essence."

A second viewpoint is much less concerned with intuition and perhaps more closely related to the old radicalism. It attacks liberalism as a *de facto* form of conservatism, and for fascism substitutes oligarchy. This persuasion carries the sense of "power" to a point now familiar—it is of course dependent on C. Wright Mills for furnishing that definition. In *The Power Elite* Mills established for the new left an historical position which served two purposes: It attacked the idea of Liberalism As Social Action made famous by John Dewey and it accounted for the hostility of new to old left. Mills' "The Conservative Mood" is about conversion; it affirms that liberalism has resolved itself into its antithesis. Since the New Deal the great object of liberalism has been power, and that has been achieved by abandoning a revolutionary movement for a conservative bureaucracy. Liberalism has become in effect an agency of the right, "American Liberalism is thus readily made to sustain the conservative mood." [15] Mills' other writings offer a nascent theory of totalitarian liberalism. The famous "On the new left" [16] states that "the end of ideology" is not so much an intel-

14. *Ibid.*, p. 60.

15. C. Wright Mills, *The Power Elite* (New York, 1956), p. 336. Used by permission of the publisher, Oxford University Press.

16. C. Wright Mills, "On the new Left," *Studies on the Left*, I (1959), pp. 63–72. Used by permission.

lectual position as it is propaganda. It enables those in power to justify their status, since no alternative to their own ideology is presumed to have force or legitimacy. It is particularly useful to those *status quo* intellectuals who are the subject of "The Decline of the Left" and "Culture and Politics." In these essays Mills attempts to revive the thesis of Benda, or rather to approximate it; the new treason of the intellectuals consists not in their adherence to ideology but in their pursuit of power. In fact, Mills concludes, the new cultural cartel is made up of blocs of "political," "military," and "intelligentsia."

Those who follow Mills argue that representative democracy no longer works, since it has become the instrument of conservative liberalism. In the terms of Irving Horowitz "the consensual society" we now have is of the same order as "the coercive society" of Soviet Russia.[17] Sumner Rosen, who is fully equipped with the Millsian rhetoric of "power structure," "power system," and "establishment," writes that the "liberal establishment" is responsible for the perversion of "authority" and "power" in America.[18] In fact, it is an error to "construe the politics of the future as a struggle by moderate liberalism seeking to prevent itself from being overthrown by reaction." That argument is designed to disguise the partnership of liberalism and the right against radicalism.

The sense of liberalism as hidden conservatism is not restricted to the followers of Mills, although his vocabulary may be retained. According to the editors of *Liberation* "the liberal accepts the existing order and wants to exploit it."[19] In *Dissent* the commitment to democracy of official liberalism is described as "more abstract than real."[20] The argument of pluralism to which liberalism appeals is simply a rationalization, for its true commitment is to

---

17. Irving L. Horowitz, "The Unfinished Writings of C. Wright Mills: The Last Phase," *Studies on the Left*, III (1963), p. 14. Used by permission.

18. Sumner Rosen, "The Case for a Radical Politics," *Studies on the Left*, IV (1964), pp. 32–38. Used by permission.

19. "Tract for the Times," *Seeds of Liberation* (New York, 1964), p. 6.

20. William J. Newman, "Official Liberalism and National Nervousness," *Dissent* (Winter, 1962), pp. 40–45. Used by permission.

power. Liberalism is on the side of "the same power structure, the same class structure, which we now possess." In *Studies on the Left* the thesis is rephrased, "For the left to view the irrational right as the major threat to freedom or progress . . . is to follow . . . [an] ultimately fatal path. Twentieth century liberalism, insofar as it is not purely rhetorical, is a system of political ideas consciously developed to strengthen the system of large-scale corporate capitalism." [21] Distortion is the natural fate of this argument. Within SDS it is held that "the broad liberal consensus . . . has developed present American society into the most 'flexible of totalitarianisms,' paralyzing human activity by its dependence on welfare capitalism and the Cold War." [22] Perhaps the most visible of these accusations has been that of Carl Oglesby, whose address at the SANE March on Washington of 1965 was a public, symbolic break between old and new left. The subject was Vietnam, although the culture as a whole is intimated by other passages:

> The original commitment in Vietnam was made by President Truman, a mainsteam liberal. It was seconded by President Eisenhower, a moderate liberal. It was intensified by the late President Kennedy, a flaming liberal. Think of all the men who now engineer that war—those who study the maps, give the commands, push the buttons, and tally the dead: Bundy, McNamara, Rusk, Lodge, Goldberg, the President himself.
> They are not moral monsters.
> They are all honorable men.
> They are all liberals.[23]

What Oglesby calls Corporate Liberalism is the generative agency. It permits the articulation of pieties while protecting the interests of imperialism. Certain assumptions are involved. One is that the policy-making bureaucrat is a stockholder beneath the skin. A second is that liberalism functions in the modern state the way the Inquisition did in the feudal state. The illustration is Oglesby's—as far as he can see the role of liberalism is precisely the maintenance of orthodoxy. And his speech refers to the now generalized experience of the new left—it is about a conversion and an illumination.

21. "Editorial," *Studies on the Left* (Fall, 1962). Used by permission.
22. *The New Radicals*, pp. 36–37.
23. *Ibid.*, p. 257 ff.

It is an apologia of the new radical for no longer being the old radical. It has been written so many times in this century as to produce no shock but only recognition. The idea of totalitarian liberalism is as useful as it is widespread. Whether the society of the Sixties is called corporate, conservative, or fascist, whether the democracy it offers is called managed, consensual, or acquiescent, the effect is to nullify political legitimacy. The connection is fairly plain between the positions of anti-liberalism and "direct" democracy—the former identifies what the latter is intended to destroy. The advantages of the totalitarian liberalism theory are also plain, it raises the possibility that cultural *lacunae* do not evolve but are created. When Tom Hayden links "the Vietnam war, segregation, poverty and university paternalism," and absolves "Birchite generals" and rednecks in favor of "Democratic bureaucrats" and "affluent liberalism," he is going significantly beyond the rather piddling issue of the radical right which has so monopolized the attentions of liberalism.[24] For one thing, he is being intensely realistic—the right has a negligible influence on the culture at large and certainly exerts very little force on "poverty" and "Berkeley." More important, he is among those now constructing a new left sociology. It is quite superficial to believe that the new left is concerned with "issues"—although nothing is more common than to find this pseudo-theory invoked by those who should know much better. Issues are certainly mentioned, but the rather imaginative yoking of Vietnam, segregation, poverty, and Berkeley is really not empirical. It is indeed theoretical, for one of the purposes of the new left is to prove the exhaustion of our culture as we know it. I think there is a reason for the particularly moral attacks on liberalism, the metaphorical language, and the avoidance of that complexity which politics brings naturally to a discussion. Anti-liberalism has another, existential side. It is concerned really with values and not with issues. The concept of totalitarian liberalism is only the first step in a dialectic.

24. Tom Hayden, "The Ability to Face Whatever Comes," *The New Republic* (15 January 1966), pp. 16–18. Reprinted by permission of *The New Republic*, copyright 1966, Harrison-Blaine of New Jersey, Inc.

# The Existential Liberal State

There is a kind of language in use on the new left with a specifically existential quality. It does not refer itself directly to either Camus, Sartre, or Marcel. Nor is its use so much intellectual as ideological. The function of this language is to oppose human values to ideas, principles or institutions conceivably hostile to them. The word "human" exemplifies this language. With its derivates—"humanist," "humane"—it is generally offered as a conclusion obviating the need for further analysis. That a thing should serve human needs allows it the status of a philosophical truth.

This language is problematic. When apprehended as a metaphor it often demands literalness. When Nat Hentoff argues for "spontaneity" [25] or James Baldwin speaks for "the force of life" [26] the phrases have to do with sensate vitality but the context is social and indeed political. An argument is implied: that there is the kind of organic sameness of individual and society which obligates the latter in a specific way. The public realm, which is in fact the subject attacked by this language, is held responsible emotionally. As moral referenda, phrases like "humanize," "sensitive," "intimate," and "passion" (used by Arnold Sachar to connote the ideal *polis*[27]) bring a necessary dimension to discourse. It would be undesirable for public life to lose consciousness of their meaning. As political referenda their use is somewhat dangerous: "In this dreary contest, then, there is needed some indication of empathy, passion, accord. But . . . one becomes sick. The spirit is drained. Hope is weakened. One sometimes feels an inevitable loss. One can almost imagine the sense behind the genocidal Cold War of the governments and their ridiculous hydrogen bombs. But I am determined not to let this sickness overtake me." [28] The subject is evidently the alienation of the healthy individual from the diseased state, but

---

25. Nat Hentoff, "Is There a New Radicalism?", *Partisan Review* (Spring, 1964), p. 188.

26. James Baldwin, *The Fire Next Time* (New York, 1963), p. 57, p. 111.

27. Arnold Sachar, "To Live as Men," *Seeds of Liberation* (New York, 1964), pp. 371–379.

28. *Ibid.*, p. 373.

the effect is to blur some important distinctions. There are many words for the bomb, but none of them includes the term that is offered. And there are many terms for the Cold War, none of which, for the sake of honesty and our lives, confuses its existence with our intentions. The point is not that life and death are trivial, but that no social discourse is directly framed by the alternatives they represent. It would be splendid if, in fact, one could make love and not war.

The existential vocabulary has been harnessed to a particular political wagon. It is designed to prove that the liberal state is inhospitable to human life. A distinction—and I think it is a false one—is being made between people and things. According to the editors of *Liberation* the early greatness of liberalism resided in its "humaneness" and its present decadence resides in its inapplicability to "private life and behavior." [29] According to Carl Oglesby, who has served as President of SDS, those whose "commitment to human value is unconditional" will abandon the liberal idea that "statements will bring change . . . or that policy proposals will bring change." [30] According to Tom Hayden, liberalism needs a "humanist reformation" because the society it has formed "is a paralyzed one, in which humane promises go unrealized." [31] The culture is, he states, "impotent" and in some psychological way unsatisfactory. Such statements appear with great frequency on the new left, and complement its political attacks on the consensual liberal state.

To an extent the statements reflect the real and honorable concern of the new left with the problems of individuals, particularly the Negroes and the poor. They are sensibly concerned with what happens to men in a technological society. But there are other aspects to this humanist style. The entire problem of new left sexual theory resolves itself around this, because the frequent connection of sexuality and politics is dialectical The two are linked in such a way as to presuppose that a satisfactory orgasm may be attained only in the humanist condition. It is only fair to say that the Pop Left alone takes this with entire seriousness. But even the more responsible have taken the position that emotional needs have

---

29. "Tract for the Times," *op. cit.*, p. 6.

30. *The New Radicals*, p. 266.

31. Hayden, *op. cit.*, p. 18.

political forms. The state, since it is a kind of larger organic version of the individual, is held to have an existential character. To take a familiar example, in the case of Cuba there is a common argument that the vitality of government transcends issues which are not so directly "human." The passions are more important than the policy. Such an essay as LeRoi Jones' celebrated "Cuba Libre" takes account of little more than the feeling of Fidelistas, and goes to astonishing lengths to show that the quality of human responses to Castro is self-justifying. The point about existential politics is not that its adherents, like the old left, would forgive authority and allow it to "skip a stage" of parliamentary democracy in order to develop the Real Thing. The stages have no meaning in themselves; what matters is intensity of experience within the state.

If the source of new left thought on totalitarian liberalism is C. Wright Mills, the principal sources of the idea of existential liberalism are Paul Goodman, Norman Mailer, and Herbert Marcuse. Mailer's Great Society speech for the VDC began with the homage to alienation which is by now ritual: "But one must speak first of alienation, that intellectual category which would take you through many a turn of the mind in its attempt to explain that particular corrosive sensation so many of us feel in the chest and the guts so much of the time—that sense of the body growing empty within, of the psyche pierced by a wound whose dimensions keep opening." [32] After this, a certain amount on cancer and depersonalization, which are in the way of being hobbies for Mailer. Like his *Presidential Papers* this essay is concerned with what he calls "essence"—the fundamental human material altered by politics. To be brief, Mailer's position is an exaggerated but not distinct version of new left doctrine. All that which is fully human, which discloses to itself the sense of human identity through sexual experience, is at the mercy of political mechanization. The Great Society is merely a synonym for the Power Elite—with this difference, the former is desexualized and incapable of responding to things human. Its primary concern is with things financial and mechanical, and to the end of promoting national profit all its energies burn. One of its objects is to make fully human existence impossible; hence its attitude toward the existential left.

---

32. "The Great Society?", *We Accuse*, p. 15.

Goodman and Marcuse, both inconceivably better thinkers, have somewhat less to say about the conspiratorial nature of the consensual society. They do write that the conditions of life at present are existentially intolerable. For Goodman and the editors of *Liberation* the liberal state is the repressive state. For example, the matter of pornography has reverberations which are expectedly cultural and unexpectedly political. Goodman's "Pornography and the Sexual Revolution" [33] conceives of the state as the ultimate form of repressive super-ego. Its combination of "police, administrators, and lower courts" (he may well add the Supreme Court in view of the recent *Eros* decision) destroys that more sensual feeling which "would ennoble all our art and perhaps bring some life to the popular culture." The problem of the liberal state is its political attitude toward what is "real" and "sexual"—it refuses to incorporate sexual relativism into custom or law. Freedom, in other words, is seen to derive neither from the rights of property nor from those of man, but from unlegislatable sexual needs. Insofar as government does not acknowledge these it is tyrannous. If this fails to convince it indicates at least why Caryl Chessman was a culture hero of the left.

The clearest statement of Goodman's position is in "My Psychology as a 'Utopian Sociologist'." [34] He differentiates the existential absurdity of our society from that of classical existentialism. French theoreticians have mistakenly concentrated on extreme and catastrophic situations—the real meaning of existential sociology is to be found in everyday life. The statement that follows is of crucial importance to the new left theory of human relations, "Both my animal and spiritual values are unquestionably worth while and justified." If classical existentialism is metaphysical and intellectual, new left existentialism is material and sexual. And the latter has a kind of certainty which permits it to deal freely with absolutes. It leads quite naturally to a theory of social displacement. The universities, which are central objects in Goodman's thought, are reclassified as places of "new," "revolutionary," and "humane" studies. Their purpose is not so much intellectual as moral—and

---

33. Paul Goodman, *Utopian Essays and Practical Proposals* (New York, Random, 1964), pp. 49–69. Copyright, 1951, © 1955, 1958, 1959, 1960, 1961, 1962, by Paul Goodman; copyright, 1950, by Arts & Science Press; copyright, 1952, by Complex Press.

indeed the last term is a recurrent one in Goodman's application of the existential to the social. His "Crisis and New Spirit" [35] centers on the new student attitudes toward sexuality, and suggests that radical freedom is a *sine qua non*. The university may attain a higher and more moral status not by imposing on individuals the Aristotelian rules of middle-class behavior, but by signifying assent to the revolution. Sexuality is not precisely an issue subject to negotiation—and here the experience of the FSM at Berkeley is clarified—but a value. The new left students "quote Wilhelm Reich. They seem to want the university to *declare* for the sexual revolution."

The academic liberalism outlined by Seymour Martin Lipset and familiar to all those who teach has for a long time been regarded as progressive—far more so than trustees and taxpayers would like. For the new left academic liberalism is hopelessly reactionary. The issue is not simply that academics are hypocrites who refuse to radicalize the structure of power at the university, although that is a donkey well beaten. As Goodman and his followers see it the matter involves the existential failure of universities. Academics represent the desexualized middle class, and make it impossible for the student to engage in real "human action" or "community." Goodman's view of the university is quite orthodox so far as the new left is concerned: It is a paradigm of outer society and a servant to its values. In existential terms the university (which is the womb of Official Liberalism) is simply an agency of repressiveness. It prefers to ignore real intellectual freedom, which is conceived of primarily as a sexual liberation. It is "Henry Miller, Genet, and so forth, who have taught acceptance of one's experience as it is, whatever it is, without regard for official values or conventional norms." The burden of Goodman's thought then is that human values are not specifically intellectual values. Sexuality becomes a political force for two reasons: Those who assert it as an ultimate value have a clearer insight into reality than those who repress it; and those who practice sexual behavior opposed to norms and conventions are in fact experiencing freedom in its highest sense. As insights these are acceptable. As revelations they leave something to be desired.

---

34. *Ibid.*, pp. 110–118.
35. *Ibid.*, pp. 274–289.

The most sustained argument on the "new totalitarianism" is that of Herbert Marcuse. His *One-Dimensional Man* is essentially a study of "the Welfare State [as] a state of unfreedom." [36] Marcuse writes from a Marxian and Freudian foundation, and it is to his work that the new left turns for a justification of its sense of alienation. The liberal Welfare State is perceived by Marcuse as an essentially ideological state; its ultimate aim is to liquidate human, sexual responses by absorbing them into a kind of pluralism which would make all differentiations meaningless. Both Dwight MacDonald and Irving Howe have remarked that rebellion is easily absorbed by society—it is really sought masochistically. Marcuse's sense of artistic rebellion is that it has been rendered harmless by a public only too pleased to be emotionally violated. The only real satisfaction offered by society is in fact sadistic and involves the pleasures of imperialistic war. It is unfortunate that Marcuse should adopt the terminology of Fred Cook, and even allow that Cook's manic idea of the Warfare State has any basis in fact.

Marcuse conceives that erotic energies are directly affected by the culture—not in the sense of Goodman, who argues that repression is consciously imposed by the agencies of legal and moral authority, but in ways that are less conscious. What he calls the universe of libidinous cathexis is reduced in the Welfare-Warfare state, or perhaps the term should be evaporated: sexual feelings are applied to mechanical rather than human objects; polymorphous eroticism has fewer objects of pleasure; sexuality becomes desublimated. On the last Marcuse is particularly obsessed. He argues that sexuality as it is represented in art is "absolute, uncompromising, unconditional," and that this reflects the simple truth that it is beyond morality and the Reality Principle. In this culture, when sexuality is either represented or experienced, it takes the form of an obscenity rather than a truth. Thus far Marcuse is not substantially different from Norman O. Brown. His political extrapolations make the difference. Sexual desublimation—taking the pleasure out of bodily experience and imposing

---

36. Herbert Marcuse, *One-Dimensional Man* (Boston, 1964), pp. 1–83. Reprinted by permission of the Beacon Press; copyright © by Herbert Marcuse.

the Reality upon the Pleasure Principle—is a form of conditioning. He calls this "institutionalized desublimation," and argues that it is "a vital factor in the making of the authoritarian personality of our time."

Those who conspire to desexualize the human personality are in charge of the liberal culture, the publishers, politicians, and corporationists who form the Establishment. There is a great parallelism, ". . . just as this society tends to reduce, and even absorb opposition . . . in the realm of politics and higher culture, so it does in the instinctual sphere." It is this parallelism—I think it would be agreed that it has the insubstantial form of an analogy— that fortifies the attitude of the new left on the evils of existential liberalism Once again we find the comparison of Eichmann to the de-ideologized liberal: in the consensual state there is no need for *political* guilt. Liberalism, Marcuse suggests, has in fact absorbed "the benefits of the Nazi scientists, generals, and engineers." The only values insisted upon in this culture are technological. If our sexual feelings are repressed in order to destroy individuality our "technological rationality" is stimulated in order to make us creatures of the state. It is the government, abetted by *Time* and the Rand Corporation, which is behind this suppression. This nonsensical view of culture as conspiracy underlies New Left dogmatics today.

Marcuse insists that the totalitarian element in the welfare state is not metaphorical. Sexuality liberated from its instinctual objects is a utilizable social force. It leads to massive cultural despair, which in turn "lends itself easily to political mobilization; without room for conscious development, it may become the instinctual reservoir for a new fascist way of life and death." For the left theoreticians of the late Fifties and early Sixties the Radical Right was almost exclusively the object of apprehension. Things are now changed, the Radical Right has been treated to the indifference it deserves, and liberalism is now the fish in the barrel. The hard ground of political dialectic has given way to the more suppositious terrain of the "human" question. It is needless to say that, given current cultural fashions, this has attracted more attention than many a saner issue.

The effect of this analytic can be seen in the operational writing of the new left. The *Dissent* symposium of 1962, "The Young

Radicals," [37] devotes a significant amount of time to discussing questions of "energies"—in the essay of Roger Hagan these "energies" are contrasted to the futile "endless theological disputation" of the old left. The premise is that the old Left is concerned with form, and the new left with the saving essence. Jeremy Larner is more specific vis à vis the opposition of doctrine and feeling: "As for old socialists . . . their limitations as people seem disastrous, and frustrate me insofar as they are my own. They appear to be tedious, tired of themselves, full of self-hate, and chained to an idealism so abstract that it precludes all love of life." This involves something more than the generational conflict, or the hostility of activist for dogmatist. Two systems of value are quite consciously being compared. One is intellectual, hence bound to the complexities of programs and politics. The other is existential, and eventually metaphysical, "the infinite visions of *possibility*" of which Larner orates have their equivalent in what used to be called antinomianism. That which is done and thought is secondary to what is felt. And it is justified by standards not answerable to the merely phenomenal order. When the mood is expressed by Staughton Lynd—"the revolutionary upsurge from Cuba to China seems to me wonderfully hopeful. . . . Perhaps we can help them most precisely by the richness and passion we can bring to creating our own synthesis"—there is a sense that politics has surrendered completely to vitalism. [38]

The remarkable histories of fascism which have been published since the war have had few readers on the new left. The work of Arendt, Bullock, Nolte, and Talmon—to say nothing of the writing of Crane Brinton—have been exceptional in their analysis of existential politics. One assumes that there is no need to go into their writing, but only to remind ourselves that the totalitarian impulse has fed on such politics. "Human" considerations have overridden all others, and have eventually overridden the truth itself. Perhaps the characteristic syndrome of totalitarianism has been the primary assumption that "community" of a mystical order is being threatened, and the consequent argument that human rights of a more basic nature than those merely constitutional or legal or cultural must be reasserted.

37. *Dissent* (Spring, 1962), pp. 129–163. Used by permission.
38. Cf. comments by Lewis Coser, *Dissent* (Spring, 1962), pp. 158–162.

## 6. The New Left (II)

# PROBLEMS OF IDEOLOGY

## Old and New Left

There is an *embarras de richesse* in making distinctions between old and new left. We are invited to see those distinctions as operating between revolutionaries and conservatives, activists and theoreticians, old and young. These and other dichotomies—Marxism and empiricism, isolation and permeation—are authentic but perhaps too simple. It may be best to observe the dialogue of old and new left, a dialogue which is now rather less diplomatic than promised by the beginning of the decade.

The prevailing tone of old left vis à vis new is irony tempered by admonition. The essay of Irving Howe in *Dissent* is representative of this mode.[1] It places the new left, or part of it, as a modern form of enthusiasm. Howe's essay, like the essays of Hal

1. Irving Howe, "New Styles in 'Leftism'," *Dissent* (Summer, 1965), pp. 295–323. Used by permission.

Draper and Michael Harrington,[2] is written from the position of
the intellectual; its sense of discipline as well as its tone, its allegiance to history and grasp of probability define at once the loyalties
of the old left and its distance from the new. The accomplishment
of Howe has been to chart the fragmented universe of the new left
and to give some sense of its cultural attitude and style. It has for
some time been apparent that a style as well as a position distinguishes the new left—in writing about this style from the conservative point of view Jeffrey Hart suggests that the actual
emotional object of "revolutionary manners" is the expression of
resentment toward the community at large.[3] In writing about
these manners from the liberal point of view William Petersen described them as Castroite and intimated their tendency toward
nihilism.[4] From the democratic socialist point of view Bayard
Rustin decried their "existential subjectivism"[5] and Howe himself
wrote of a "rigid anti-style" dependent on the pleasures of shock-
ing. As seen from the right—and this includes the liberal left—the
new style defines the difference.

In a phrase widely resented by his subjects Howe wrote of the
new "kamikaze radicalism . . . white Malcolmism . . . black
Maoism." Ideology and intellectual positions seemed to him subor-

2. Hal Draper, "In Defense of the 'New Radicals'," *New Politics*
IV (Summer, 1965), pp. 5–28; Michael Harrington, "Is There a New
Radicalism?", *Partisan Review* (Spring, 1965), pp. 194–205; *ibid.* (Sum-
mer, 1965), pp. 366–372.

3. Jeffrey Hart, *The American Dissent* (New York, 1966), pp.
131 ff. Cf. Bruce Payne, "SNCC: An Overview Two Years Later," *The
New Student Left*, Mitchell Cohen and Dennis Hale, eds. (Boston,
1966), pp. 86 ff. Payne, a former member of SNCC, writes that it
"is capable of heaping great abuse upon, and treating as its greatest
enemies, those with whom it is in only minor disagreement." He gives
as an example of "the constant attack on middle-class values" an excerpt
from a SNCC letter: "we crap on the clean antiseptic decent middle-
class image. It is that decency we want to change, to 'overcome.'"

4. William Petersen, "What's Left at Berkeley?", *Columbia University Forum* VIII (Spring, 1965), pp. 39–44.

5. Bayard Rustin, "The New Radicalism," *Partisan Review* (Fall,
1965), pp. 526–542.

dinate to personal style, and it was that style, of speech, dress, demeanor, which expressed the impotence of new radicals. The central point of his argument is that those who would reform society must be part of it. If his program is coalitionism his mode is pragmatism, what has, on the intransigent left, been unflatteringly called *Realpolitik*. Those who abandon the social dialogue—"Ideologues" and "Desperadoes"—have carried radicalism to a cul-de-sac. The former were prefigured by Malcolm X and are caricatured by LeRoi Jones. Malcolm X never attempted to put his ideas into programs and Jones, the "pop-art guerilla warrior," simply has no conception of programs. The desperadoes are the militant alienated, whose condition has passed from an affliction to a value. They live in that world of social myth which may be the principal imaginative construction of Norman Mailer. The composite type, granted such a one, is as much attracted by sensation as ideology. Drugs, sexual behavior *à la outrance*, sick comics who say the words in nightclubs that are iconized at universities, these are essential to the life-style. But it is rarely remarked, Howe notes, that the lifestyle is quickly absorbed by mid-cult; the bourgeoisie engages in happy complicity with those who try to rape it. A useful remark by Trotsky is adduced—the writer who thought to frighten the bourgeoisie by making scenes discovered that the bourgeoisie was delighted, it adored scenes.

Howe writes of another aspect of style too little observed. There is on the new left *"a vicarious indulgence in violence, often merely theoretic and thereby all the more irresponsible."* Thus far, in the civil rights sector of The Movement, violence has been principally on the side of the state, although in the North riot has been elevated to the status of rebellion. There are those who claim violence as a value—whether, as in the cases of Robert Williams and William Epton, as a precipitate of revolution or, in the case of others, as an instrument, threat, or apocalyptic vision. Bayard Rustin's comment on such a vision, that of Staughton Lynd, is worth remarking. The demonstration of Vietnam Day in Washington impelled Lynd to write "it seemed that the great mass of people would simply flow on through and over the marble buildings, that our forward movement was irresistibly strong, that had some been shot or ar-

rested nothing could have stopped that crowd from taking possession of its government. Perhaps next time we should keep going." [6]
This, Rustin saw correctly, was merely ideological language for a
*coup d'état.* One suspects that Lynd was speaking metaphorically,
or hopes so; the threat of violence from the new left is about as
material as from the ineffably ridiculous Minute Men.[7] Even after
the barricades were raised at Berkeley, the affair reached its climax
when Mario Savio bit a policeman in the leg. Emphasis should be
on the "theoretic" violence remarked by Howe, and on what I
should call the Robespierre syndrome, an attitude of furious morality which expresses itself in absolute terms. If those to the right of
the new left are in fact fascist, totalitarian, and otherwise involved
in cultural treasons; if the only adequate comparisons to be made
are those between liberals and Eichmanns; then it would appear
that, given power, those who sense the crime would devise the
punishment. There is after all a point where argument ceases to be
metaphorical, and the intense strain in new radical thought centering on the crimes of liberalism would seem to demand a fitting
punishment. This is the violence which might be noted; it is
couched in rhetoric of an absolute and moralizing kind which
makes demands only too familiar to our century. Violence, in other
words, may be dialectical, at least in its preliminary form. It is really
what many on the new left are proposing, whether it takes the
form of rhetorical fury, of Lynd suggesting that demonstrations
become revolutions, or of Marcuse urging that the right be forcibly suppressed.[8] The dialogue of the left comes more and more
on this issue to resemble that of Cleon and the sausage-seller.

Hal Draper's attack on the new style proceeds from different
grounds but is no less obdurate:

> Berkeley was treated to a costumed charade on the meaning of
> this type in a strange interlude at its Vietnam Day Rally on
> October 15, when, in the course of serious political attacks on
> U.S. foreign policy, the novelist Ken Kesey came on, in army

6. *Ibid.*, p. 536.
7. For a view that takes seriously new left violence see Phillip
Luce, *The New Left* (New York, 1966), pp. 103–118, *passim.*
8. Herbert Marcuse, Barrington Moore, Jr., Robert Paul Wolff,
*A Critique of Pure Tolerance* (Boston, 1966), pp. 108 ff.

garb with helmet, to deride the previous speakers for discussing the Vietnam war politically and to show how it should be done. His contribution consisted essentially of repeating "Fuck it" with great emphasis, in-between playing the harmonica.

Comparisons are legion—Bob Dylan accepting the Emergency Civil Liberties Award, Norman Mailer immortalizing John Kennedy as the man with *cojones*. LeRoi Jones being interviewed by *Esquire*. The hip left is hypnotized by gesture: suspicious of coalition, contemptuous of their old left predecessors, fascinated by an idea of the moral while they live in the world of the political, its protagonists represent a withdrawal from reality into style. Indeed, according to Draper, style is an alternative to ideology, and an excluding one at that. The point of his argument is that the new left has come to the time of decision. Ahead lies either a series of ever less meaningful exhibitions or a systematic strategy and form.

The style is based upon an ethic, and the old left has been alert to the religious element in the thought of its successors. The term "mysticism" was used to good purpose by Michael Harrington, not without sympathy, "as disestablishmentarians, the young radicals . . . identify precisely with the *lumpen*, the powerless, the maimed, the poor, the criminal, the junkie. And there is a mystical element in this commitment which has nothing to do with politics. By going into the slum, they are doing penance for the sins of affluence." [9] Harrington remarks the same kind of moral dilemma in these circumstances as does Draper vis à vis style, that is that the intention is of more consequence than the effect. When the new radical shares the life of the poor it sometimes does not matter whether the community organization works or not. There is indeed a fear of success based on the suspicion that the oppressed will be integrated into the corruption of culture. Harrington sees mysticism as a strength morally but a weakness politically; it is really an obstacle to discussion, strategy, organization. These are necessary "if the conflict of mysticism and militancy is to be resolved. For if the poor are seen as Dostoevskian peasants whose

9. Michael Harrington, "The Mystical Militants," *Thoughts of the Young Radicals* (New York, 1966), pp. 65–73. Used by permission of *The New Republic*.

beauty is their suffering, then politics and the inevitable alliances with others is a contamination; but if they are to be a social force, then coalition is a necessity."

Howe argues for coalition, Draper for ideology, Harrington for programs. Their respondents prefer an attitude over such purposiveness. For them the old left represents a classical failure of nerve, and they prefer to draw their own strength from other altars. There is a substantial literature on the hiatus between old and new left, part of that literature of disappointment which characterizes the decade. In attacking Bayard Rustin, Norm Fruchter refused to admit that the "subjective" new left was disabled by its style and ethic.[10] These were precisely the source of its abilities, and those "charged with elitism, subjectivism, and arrogance" were in fact equipped to a far better degree to cope with reality than those who are disabled by ideas. As for mysticism, Fruchter prefers the "transcendence" of new left totalism to the corrupt *Realpolitik* of the organizers. Harrington uses the idea of mysticism, Fruchter of transcendence, and David Bazelon, forced also into quasi-religious terminology, surveys the "idealism," "piety," and "moralism" of the new radicals. But the religious apparatus, he notes, is as common to old as to new left. It was the Marxist idea of socialism that was once "enshrined" on the left, and a system of ideas rather than feelings that had the place of dogma. His conclusion, like virtually all such conclusions on the part of the old left, is ironic and ambivalent:

> They come from the pacifist tradition, and other remnants of Christian idealism. A lesser tradition? One that we were raised to believe Marx had laid low long ago? You betcha. Suckers for another Popular Front gang-shag? You betcha. So what should we do about it? Weep, brother, weep.[11]

If the old left finds that the new is somewhat more sectarian than is politically desirable the new left sees in the old a kind of apostasy. It is not merely that the old left is dogmatic in orientation

---

10. Norm Fruchter, "The New Radicalism," *Partisan Review* (Winter, 1966), pp. 34–43.

11. David Bazelon, "The 'New Radicalism'," *Dissent* (Autumn, 1965), pp. 484–486. Used by permission.

encumbered by ideas as troublesome as anti-communism, but that the old left has become the liberal left. The attack on liberalism from the new left necessarily includes the old. Howe notes that the militants make increasingly clear their distance not only from Lionel Trilling and Sidney Hook but from Martin Luther King and Bayard Rustin. Draper makes even clearer their distance from such as Howe himself; it is "the odor of decayed radicalism" which he perceives in the ideological persons of Howe, Hook, and even such latter-day leftists as Tom Kahn and Robert Pickus. The decayed radicals are the objects of Draper's attack on behalf of the new left; "what enrages Howe," he concludes, "is the new-radicals' far-from-vague enmity against the Establishment, including the Establishment liberals (the living ones), including the lib-lab coalition leaders who are today truckling to the Establishment."

The great theme running through new left attacks on the old left is that of the treason of the intellectuals. Hook and Trilling have compromised themselves by their anti-communism; Howe, Harrington and Rustin have become members of the establishment. On other fronts, other accusations. According to Sidney Lens, the new left is the product of a discontinuity in American radicalism. The old left declined not because of McCarthyism but because of its own vulnerability. "It was a false estimate of the future, a narrow and outmoded Marxist projection of the American economy, which doomed the Old Left and created the vacuum which the New Left now tries to fill." [12] Finally, the lengthy explanation of new left hostility by Nat Hentoff in the *Partisan Review* symposium. "Is There a New Radicalism?" centered conclusively on the sins of the fathers.[13] It was Hentoff's contention the old left is not ready to move beyond meliorism. It has been compromised in labor by the notorious post-war conservatism of the unions; it has been compromised in civil rights because the leadership in that movement has chosen coalition over purity; it has been compromised most bitterly of all by those who have surrendered to

12. Sidney Lens, "The New Left—and the Old," *The Progressive* (June, 1966), pp. 19–24.

13. Nat Hentoff, "Is There a New Radicalism?", *Partisan Review* (Spring, 1965), pp. 183–193.

the attractions of the Democratic Party. Hentoff's piece—later heavily criticized by Michael Harrington and Stephen Rousseas—was based in part on a stupendous irrelevance the source of which he identifies as U Thant. It is that the kind and scale of resources that a nation determines to have is what that nation can have; the only problems are decision and allocation. That this is economically absurd is no more obvious than that it is morally instrumental; if reform is only a matter of allocation then the guiltiest nation on earth must be the United States. It is an enabling proposition, one which permits the new left to view human activity as mensurable, controllable, subject to usefully simplistic ideas of guilt and innocence.

Hentoff is somewhat more convincing when he analyzes the difference in modes between old and new left. He makes a necessarily sharp distinction between new left activists and *enragés*—between the preaching of Baldwin and fire-eating of Jones and those who involve themselves in welfare, housing, unions, bureaucracies. The activist radicals are thoroughly involved in the problems of community. It is they who man the live-in projects and fight the battles of welfare, who contact alderman and wait patiently for City Hall machinery to turn. These activists are no longer in sympathy with the *enragés*—nor do they have patience "with those older utopians who are not interested in politics." Their interests are political rather than ideological. "Retired radicals" and "utopian rhetoricians" strike them as being simply frivolous. They view the old left, in short, as prisoners in a library.

## Ideology

The decade opened with the proposed end of ideology in the West.[14] According to Daniel Bell, the radical tradition had reached the point of exhaustion, for questions of substance no longer

---

14. Daniel Bell, *The End of Ideology* (New York, 1960).

evoked truly divisive responses in the West. The ideologue as a figure of passion—that figure remarked by Benda as betrayer of the intellectual cause—no longer had a field in which to operate. History itself had denied him; the corruption of ideals by the one-party state proved that the old ideologies had lost their truth. The new radicalism was at the beginning of the decade in an invidious situation. "One finds, at the end of the fifties, a disconcerting caesura. In the West, among the intellectuals, the old passions are spent. The new generation, with no meaningful memory of these old debates, and no secure tradition to build upon, finds itself seeking new purposes within a framework of political society that has rejected, intellectually speaking, the old apocalyptic and chiliastic visions." The play of radical ideas in the Sixties has been around this subject; it is not too much to say that the central intellectual issue of the new left is the validity of ideology, indeed its very identity.

Both old and new left reacted strongly to Bell's argument, as did the new conservatism. Henry Aiken read in the theory simply the willingness of its author to accommodate himself to our illiberal culture.[15] To grant that ideologies were no longer significantly different was to take a position hostile to those intellectuals who sought to modify Western political structures—and to intimate that their peculiarly *moral* tone was simply an excess of rhetoric. Bell's position was seen as a form of mock-pragmatism based on nothing more than indecision; his pluralism was simply a device which permitted him to denigrate those on the left whose passions and truthfulness were authentic. The representative position of Bell is that of the moderate left; no matter how qualified his responses to this argument he was still cast in the role of Judas. Yet his analysis of modern radical rhetoric seems to me to be honest and acute—he objects to the moralistic mode, to the excess and overstatement, to the verbal fetishism that is so often cultivated. His distaste for anti-establishmentarianism, an awkward but necessary term, seems based on fact. Perhaps the best evidence for his position is that the new left has gravitated inexorably toward the "establishment" in its successful attempts at social reform. He represents, in short, the

15. Henry Aiken, "The Revolt Against Ideology," *Commentary* (April, 1964), pp. 29–39.

case of the moderate left; while keeping in mind the need for change that position asserts "the commitment to action must proceed from the ethic of responsibility." [16]

The statement is something like a red flag to a bull. Perhaps the most famous antithesis was generated by C. Wright Mills:

It is no exaggeration to say that since the end of World War II, smug conservatives, tired liberals and disillusioned radicals in Britain and the United States have carried on a weary discourse in which issues are blurred and potential debate muted; the sickness of complacency has prevailed, the bi-partisan banality flourished. . . . the fashion I have in mind is the weariness of many NATO intellectuals with what they call "ideology," and their proclamation of "the end of ideology." [17]

The passage is from Mills' "On the New Left," which, on the subject of ideology at least, has become *Das Kapital* of the present radicalism. The argument of Mills has been accepted with some qualifications. His main points ought to be outlined if only in order to recognize them as they reappear in new radical writing: (1) The "end of ideology" is essentially a strategem of liberalism to attack Marxism; (2) its reasonableness is in reality the complacent acceptance of the corporate liberal establishment; (3) it assumes that great issues no longer agitate the West, thereby ignoring the legitimacy of new left criticism; (4) it is principally the self-image of a group of exhausted academic intellectuals; (5) it masks the complicity of these intellectuals in the crimes of their culture. Mills' conclusion has become familiar as the *raison d'être* of the student left, that is, if ideology, far from being dead, is on the verge of a new birth, then its "immediate, radical agency" will be the left intelligentsia. It is from this point that the debate on the ideology of the new left takes its origin.

Shortly after the essay by Mills appeared the question of what ideology to assume was raised. David Riesman wrote in 1962 that those beliefs then in evidence were unsatisfactory: "Among the

16. "Ideology—A Debate," *Commentary* (October, 1964), pp. 69–76.
17. C. Wright Mills, "On the New Left," *Studies on the Left* I (1959–1962), pp. 63–72. Used by permission.

sit-in and disarmament groups, there is often a rejection of ideology and complexity and a preference for a single issue simply seen." [18] Like nearly every older academic writer on the left Riesman was *for* ideology, and he helped to inaugurate a sense that the new left operated from a reserve of feeling alone. While the decade was still young this seemed to be essentially correct—one of the triumphs of feeling was Dale Johnson's "On the Ideology of the Campus Revolution," an essay which attempted to find a theory of radicalism in the notion of dissent itself. Castro was then not only respectable, he seemed to fulfill the Millsian canons of radical identity. He was chosen by Johnson, in an early issue of *Studies on the Left*, as an exemplification of the new empirical ideology:

> To a remarkable degree there are ideological similarities between the Cuban and Campus revolutions. Both Cuban and Campus rebels are *strong* dissenters, firm in their convictions and willing to speak out and act militantly in spite of the mighty coercive powers of the American state. Both are pragmatic, always putting first things first, with rarely an eye to ultimate ends. . . . Organizations form almost overnight to work on specific questions— civil liberties, academic freedom, ROTC, the death penalty, civil rights. . . . Most important, their motivating ideologies are neither socialism—Marxian or otherwise—nor liberalism, although they combine elements of both. Rather, the ideology of both the *Barbudos* of Cuba and the campus revolutionaries is a refreshing combination of humanism and rationalism. The Fidelista *knows* the meaning of misery and exploitation, of disease and illiteracy, of unemployment and squalor in the midst of plenty, of graft and corruption—he has lived it; the campus rebel, lacking the Cuban experience, nonetheless *feels* it—it violates his sense of values.[19]

The ironies involved are plain. The revelations of Theodore Draper and others simply invalidated this, and removed from the new left

18. David Riesman, "The Intellectuals and the Discontented Classes," *Partisan Review* (Spring, 1962), pp. 250–262. Riesman's own exposure to ideology was not a happy one: "more and more the Right Wing students are armored with facts and they throw arguments in the way that the pre-War semi-Fascist hoods would throw punches." He was evidently on the losing side.

19. Dale Johnson, "On the Ideology of the Campus Revolution," *Studies on the Left* I (1959–1962), pp. 73–75. Used by permission.

any chance to view ideology as reason in action in Havana. At the beginning of the decade then, ideology was much to be wished, but its consummation in Cuba could satisfy only the existential left, those for whom the exhibition of energies forgave totalitarianism.

"Humanism" seemed a dead end, at least as practiced in Cuba. This is a blow from which the new left has never really recovered. The realists were introduced by the Cuban experience to the knowledge of the gods that fail; the fantasists were reduced to a hopelessly mythological view of politics. Philip Luce wrote that the appeal of the Cuban Revolution for this generation was much like that of the Russian Revolution for the generation preceding it —and the disappointment as well.[20] Cuba, like Hungary, splintered the left and created the first major problem in ideology for the Sixties. The idea that Castro was a philosopher who had modified Marxism, who was "empirical" and "pragmatic" in policy, simply could not survive the imposition of one-party authority. The democratic left was repelled. Those who remained to admire the ideology exhibited by Cuba were Progressive Labor automatons, *enragés* like LeRoi Jones, and those whose ignorance of political history made them hopelessly inadequate judges.

The next effort of new left ideology centered on civil rights. But this was the second god to fall within a short time. In terms of leadership alone the accommodation of Martin Luther King was a disappointment. In terms of strategy there were serious shortcomings. The demonstration was one of the most satisfying social gestures of the early Sixties, it offered visible solidarity with the oppressed; it affronted the right people; it seemed to incarnate the idea of commitment. When the demonstration was abandoned as a strategy by Negro leaders (some, like Rustin, saw it as an introductory rather than as an ultimate mode; others, like Wilkins, objected to forced association with a very mixed bag of radical opportunists) and when the issue of civil rights began to involve political compromise it seemed as if ideology would have to find a new correlative. It certainly could not be sought within the Democratic Party, for after the failure to recognize the Mississippi Freedom Democratic Party the Democrats were written off as liberal oligarchs.

---

20. Luce, *op. cit.*, pp. 61–80.

Nor, for many on the new left, could it be sought in coalitionism. When Bayard Rustin brought this idea to consciousness he split his readers into two groups: those who recognized that politics were impure, but who, at least nominally, were willing to work with other interest groups like labor, and those who resented the dilution of revolutionary purity. I have mentioned the turbid reaction of Staughton Lynd to this proposal; it was no more than typical of a great many. Their position is lucidly put by Steven Kelman's "The Feud Among the Radicals":

> Existing groups, in the words of the Can't publication *Freedom North* are "so integrated into the existing structure that they function as enemies of social change." Can'ts specialize in making comparisons between America today and Nazi Germany. Many agree with Staughton Lynd that "socialism . . . is likely to come by way of resistance to fascism." With Armageddon approaching, Can'ts feel it is frivolous to do anything basic about our problems now . . . [they are] unclear as to whether they want to *take* power or *annihilate* it. This double attitude becomes apparent in the actions which New Left thinkers have proposed as alternatives to Rustin's coalitionism. Sometimes their purpose seems to be to *escape* from power, sometimes to *grab* power by a minority putsch, sometimes merely to *test* the purity of their forces against temptations to "cop out" by the power structure.[21]

Coalitionism was the central topic of the *Partisan Review* symposium "Is There a New Radicalism?", and, due either to the fact that the old left was heavily represented, or to the intellectual preeminence of the defenders of the doctrine, it evidently carried the day. To be sure, the viewpoint of the anti-coalitionists was made plain by Nat Hentoff, who argued that the impurities of the social structure made cooperation impossible. When he stated that "the failure of the unions to protest our appalling adventures in Vietnam and the Dominican Republic hardly gives the new Left confidence in organized labor as an ally," he revealed unconsciously the qualifications of his position. That the new left should *expect* labor to have such a viewpoint is unrealistic. His attack on labor, like the attack on liberal intellectuals by Stephen Rousseas, is a form of

---

21. Steven Kelman, "The Feud Among the Radicals," *Harper's* (June, 1966), p. 68. Used by permission of the author.

ideological purity and innocence. When Hentoff complains that the Democratic Party and the unions are self-interested he is not aware that he is making a definition. When Rousseas accuses intellectuals of retreating "into their specialties" he seems similarly at odds with what is normative. The counter-statements by Harrington and Rustin are more literally political. As the former puts it, "one has to make political alliances *on domestic issues* with forces which one might regard as confused, or wrong."

The premises of the coalitionists ought simply to be listed, even as we remind ourselves that men like Howe, Draper, Harrington, and Rustin, while supplying to the new left its structure of *theory*, by no means exert the powers of *dogma:* (1) Moral outrage is no longer sufficient. (2) "Style" and "alienation" have no political correlatives. (3) The idea of the "power structure" and "establishment" serves to close argument rather than open it. And, as Harrington shows in a *reductio ad absurdum*, the latter eventually includes anyone to the right of the Red Guard. (4) The search for a model of ideology in the Third World ends too often in the admiration of tyranny. In any case, it confuses domestic issues. (5) The new ideologues reject the old left out of hand; the error here consists in cutting off the most likely sources of support and ideology. (6) The search for a new proletariat among Negroes and the poor is misleading since they do not constitute a genuine proletariat nor one equipped for intensely political modes of social change. (7) Ideological purity is possible only in a revolutionary situation which does not now obtain. (8) The politics of gesture which center around movements like the Mississippi Freedom Democratic Party express feeling and accomplish very little. (9) The ideology of "corporate" or "fascist" liberalism overlooks the crucial existence of American political democracy. (10) Finally, ideology as it develops on the new left tends ever more toward the condition of revelation. It requires less and less evidence, and becomes divorced from the actual change that coalition makes possible.

Of the alternatives to coalition the ideas of "direct" and "participatory" democracy have become most important. On the estranged left—among the Communist fronts, the *enragés*, the disaffiliates—these pass for the ideology needed to justify isolation. The need for "participatory" democracy is variously expressed. According to Staughton Lynd, since the establishment is inherently corrupt, existing institutions cannot be transformed. Coalition means "co-optation" or assimilation into the establishment; hence "parallel institutions" must grow into a new society.[21] We must cultivate disobedience to the ordinary cultural forms and create schools, courts, and legislatures of our own. Lynd suggests a new Continental Congress; Bertrand Russell, acting also on this principle, proposes an international War Crimes Tribunal of his own. Its purpose will be to judge the United States in Vietnam, and it will have every attribute of a court except authority.

According to a statement of the DuBois clubs, since "order" and "democratic institutions" are on the side of the *status quo* they may legitimately be transcended.[22] A more realistic arrangement must be contrived, dependent not on forms but on ideological "function"—even if that is to be secured through "power." Between this position and that of Lynd there is no place for representative democracy as we know it. They would either by-pass the democratic process or overpower it. The strain of theoretic violence is most apparent around this subject. Civil disobedience, itself once an ideology, becomes magnified into something more formidable: ". . . our most elementary power lies in our bodies and our numbers." [23] The demonstration, if one follows the drift of the DuBois statement, must in fact lead to the barricades where "force of numbers" will "wrest concessions from [the] power structure." To revive an inauspicious phrase, it is no accident that this ideology tends to confirm itself by comparisons with the totalitarian democracies of the Third World.

A reasonable example of this may be found in *Liberation*, which as late as the mid-Sixties was carrying pieces on the democratic virtues of Castro and Sukarno. Louis Jones wrote one essay on the *"de facto* democracy" of Cuba, in which historical ignorance of the most phenomenal kind was joyfully yoked to the adoration of force. Since "the people *feel* [my italics] that they do have an

---

22. "Statement of the W. E. B. DuBois Clubs . . . to the Platform Committee of the Democratic Party," quoted in *The New Radicals*, Paul Jacobs and Saul Landau, eds. (New York, 1966), pp. 192 ff.

23. *Ibid.*, p. 196.

effective and decisive voice" in government; since that government is "dynamic" and "responsive"; since Castro communicates directly with the public, there is no need to worry about "failings of the present formal schemes of representative government." [24] Comment must surely be superfluous, as it would be over the argument of Sidney Lens that "democracy has moved forward in Cuba" and that "the common man *feels* [my italics] a greater control over his personal identity" under Sukarno than ever before.[25] It is remarkable how far sensibility may substitute for freedom, at least in the eye of the beholder.

One of the better accounts of this ideology is that of Arthur Waskow, whose "New Student Movement" suggests that the idea of totalitarianism has itself undergone an ideological change.[26] For the old left it means the apparatus of secret police and thought control, the imposition of fake constitutional rights on actual servitude. But for the new left, totalitarianism means something else: the difference in "power" between the middle class and the poor; the structure of corporations; the nature of bureaucracy; the disciplinary powers of the university. The issue is complicated by the fact that political authority, if it seems sufficiently benevolent in essence, may be forgiven failures of form. That is why the new left can damn the University of California as totalitarian while praising Cuba as democratic. The new ideology, as Waskow sees it, would choose suppression over repression. The psychology of this view accounts for the fixation of the new left on the uses of power. The new definition of totalitarianism may be psychologically satisfying, but it leads unerringly into the world of myth. When we look over the operational writing of the new left—the pamphlets, manifestos, editorials, position papers, and theories of action—it becomes plain that ideology has lost its centrifugal control. Particularly on the estranged left that theory

24. Louis Jones, "Aspects of Cuban Democracy," *Liberation* (June–July, 1965), pp. 23–27.

25. Sidney Lens, "The New Left and the Establishment," *Liberation* (September, 1965), pp. 7–10, 31. Used by permission.

26. Arthur Waskow, "The New Student Movement," *Dissent* (Autumn, 1965), pp. 486–493. Used by permission.

which is brought to bear in order to explain action rests on a freedom of interpretation both logically and politically disastrous.

I have chosen a variety of subjects to be illustrated below. What unites them is a characteristic freedom of assumption. The passages fulfill the basic requirement of ideology—that conviction "systematically 'inverts' the whole relation of thought to being." [27] In Marxian terms, ideology stands for "objective social conditions," that higher system of reality which permits fact to be viewed not in itself but as part of a process which forces its reinterpretation:

> My generation had one good fortune. It escaped the afflictions of ideology which still possess our elders. When we reached consciousness in the Fifties, we faced McCarthy and Stalin, and saw both as rotten; but Stalin as no more rotten than McCarthy. That's important—to see just precisely how equal things were.[28]

> But the brute reality is that for most Americans the reins of power —control over elemental life decisions—are remote. Most of us are reduced to apathy. . . . Political free enterprise is as illusory as the economic, largely *because* the economic model is a fraud. The dual engines of industrialization and war have created a tightly-planned corporate complex that dominates the economy. . . . Much of the sham of pluralism stems from the unchallenged domination of the values of the marketplace.[29]

> I would support such a leader as Lumumba wholeheartedly unless I could learn that he was nothing but a self-seeking totalitarian. We have seen what hope parliamentary democracy *alone* is in the Congo. . . . To begin with, I would still press for democracy, but on all fronts, not just the political, so that the organism could grow whole. I would expect deviations. . . .[30]

---

27. Aiken, *op. cit.*, p. 32.

28. Milton Kotler, "Notes on the Vietnam War," *Liberation* (June–July, 1965), pp. 12–15. Used by permission.

29. Todd Gitlin, "Power and the Myth of Progress," *Thoughts of The Young Radicals* (New York, 1966), pp. 17 ff. Used by permission of *The New Republic*.

30. Roger Hagan, "The Young Radicals," *Dissent* (Spring, 1962), p. 131 ff. Used by permission.

In all these cases the *impasse* of the new left is clearly figured, the confrontation of what Hal Draper called the Ideological Hang-up and the Non-Ideological Hang-up. If no group of ideas means any more than its alternatives the new left will find itself without historically adequate standards of judgment. If any group of ideas may be asserted in spite of those standards, the new left will fragment into groups who differ solely on the basis of the amount of evidence they require to reconcile belief and reality. The possibilities are not mutually exclusive. Apart from those who quietly drop the entire matter of ideology in order to work within coalition, there remain those for whom it is possible to give an infinitely subjective account of reality. The irony is that the Marxian idea of ideology was based on a limited set of "objective" social conditions. On the new left in the Sixties the very idea of what is objective is subject to definition.

# 7. The New Left (III)

# PROBLEMS OF ACTIVISM

## The University

The university is the natural habitat of the new radicalism. It is the one institution in America which offers self-sufficency. It offers a form of community, but one uncommonly free of the restraints of authority. Its sanctions are ritualistic and habitual, hence they are easily permeable to the critical mind. Its milieu of enforced equality permits money to have only the slightest social leverage. As an independent institution it shelters the single largest group of left intelligentsia in the culture. As matters of principle and custom it encourages radical expression; on its perimeter flourish those marginal ideas and groups which have no hope of sympathetic reception elsewhere. Within its extra-curricular structure there is a recognized place for the politics of dissent; indeed, the most firmly established of the new left groups are specifically organized around the campus. As the recent history of the decade makes plain, the university supplies the manpower for the student movement. If the process of ideological conversion may be said to have had a locale from the Thirties to the Sixties that has been the university. The ambivalence of the new left to the university follows from the character of educational structure; when perceived as a microcosm of outer society the campus seems to groan under the dead weight of bourgeois culture. When perceived as the natural ideological center that it is, and as the very source of student identity, it evokes the deepest sympathies. The university has, in short, held for the new left sometimes the character of the Inferno, and sometimes that of Utopia.

Nothing is more common than to find "alienation" and "bureaucracy" invoked to explain the attitude of the new left towards universities. This is particularly true of new left apologetics as well as of the bandwagon analysis of the mass media. Such explanations are generally accompanied by the statement that the Berkeley riots of 1964 exemplified student action against those conditions. It is a partial truth and hence a disabling one. At the very least the idea of "alienation" has become so subjective as to remove it from the realm of usable ideas. It may extend from the most abysmal despair to a contempt for Deans. In purely historical terms the Berkeley affair was preceded by several years of theorizing about the nature of the university. If the affair at Berkeley was first perceived as a confrontation between human essence and the machinery of the state it was later seen in more pragmatic terms. The general position of the new left vis à vis the university has to do with other matters: the nature of scholarly objectivity; the nature of freedom; the social function of the university; the distribution of power.

As with so many other aspects of new left thought the idea of a university proceeds from a sense of intellectual betrayal. This was clear as early as 1960 when Andrew Hacker's essay on "The Rebelling Young Scholars" appeared in *Commentary*.[1] It was written from the point of view of an academic liberal; its author was removed by age, moderation, and professional inhibitions from his subject and was well aware that this compromised him. His point

1. Andrew Hacker, "The Rebelling Young Scholars," *Commentary* (November, 1960), pp. 404–412.

was that "today's graduate students are substantially to the left of the men at whose feet they have chosen to sit." Whether the professors are enlightened conservatives or mild liberals there is strong dissatisfaction with their political inertia. These professors seem disinclined to take direct political action. They persist in teaching their specialties rather than "the main controversies of the time." They appear to the student to be classical cases of the liberal mind come to terms with inherently conservative social status. As such, the professors are at least as culpable as those administrations which customarily figure as tyrannies. Thomas Hayden's review of a group of academic figures reveals this sense of intellectual betrayal:

> There is, I find, an inhibiting, dangerous conservative temperament behind the facade of liberal realism which is so current: Niebuhr in theology; Kornhauser, Lipset, and Bell in political science and sociology; the neo-Freudians in psychology; Hofstadter in history; Schlesinger and other of the ADA mind . . . always the same impressions emerge; Man is inherently incapable of building a good society. . . . ideals have little place in politics.[2]

Against this failed tradition there is that of the present radicalism —utopian, critical, anti-establishment, free of the treasons of liberalism, informed with moral energies.

The legacy of the old left is seen to be ideologically and methodologically useless. For truth it substituted scholarly objectivity. An important statement on this opened the decade; it is in the first issue of *Studies on the Left*.[3] In the editorial "The Radicalism of Disclosure" it was asserted that the mode of objectivity was at best incomplete and at worst an ideological fallacy. Objectivity in history and political science was seen by the new left not as a method approximating that of physical science but as an imposition of dogma. To review the argument, it was first stated that objec-

2. Thomas Hayden, "A Letter to the New (Young) Left," *The New Student Left*, Mitchell Cohen and Dennis Hale, eds. (Boston, 1966), pp. 2–9. Copyright 1966, 1967 by The Activist Publishing Company; used by permission of the publisher, Beacon Press, and the editors.

3. "The Radicalism of Disclosure," *Studies on the Left*. Quoted in *The New Radicals* edited by Paul Jacobs and Saul Landau (New York, 1966), pp. 90 ff. Used by permission.

tivity was the intellectual equivalent of consensus politics. Emotionally, it inhibited the "impassioned" search for truth. As a social device it assured that those who accepted it would find a place in the academic hierarchy. As an inherently *political* mode, objectivity was "a way of justifying acceptance (either active or passive) of the *status quo*." It is plain that a restricted sense of objectivity was intended. The term connoted at once conspiracy, social climbing, and the failure of the standards of scholarship. The act of definition had a heavy emotional residue; it is significant that the very idea of "dispassion" was profoundly unpleasing. Since it "is not easy to be dispassionate about racism, or the creative process, or the galaxy, about war and peace, and the fate of man" it becomes implicit that the objective account is guilty of inhumanity. The signatories of this essay, in other words, held that it was necessary not only to comprehend these matters but to declare for them.

In response to objectivity it was proposed by *Studies on the Left* that a radical scholarship be instituted. This would be objective *because* of its "partisanship" and "bias." The character of this scholarship would be fixed by its orientation: opposed firmly to "established institutions." This approach was to be formulated in another important sense, involving not only conclusions but attitudes. It was a theme often repeated in the essay that excitement and passion were in themselves at least as valuable as method. That false distinctions were being made seemed not to be noticed; the stance of attack is no more productive of truth than that of defense. As for passion, in the realm of scholarship it is much the same as in that of sex. The contemplation of ideas—and it is surely unnecessary to invoke piously the great philosophies—may properly be thought of as generating its own excitement. Intellectual excitement, in fact, is radically unlike the feeling that arouses groups and supplies effervescence to ideologies. In any event, this position taken early in the decade has furnished the new left with one of its *points d'appui* on university education. It was not entirely the structure of administration which inhibited the learning of radicals but the nature of curriculum and inquiry. And it was essentially the role of intellectuals which estranged students on the new left. When some of the defenders of the Berkeley riots wrote about the "yearnings and commitments of the present generation of students"[4] they referred, in existential shorthand, to the central criticism of objectivity by the new left. In brief, what is taught at the university has no relationship to what is real. Objectivity is a mode that deals with the dead issues of history. It involves no political imperatives. The passions of "yearning" and the politics of "commitment" demand another mode entirely.

The passions which are so often referred to and which have a kind of moral status of their own take as their object a more visionary university than now exists. New left writing often describes the ideal university as a place in which these passions ought to be cultivated. The student movement, according to *The New Radicals*, is in search of "a psychic community, in which one's own identity can be defined, social and personal relationships based on love can be established."[5] Much the same point is made by the SDS *Port Huron Statement*, in which the present university system is intensely criticized for failing to capture the private energies of students.[6] It is a theme often stated. Some of this thought can be traced to the existential philosophers, some to the justified disappointment of students in oversized, over-endowed, over-centralized learning. A certain amount can be traced to the work of Paul Goodman, whose *Community of Scholars* furnished a utopian model of personal relationships. The important distinction for Goodman was that between a "community of scholarship" and "a community for living."[7]

Goodman and his followers on the new left believe that the university exists for more than intellectual reasons. In this they would appear to be perfectly justified. It is in certain corollaries that dissent may be produced. The passion which is so valued as an atti-

---

4. Sheldon Wolin and John Schaar, "The Abuses of the Multiversity," *The Berkeley Student Revolt*, Seymour Martin Lipset and Sheldon Wolin, eds. (Garden City, 1965), pp. 357. I am indebted to this book for its coverage of the subject.

5. *The New Radicals*, p. 4.

6. *The Port Huron Statement*, Students for a Democratic Society (New York, 1964).

7. Paul Goodman, "How to Make a College," *The New Radicals*, p. 243.

tude loses its integrity as an action: one of the most common de-
fenses of the student demonstration is that its use of force is a
sign of sincerity. It is defended as a mode of passionate argument,
and one of the less hopeful consequences of Berkeley was the
theory that such demonstrations be accepted as normative. As a
theory it demands qualification: as an action it is simply the violent
suppression of opposition views.[8] Finally, that passion which is so
abstractly expressed and that community which is so intensely defended have forms of being which appear to be removed from the
life of intellect. It ought to be pointed out that "passion" and
"community" have rather heavily sexual referents in new left educational theory. As one member of SDS put it, "In SDS, fucking is
a statement of community, and there's a lot of inter-fucking, but
it's not casual. Sex comes out of a relationship and is used to build
a relationship stronger."[9] This may be pleasing or displeasing according to one's morality; it can only be irrelevant to the university.

In the case of the following I refer to no published sources but
simply to conversations with new left students at the University
of California. The argument that ensued was based neither on ideas
of law nor sin, but simply on the character of sexual modes. That
admittedly constituted a philosophical weakness, but it turned out
to supply the only dialectical point of encounter. I took the position that sexual passion was private and that the university had very
little business investigating it so long as it remained private. To my
interest, this fairly libertarian view was judged to be inadequate
and ideologically suspect. The point my respondents made continually was that undifferentiated sexual behavior, the pursuit of
"passion" and "community," must be specific objects of university
concern. The sexual relationship would have to be recognized by
the university as a primary part of its function. The students objected strongly to the sense that sexuality was in fact private and
insisted that all restrictions on its public practice be dropped.
That this would have involved the university in complicity with

---

8. See Lewis Feuer, "The Decline of Freedom at Berkeley," *The
Atlantic Monthly* (September, 1966), pp. 78–87; Sidney Hook, "Academic Freedom and the Rights of Students," *The Berkeley Student Revolt*, pp. 432–442.

9. *The New Radicals, op. cit.*, p. 176.

felonies (statutory rape, homosexuality) exerted no force. So far as they were concerned sexuality produced community and was a cure for alienation. It supplied that strength of feeling naturally inhibited by the conditions of mass intellectual life. Sexuality, in short, was to serve an instrumental purpose—it did not exist for its own sake so much as it did for a symbolic reason. It is a curious and political definition of passion toward which this leads, and something, I would think, of a loss. I began by feeling myself to be something of a libertarian and ended, faced by their ideological purity, by feeling something of a decadent. I had not thought, frankly, that the Pleasure Principle could ever be the concern of more than two people at once.

The existential failure of the university is frequently linked to its social function, ostensibly the continuance of liberal oligarchy. For the new left the university is part of the power structure, that part which acculturates and propagandizes. A good deal of published theory on this subject has appeared, Bradford Cleaveland's "Education, Revolutions, and Citadels," John Weiss' "The University as Corporation," James Bauerlein's "The Social Function of the University," Mark Shechner's "Cold War and the University of California." [10] It is the burden of these pieces that the university —specifically the University of California—has the dual function of producing human materiel for the economy and inculcating a Cold War mentality.

Perhaps the most famous of these essays is Bradford Cleaveland's "A Letter to Undergraduates," which appeared on the Berkeley campus a short time before the demonstrations began. If there is an official version of new left thought on university education it is this essay, which, throughout the movement, has been the subject of admiration and a certain amount of spoliation. Cleaveland builds from a premise now familiar in new left thought: The world is in

---

10. Bradford Cleaveland, "Education, Revolutions and Citadels," *The Berkeley Student Revolt*, pp. 81–93; John Weiss, "The University as Corporation," *New University Thought* (Summer, 1965), pp. 31–45; James Bauerlein and Jan Diepersloot, "The Social Function of the University," *Alternatives* (Summer, 1966), pp. 20–24; Mark Shechner, "The Cold War and the University of California," *Frontier* (August, 1966), pp. 5–11.

the process of a revolution which transcends merely national interests and which makes the antiquated idea of scholarly detachment a political danger. The institutions of the university are in fact political and corrupt. Fraternities and sororities, for example, are simply undemocratic distractions which serve to keep the student mind off reality. As for the structure of the system, the ceremonies and rituals of the university are silent forms of persuasion. They sanctify the oppression of intelligence by authority. The use of grades entails a Pavlovian system of rewards and punishments—those who fail constitute by their independence a danger to authority while those who do not fail learn that success in this culture is attained by hypocrisy. The extra-curricular life of lectures and arts, recreation and debates is simply a new form of bread and circuses. The heart of the matter is that "the multiversity is not an educational center, but a highly efficient industry: it produces bombs, other war machines, a few token 'peaceful' machines, and enormous numbers of safe, highly skilled, and respectable automatons to meet the immediate needs of business and government." [11]

Once the conspiracy theory has been broached, an enormous amount of conjecture may be released. If the university is in fact a silent partner of the cold war it acts directly in the service of capitalism. Cleaveland's list of the corporate attachments of the Board of Regents has become famous. He lists the directorships and stockholdings in such a way as to intimate that the corporations benefit directly from the operation of the university. The function of the university and the desires of the Regents are one: "as corporate men of power, the Regents are getting precisely what they most desire—enormous numbers of highly skilled graduates to fill the corporate structure and to keep it running smoothly." This is surely no place in which to indulge in defense of the Regents—it might simply be noted that they fulfill the traditional role of the American trustee, which is to attract money to the university and make it responsive to the community of private taxation upon which it depends. It is possible that the new left at Berkeley has been driven to see corporations as the enemy because they offer a more precise target than the real opposition, which is the middle class of California.

---

11. *The Berkeley Student Revolt, op. cit.,* pp. 66–81.

The accusation that the university is the intellectual arm of the state appears with regularity. One view holds that the university is the instrument of "the military-industrial establishment." [12] Generally, the university serves as one of the resources of this complex; specifically, it trains an intellectual elite for purposes best revealed in *Brave New World*. A second view declares that the corporations "reproduce in the heart of the University itself their own goals and values." [13] In order to accomplish this the administration models its own structure after that of holding companies. On top is the final authority of the Chairman of the Board; at the base a mass of students and faculty with no rights "except those they can extort by the threat of direct action." A third view claims that the universities no longer distinguish truth from national defense because their values derive in fact from the Pentagon.[14] Behind these statements lies the microcosm theory, which adapts for the new left the now moribund idea of the ivory tower. For most of the twentieth century the universities have been criticized because of their distance from social realities. It has been public sentiment that a university education disqualified one for knowledge of, let alone success in, the actual world. The new left agrees that the university deals with mythology rather than reality. It emphatically disagrees with the notion that education prevents social success.

As seen by the new left the universities act as the agency of the culture in shaping our ideas of democracy, capitalism, and nationalism. If the universities were once lost in the past they are now the slaves of the present; ideological microcosms of the outer society. The new student left views the American university as we would once have viewed the Prussian university. There have been two positions. The first of these holds that the influx of federal funds and the emphasis on technology have made the universities direct agencies of the state. It is no longer the power of taxation which has the power to destroy but the power of donation. An

12. Bauerlein and Diepersloot, *op. cit.*, p. 23.

13. Marvin Garson, "The Regents," in Hal Draper's *Berkeley: The New Student Revolt* (New York, 1965), pp. 215–221. Used by permission of Grove Press, Inc.

14. Shechner, *op. cit.*, p. 5.

enormous amount of university financing is dependent on federal aid; as a consequence there are vast programs of research, building and training which are directly related to the needs of the state. Insofar as a great deal of this relates to military needs, the new left, in its pacifist aspect, is much disturbed. Particularly at Berkeley the anomaly of the largest system of federal research cohabiting with the largest single group of left intelligentsia has made itself exquisitely plain. The second position, unlike the first, seems not to have a basis in fact, it is that the university offers an apologetic in its teaching for the totalitarian liberal state. Both positions are expressed in the important FSM document, "We want a University." [15] Here is a sense of the economic entente: "Current federal and private support programs for the university have been compared to classic examples of imperialism and neocolonialism. The government has invested in underdeveloped, capital-starved institutions, and imposed a pattern of growth and development upon them." Here is a sense of the ideological entente: "the main concern of the university should not be [as it now is] passing along the morality of the middle class, nor the morality of the white man, nor even the morality of the potpourri we call 'western society'."

The suspicion with which the new left regards federal influence on the schools can only be shared by critics of whatever persuasion. On this particular issue the bulletins of the FSM have some resemblance to those of the *National Review*. The neutral critic will share the feeling of the new left toward educational gigantism. He will be less inclined to believe that the university and the corporate liberal oligarchy are in cahoots. He will give absolutely no credence to the theory that the university intentionally prevents radicalism from seeking truth. As for the charge that the university represents western thought—he is likely to approve highly of that. Since the days of the Platonic Academy the university has been identical with western thought. Since the medieval foundations of learning it has been concerned profoundly with morality. Purely as a consequence of American custom and fiscal practice it has been responsive to the middle class. If there is a particular weakness in new left educational theory it is that dialogue is conducted in ignorance of this.

---

15. Draper, pp. 188–196.

What is most objectionable to the neutral critic is that moral voluptuousness permitted itself by the new left. No one who has taught a term at any college much to the left of Bob Jones can fail to be aware of the almost crippling liberty of the campus. The odd thing is that "participatory" democracy, far from being found within the enclaves of radicalism, is the gratifying, maddening possession of most faculties. As a matter of form, all ranks of the University of California (from Assistant Professor up) have equal voting rights. As a matter of practice most academic discussions attempt a consensus rather than depend on a strict majority vote. As for the teaching process itself, the intellectual freedom allowed is proverbial, and there are watchdog committees which exist for the sole purpose of extending that freedom. One notes at this point that the idea of academic freedom for the new left has more than intellectual connotations.

Before considering this as it developed from the Berkeley experience it remains to adduce the matter of power. I have noted in an earlier chapter the intense disappointment of intellectuals in their public role; the student left shares this very nearly by definition. The single most obvious thing that may be said is that the cultural impotence of intellectuals has been translated into a new and factitious idiom. The relative inefficacy of ideas has caused the new left to assert that actual power is being denied them. In other words, *the fact that intellectuals have little social influence is ascribed not to the nature of thought but to the structure of university policies.* This has led to some tragicomic statements, notably that of the *Port Huron Statement:* "With administrators ordering the institution, and faculty the curriculum, the student learns by his isolation to accept elite rule within the university, which prepares him to accept later forms of minority control." [16] What this really means is that no one can be conscious of truth unless he is in administrative charge of the institution which studies it. It is not necessary to go deeply into the matter of elite rule, except to note that it is demanded by any organization, and by the nature of professional standards. What matters more essentially is the translation of power, which first referred to the condition of intellectuals and then to their influence.

---

16. *The Port Huron Statement,* p. 11.

One of the most illuminating statements on this issue was made by Paul Potter of SDS in 1964. He then wrote that "Intellectuals want direct power. They no longer want to deal with power as an abstract symbol of the classroom and of lectures. They want to utilize power for social ends." [17] The confusion between the power of ideas and actions is quintessential. A corollary of this might read, "ideas themselves, having no social power, may not be trusted to the ponderous mechanism of historical dispersion. The power that should be sought by intellectuals is of another order: the direct exercise of ideologies in a political context." When Potter added that the new radicals "think of the university very concretely as a mechanism they can utilize, that they can manipulate to gain certain ends," he expressed the strategy of Berkeley.

## Berkeley

Although the affair at Berkeley began over a highly local issue it ended by bringing to consciousness some of the great oppositions of the Sixties: radicalism against liberalism; direct against legal action; moralized politics against the rule of custom. It was not entirely a unique event. Several years before, when a group of Japanese students made a particular issue into a profound attack on their culture, the same sides were taken and the same ambiguities came to rule. The organization of Japanese students called Zengakuren demonstrated with great feeling and some ferocity against the visit to Japan of President Eisenhower, and became the center of some conflicting analysis. Some Japanese liberals believed that the students were inspired by Communism, others that they were existentialists. They seemed to be too privileged, or too poor to have any feeling but resentment toward society. They were either sexually repressed or licentious. They were innocents misled by radical doctrine, or rebels against the timid, shopworn liberalism of

---

17. Paul Potter, "The Intellectual and Social Change," *The New Student Left*, pp. 16–21.

their professors.[18] One of their American apologists claimed that they were overthrowing a culture morally bankrupt; ironically, he was to become the principal antagonist of the students at Berkeley.[19] The critics of the Zengakuren noted its anarchism, its diffuse hatred of society, its attachments to pacifism and unilateralism. They were surprised that the students were members of a class enjoying privileges entirely novel in its history. They were at a loss to explain the disparity between the ends and means of the demonstrations. One important conclusion was that the ultimate object was social predominance by an intellectual elite.[20]

The revolt at Berkeley was to a certain extent prefigured by that of the Zengakuren. Its theoreticians recognized resemblances to the revolution in Cuba and indeed cultivated the theme of Third World rebellion. It was decidedly part of the worldwide praxis of the intelligentsia. I have suggested that the intellectuals feel themselves not so much alienated as declassed; that they are fundamentally disoriented between Enlightenment and modern views of human possibility; that they are bitterly disappointed by the fate of intellect in power. These general feelings found expression first in the experience of the civil rights movement and then in the local issues of the Berkeley affair.

The local issues were transcended almost instantly. The real issues were the rights of man—for intellectuals. What I consider to be the ultimate subject was the power of intellectuals in the state. The following first considers the issue of the true heirs of the Enlightenment.

In this as in the general argument over ideology the central matter was the viability of liberalism. The ideological issue should take precedence, in fact, over that of the real ownership of the Bancroft

---

18. See Kenichi Koyama, "The Zengakuren," *New Politics* (Winter, 1962), pp. 124–134; Edward Seidensticker, "An Eastern Weimar Republic?", *New Leader* (5 September 1960), p. 7 ff.; Lewis Feuer, "A Talk with the Zengakuren," *New Leader* (1 May 1961), p. 16 ff.; and response by I. I. Morris, *ibid.* (3 & 10 July 1961), p. 28 ff.

19. See Lewis Feuer's "Rebellion at Berkeley," *New Leader* (21 December 1964), pp. 3–12, and "The Decline of Freedom at Berkeley."

20. Feuer, "A Talk with the Zengakuren," *op. cit.*

strip, and over the matters of advocacy and tactics. From the liberal point of view it appeared that the conflict was between Jacobins and Girondists, but from the inside it seemed to be a classical opposition of the left and reaction. According to Seymour Martin Lipset and Paul Seabury "Universities are probably more vulnerable to civil disobedience tactics than any other institution in the country precisely because those in authority, whether administration or faculty, are liberal." [21] The objective truth of this and the fact that the rebels evoked the *sympathies* of their antagonists exerted no force in an ideological situation. Another view became more prevalent, one best expressed by Hal Draper: " . . . the bitterest and most virulent enemies of the FSM among the faculty were not the conservatives or rightists, and not Kerr's admirers, but rather a hard core of ex-radicals who had made their own peace with the system." [22] The system was in fact that of the totalitarian liberal state:

> What the Berkeley students have exposed is not merely a vast and inept bureaucracy, but a coherent ruling-class structure. It runs all the way from the agro-business, banking, mining, railroad, utility, and newspaper capitalists and their direct representatives on the Board of Regents, through the Democratic governor and the university administration down to the point of application, the police club.[23]

The variety of attacks—on police, Regents, administration, and, most interesting of all, on faculty—were integrated by this version of outer reality.

The transvaluation of liberalism was the theme of James Petras and Michael Shute, who wrote in *Partisan Review* of the liberal "New Conservatism." The essay began by disavowing the traditional liberal modes of political address. In a maneuver sadly familiar they argued that "there are times when events make liberal

---

21. Seymour Martin Lipset and Paul Seabury, "The Lesson of Berkeley," *The Berkeley Student Revolt*, p. 349.

22. *Berkeley: The New Student Revolt*, p. 168.

23. "Pluralistic Society or Class Rule," *Spartacist*. In *The Berkeley Student Revolt*, p. 232.

goals incompatible with liberal means. . . ." [24] Paul Goodman has approvingly called this "existential politics." [25] It means that the "moral struggle" and the "commitment" which imbues it are self-justifying. From this beginning it was not so difficult to discern in the older liberalism the shape of the *ancien régime*. The attack on conservative liberals was in a sense an attack on status; like many on the new left the authors disapproved of the fact that their antagonists were "committed to certain institutions." It was an attack on a frame of mind. Draper initiated the *tu quoque* argument of "paranoia" when he insisted that the old left was expressing self-hatred of its own guilty past when it criticized the students at Berkeley.[26] It was an attack on pluralism which may be traced without much difficulty to C. Wright Mills. Pluralism, the doctrine that the conflict of interest groups is the essence of the democratic process, is for a great part of the new left a moral and strategic heresy. It is morally so because it leads to the compromise of ideology. Strategically, the new left, particularly the student left, does not have the political organization to exert public force.

The most visible part of this issue has been the rhetorical excess. The loyalty of men like Lipset and Glazer to the university temporal and ideal was translated into slavish acceptance of authority. Their sense of democratic process was translated into the worship of bureaucratic order. But the hidden issues are conceivably more important. At the heart of the contention between old liberals and new radicals was the definition of political change. This goes somewhat beyond the matter of tactics, which has been given a surplus of attention. The FSM based its position on the orthodoxies of the Enlightenment, that is, that institutions framed by society had little authenticity when compared to the intentions of nature; that reform needed little justification of its means; that no limits could be set on the possibilities of change. Their image of Berkeley was

---

24. James Petras and Michael Shute, "Berkeley '65," *Partisan Review* (Spring, 1965), pp. 314–323.

25. Paul Goodman, "Berkeley in February," *Dissent* (Spring, 1965), pp. 161–183. Used by permission.

26. *Berkeley: The New Student Revolt*, p. 169.

the heavenly city of the twentieth-century philosophers.[27] It is of interest that their primary antagonists were sociologists. Throughout the arguments of Lipset, Seabury, Feuer, and Glazer there reverberate appeals to law, custom, and those self-imposed limitations which govern the conduct of politics. They appeal to historical experience and to normative values. It is not simply decorum and order which dominate their thinking but a sense of freedom qualified by human experience. They have been accused of reading Burke, but one suspects that they have also read Kierkegaard and Dostoevsky.

James Burnham has written of liberalism that it is living on "inherited moral capital" and that, because of this, it has great difficulty in utilizing sanctions. The affair at Berkeley qualified this. Norms, values, tradition, and experience were appealed to with such rapidity and force as to suggest that the new left was correct about the conservative tendencies of liberalism. It must be acknowledged that in terms of tactics the liberal administration and faculty were very much at a loss. They hesitated, they equivocated, they repeatedly failed to come to grips with their opponents. The very nature of the bureaucracy made it possible for its different elements simultaneously to give different responses to the FSM. This naturally was infuriating. But the remarkable series of essays and rejoinders by faculty and other interested parties indicated that liberalism was by no means ready to give up on sanctions. Sidney Hook affirmed that academic freedom had no relationship to the *civil* situation of the student, who was under the obligation to submit to university authority.[28] Lewis Feuer argued that the demonstration was a totalitarian form of political expression.[29] Nathan Glazer, perhaps most involved in controversies with the FSM, wrote that sanctions were inherent in the nature of the university:

> I do not think a political democracy and a university are the same thing. I think there are matters in a university which cannot be

---

27. Cleaveland's "A Letter to Undergraduates" calls for an end to courses, units, grades, dormitory regulations, and so on.

28. Sidney Hook, "Academic Freedom and the Rights of Students," *The Berkeley Student Revolt*, pp. 432–442.

29. Feuer, "Rebellion at Berkeley," p. 8.

determined by majority vote of its elements, for the simple reasons that inevitably and necessarily a university involves two classes, at least, with very different rights and privileges. By its very nature, one must assume that in a university one of these classes has greater rights and privileges and authorities than the other.[30]

Glazer's second major point was that political action, by definition, occupied a very inferior place on the list of university priorities. Before it came the conduct of classes and research; even the maintenance of civilized order. These rejoinders were mistaken by the FSM, which took them to be not the sanctions governing intellectual life but the expression of the power of the state.

In some important ways Mario Savio's "An End to History" confirms this misunderstanding. What I think is most meaningful is its quality of representing the monism of the new left. This monism has become habitual; it consists in the practice of drawing all aspects of social life into an integrated whole. Those faculty liberals antagonistic to the FSM conceived of the issue as restricted to the rights of advocacy, the nature of protest, and the values of an institution. Savio and the members of the FSM perceived a larger cultural meaning. The synthesis for which the new left had been searching since the early years of the decade is presented in his opening:

> Last summer I went to Mississippi to join the struggle there for civil rights. This fall I am engaged in another phase of the same struggle, this time in Berkeley. The two battlefields may seem quite different to some observers, but this is not the case. . . . it is a struggle against the same enemy. In Mississippi an autocratic and powerful minority rules, through organized violence, to suppress the vast, virtually powerless, majority. In California, the privileged minority manipulates the University's bureaucracy to suppress the students' political expression.[31]

The microcosm theory, advanced earlier in the Sixties, attempted to define the university as a moral reduction of the society at

---

30. Nathan Glazer, "FSM: Freedom Fighters or Misguided Rebels?", *The Berkeley Student Revolt*, pp. 333–339. Used by permission of the author.

31. *Berkeley: The New Student Revolt*, pp. 179–182.

large. With the delivery of "An End to History" it was asserted as the principle of the Berkeley rebellion.

This monistic reasoning became the mode of new left response to Berkeley. Hal Draper wrote of the connections between Berkeley and the failure of the Great Society "with its fraudulent non-war on poverty, its fraudulent crypto-war in Vietnam, and its fraudulent civil-rights laws." [32] The FSM manifesto "We Want a University" stated, astonishingly, that "the parallels between the university and the habits of the society are many; the parallels between our academic and financial systems of credit, between competition for grades and for chamber of commerce awards, between cheating and price rigging, and between statements of 'Attendance is a privilege, not a right,' and 'We reserve the right to refuse service to anyone.' " [33] The Progressive Labor Movement moved in on the action: ". . . the university officials represent the same financial interests that control the government, that determine domestic and foreign policy, that profit from the cheap labor of colonial peoples and the Negro people." [34] In short, the issues were quickly overlaid by icons and ideology; the affair became, as seen by Michael Shute, "a symbol of the efficacy of mass struggle against authoritarianism." [35]

It is my own opinion that this kind of synthesis is unintelligible. It is enthusiastic—indeed manic—but seems to be unconcerned with evidence. Civil rights have given the Berkeley movement its organization and tactics, and certainly its moral energies. It has given it also a kind of intellectual confusion. Savio's reconsidered apologetic, written in the year after the riots, reads as follows: "What oppresses the American Negro community is merely an exaggerated, grotesque version of what oppresses the rest of the country—and this is eminently true of the middle class, despite its affluence. In important ways the situation of the students at Berkeley is an exaggerated respresentation of what is wrong with

---

32. *Ibid.*, p. 155.
33. *The Berkeley Student Revolt*, pp. 208–216.
34. *Ibid.*, p. 233.
35. Michael Shute, "Berkeley Campus in Revolt," *New Politics* (Fall 1964), p. 44 ff..

American higher education." [36] This is foggy, but I take it to mean that the Berkeley students exist in the same conditions of servitude as American Negroes. Such a meaning does not invite rational comment. There are two intellectually distressing aspects to the Berkeley affair. I have mentioned the first, which is the confusion between the power of ideas and that of intellectuals. The second is the confusion between the civil rights of a social minority and intellectuals as a political minority. It is a confusion consciously developed by the new left. It is painfully true that Negroes are deprived of their rights in this country. It is equally obvious that political ideas are not "deprived" in the same sense. No one doubts that the FSM was inhibited from expressing its ideas at Berkeley. But, it hardly seems that these rights were otherwise unavailable.

I view the real issue as ideological and strategic. The FSM wished to secure a base for its operations and do so was prepared to halt the university's operation. More important, it undertook to convert the university into a field of self-interested political expression. To go back to the statement of Paul Potter, intellectuals want power. They want it directly. The candor of Stephan Weissman, a leader of the FSM, appears to substantiate this vis à vis Berkeley. Weissman undertook to defend the FSM against the criticism of Lewis Feuer, and in the course of discussion made the statement that campus life would be more and more determined by the civil rights movement. Since civil rights were to furnish the ontology of learning it was only to be expected that "contradictions" would appear between the new ends of education and their old mechanisms. These would be resolved once more by the direct power of intellectuals—which I take to be the meaning of the following euphemism: "Armed with a variety of weapons and encouraged by a new sense of community, there is little reason to predict a passive return to the isolation and fragmentation which formally [*sic*] characterized campus life." [37] The monism of new-left thought permits a highly synthetic view of cultural life. It offers ideological conveniences—and disables the conduct of particular dialogues. The tactics of Berkeley reflected this; they were not simply the

36. *Berkeley: The New Student Revolt*, p. 1.
37. Stephan Weissman, "What the Students Want," *New Leader* (4 January 1965), pp. 11–15.

inheritance of the civil rights movement. Since they were attacks on a system rather than on an issue their language could only be gesture. And the strategy at Berkeley reflects this monism as well. Time and again the tactics were validated by a sense that they were morally appropriate. In the last analysis, the often-quoted theme of mass action seems nugatory. What comes to mind instead is elitism, the sense of a class of intellectuals that they ought to exercise that power now in the hands of a class unworthy and antagonistic to them.

## The Peace Movement

In 1961 Nathan Glazer, writing in praise of SANE, nevertheless stated that the peace movement in America was destined to fail because of public indifference.[38] In 1962 Michael Harrington balanced the energies of the movement against its chaotic structure and the "fierce, fratricidal struggles" of its elements.[39] As late as 1966 Homer Jack noted that "there is no peace movement, sociologically, in the U.S. today." [40] From every branch of the left, whether from *Commentary*, *Dissent*, or *Studies on the Left*, the self-appraisals of the movement have been critical and dejected. One of the principal objects of criticism has been the carnivorous mutual relationship of peace groups.[41] A second has been the strategy of the movement, which divides those who seek nuclear controls from unilateralists, absolute pacifists, and sympathizers of the Viet Cong. Perhaps the most serious division is ideological, between those who accept the war in Vietnam as a political fact and those who view it as only the most recent evidence of our cultural exhaustion.

---

38. Nathan Glazer, "The Peace Movement in America—1961," *Commentary* (April, 1961), pp. 288–296. Used by permission of *Commentary* and the author.

39. Michael Harrington, "The New Peace Movement," *New Leader* (20 August 1962), pp. 6–8.

40. Homer A. Jack, "Toward a U.S. Peace Movement," *War/Peace Report* (January 1966), pp. 14–16.

41. See Jack on the "sorry, wasteful experience of coalition," *op. cit.*

The peace movement in America is exceptionally varied. It ranges from established structures like the American Friends Service Committee and The Women's International League for Peace and Freedom, to the Vietnam Day Committe. It is divided by religion, by policy, and by social status. Because of this its central problem has been amalgamation. The case of SANE indicates how difficult a program of coalition may be. It was formed by the union of pacifists and federalists; while it held a position of undeniable moral strength it was in fact "relatively weak in attracting persons expert in the analysis of international affairs." [42] Those whom it did attract were quite the opposite; among them the fellow-traveler mentality flourished.[43] By the beginning of the Sixties the peace movement had been endowed with one of its central problems:

> Since the issue McCarthyism raised—i.e., the actual role of Communists in American culture and government—was never really clarified among liberals, but rather buried by Eisenhower's benevolent obtuseness, any attack on Communism, any attempt to dissociate oneself from and indicate one's loathing for dictatorship and lies, now appears to many old-time peace workers—and to many young people in the movement—as conformist, fearful, selfserving, a "concession to McCarthyism." By extension, even patriotism or the defense of American institutions may be seen in the same way.[44]

If anything the problem was magnified by the passage of time— the demonstrations at Berkeley in 1965 were accompanied by some fairly outrageous abuse of men like Robert Pickus, who presumed to suggest that the movement should divest itself of those attached to totalitarian politics.[45]

The first great problem of the movement was the construction

---

42. Glazer, "The Peace Movement in America—1961," p. 291.
43. *Ibid.*, p. 291 ff.
44. *Ibid.*, p. 294.
45. See *We Accuse*, edited by The Vietnam Day Committee (Berkeley, 1965), p. 1 ff. James Petras, speaking for the editors, writes that the real issues are "action" and "commitment." He upbraids Pickus for attempting to exclude communists, and calls for "realigning" the movement in order to accommodate all those against the establishment.

of some common ground for Quakers, pacifists, unilateralists, federalists, and those who were oriented simply to issues of testing or shelters. The second, as Glazer noted, was the permeability of the movement to Communism. The third great problem arose in the mid-Sixties to split once again the community of interest, this was the divergence between democratic and nondemocratic pacifism.

It will seem unnecessarily hostile for the divergence to be so named, but the terms have a basis in fact. The difference is not only over tactics, although the distance between those who take the route of political expression and those who choose demonstrations is very great indeed. As seen by the democratic socialists of *Dissent* the peace movement has been compromised by the ideology of the new left. The 1965 statement of Michael Harrington, Bayard Rustin, Lewis Coser, Penn Kimble, and Irving Howe draws the line between pacifists and apocalypsts.[46] The latter intend to transform the Vietnam protest movement into a revolutionary movement against the "power elite" and the "fascist" state. The confrontations they seek are in fact violent and seem intended to create martyrs rather than reasoners. As far as strategy is concerned, this groups seeks "to give explicit or covert political support to the Vietcong," rendering suspicious both their insight into the nature of pacifism and their personal morality. In contrast to this the democratic pacifists urge that the Vietnam war be subject to normal political protest; their program includes neither an ideological attack on imperialism nor a demand for unilateral withdrawal.

The events of the mid-Sixties, especially those concerned with the demi-hysteria of the Berkeley movement, has caused the democratic left to take a new view of protest. The authors of the statement question the idea of direct action; even the recent attempts to detain troop shipments seem to them to be undemocratic in the sense that a self-appointed elite takes into its own hands the power to revoke the decisions of a democratically elected government. Kenneth Boulding, an originator of the first teach-in at Michigan, admitted that "a protest movement needs to be shrill, obstreperous, undignified, and careless of the pattern of existing legitimacy which

46. "The Vietnam Protest Movement," *Dissent* (January–February, 1966), pp. 7–9. Used by permission.

it is seeking to destroy." [47] In an important paper delivered at a conference of Turn Toward Peace, Tom Kahn stated that direct action was too often a gesture of anarchy. It should, he said, be subordinated to legislative action—that it has not been is plain:

> Direct action which is not related to a strategy for building a mass movement has within it a tendency towards elitism. Direct action which alienates potential allies, which aims to differentiate itself rather than to attract others, soon succeeds in isolating itself. It is then prone to accept the notion that given the relative passivity or indifference or cowardice of the liberal or reform movements, it must act in place of them. . . . Staughton Lynd . . . helped crystallize the subtle putchism [*sic*] that characterizes this mood. . . . his ideas may count for something in the "new left," particularly among the counter-institutionalists. They surely have implications for the relationship of direct action to democracy, and not merely bourgeois formalist democracy, either.[48]

The controversy has reached the pages of *Studies on the Left*, which has been doctrinaire on the subject of American imperialism. An essay by Herbert Gans took the dissenting position that coalition with communist groups and the expression of pro-Viet Cong sympathy could only impair the movement.[49] Like many on the left, he saw no reason to praise an authoritarian state simply because it opposed this country. Gans demolished one of the pet theories of the new left, which was that the Vietnam war was identical to the battle for civil rights. Both, presumably, evinced imperialism by whites against blacks. The essay drew forth some indignation on the part of Lynd and James Weinstein, who were content to ignore the analysis in favor of strikingly diffuse accusations of foreign policy, General Motors, old leftists, and so on.

The most intelligible policies of the peace movement are now concerned with defining goals, creating a responsible public, and influencing legislation. The most dubious policies emanate from

47. Kenneth E. Boulding, "What the First 'Teach-In' Taught Us," *Dissent* (January–February, 1966), pp. 10–15. Used by permission.

48. Tom Kahn, "Direct Action and Democratic Values," *Dissent* (January–February, 1966), pp. 22–29. Used by permission.

49. Herbert J. Gans, "Rational Approach to Radicalism," *Studies on the Left* (January–February, 1966), pp. 37–46. Used by permission.

the new left; for absolute pacifism they substitute a program which can only be described as intellectually depressing. The speech of Paul Potter at the March on Washington (17 April 1965) comes out for the conspiratorial theory of the Vietnam war, "It is the testing ground and staging area for a new American response to the social revolution that is sweeping through the impoverished downtrodden areas of the world." That is to say the American counter-revolution, led by the President and the Pentagon, abetted by Herman Kahn, is concerned with maintaining orthodoxy throughout the world. The premises of Robert Wolfe in *Studies on the Left* invigorate his argument even as they dislodge it from reality.[50] The embarrassing fact that this country has no colonial interests in Vietnam and other localities in contention leads to a new definition of imperialism. What Wolfe calls neocolonialism is the product of our political pathology. Our foreign policy springs from "hysteria," "racism," and "lust for power"—as well as from the inherent McCarthyism of liberal America. The depths of new left historiography are raked for a reasonable analogy, which turns out to be "a strict historical parallel between [Vietnam] . . . and Hitler's Final Solution." New left pacifism has for some reason been vulnerable to pseudo-ideas, one of the worst of which is that capitalism is not so much interested in money as in intellectual assent. The "image" gossip of the last decade or so has been as bad for the left as for the rest of us. As Wolfe applies it, "the real goal of American imperialism today is not so much to preserve capitalist holdings abroad as it is to preserve and give substance to the myth upon which capitalism at home now rests." The reader may prefer to take his Marxism straight, and surmise that that is a very rarified view of class motives.

A survey of new left thought on this subject must necessarily include that of Herbert Marcuse, who believes that the alienation of the individual in the Great Society forces our aggressive energies into warfare.[51] Behind pacifism lies revolution; the only way

---

50. Robert Wolfe, "American Imperialism and the Peace Movement," *Studies on the Left* (May–June, 1966), pp. 28–43. Used by permission.

51. Herbert Marcuse, "The Individual in the 'Great Society'," *Alternatives* (March–April, 1966), pp. 14–16, 20.

to stop warfare is to change the nature of the society that permits
it. His sense of the war in Vietnam is that our repressions are being
taken out against the most primitive and innocent scapegoats.
Marcuse is singularly short on evidence, but his assertions have
great mobilizing power for the new left. What makes them attractive is the world-view they furnish, a sense that the dance of the
centuries is over for the west, and a new, more ideal cycle of history is to begin. The "alienation" which permeates his theories is
an added attraction. Milton Kotler, writing in *Liberation*, surmised
that "opposition to the war will be crushed" and that "civil rights
workers . . . pacifists, students, scholars, and critics" will all go
under in a general purge of the left intelligentsia.[52] From this
point, traveling leftwards, one finds himself in the tartarean lands
of the *enragés*. There is Norman Mailer, with his bellowings about
cancer and the cult of *machismo* which consorts so oddly with
his politics. His speech for the Vietnam Day protest might have
had the moral nobility of its subject, but it is another of his land-
marks of intellectual decomposition.[53] There are those like Don
Waskey, who wrote in "A Violent Peace Movement" that the political impotence of the movement could be converted into power
by the use of guerilla tactics.[54] And there are those others who redefine pacifism as a form of revolution.

Perhaps the best overview of the new left's involvement in the
peace movement is supplied by Edward Richer. His self-accusation is that of the radical without a program:

> Our talk of "peace candidates" in 1966, our pins, teach-ins, bumper-
> stickers, sloganeering, newsletters, marches, self-immolations, gov-
> ernments-in-exile, assemblies of unrepresented people, pickets, con-
> ventions, workshops, conferences, letters-to-the-editor, encounters
> with newspaper lies and police brutality, our fertile field of or-
> ganizations . . . are all symptoms of fear. . . . We have been
> maneuvered, with some cooperation of our own, into a position

---

52. Milton Kotler, "Notes on the Vietnam War," *Liberation* (June–
July, 1965), pp. 12–15. Used by permission.

53. *We Accuse*, pp. 6–22.

54. Don Waskey, "A Violent Peace Movement," *The Realist* (October, 1965).

analogous to what the White Liberals were to the civil rights movement. *We are the Vietnamese people's White Liberals!* [55]

This kind of sorrow is part of the inheritance of American radicalism. After the conversion, the awakening. If the tactics are the subject of Richer's despair the strategy arouses that of David McReynolds:

> To more than one of the editors and associate editors of *Liberation* —and they are symptomatic of a current within the radical pacifist movement—the "New Left" was made to order. It is nihilist, anti-American, courageous, anti-political, anti-ideological, oriented to spontaneity, given to substituting moral clichés for political analysis, deeply moral and, yet, capable of profound unconscious dishonesty.[56]

McReynolds is extremely perceptive on a major point, the connection between pacifism and democratic action. His essay ends with the recognition that the Third World, once the utopian dream of the left, has come to life by means that confound its well-wishers. The reforms in Cuba, China, Algeria, and Indonesia have all been, from the new left point of view, for the better—yet they have all been nakedly totalitarian. The question to which the new left must now address itself is this: to what extent can revolutionary violence replace pacifism? Revolutionary violence evidently *works*, no matter what the cost. McReynolds soberly notes the departure of pacifists from pacifism—Dellinger endorsing Cuba, Lynd "disengaging from his pacifism as it applies to Vietnam"— and concludes that the real dilemma of the peace movement is its choice between change and violence. He indicates that the choice will probably split the left; one part addressing itself to traditional pacifist modes, the other seeking peace through war. The latter possibility is highly intelligible, at least given the theoretical basis supplied by Herbert Marcuse, Staughton Lynd, and those others who view the problem of pacifism as subordinate to that of destroying the totalitarian liberal state.

---

55. Edward Richer, "Peace Activism in Vietnam," *Studies on the Left* (January–February, 1966), pp. 54–63. Used by permission.

56. David McReynolds, "Pacifists in Battle," *New Politics* (Summer, 1965), pp. 29–35. Used by permission.

Some years ago Reinhold Niebuhr made some remarks on pacifism that were, considering the events that have transpired, surprising in their prescience. The perfectionism cultivated by liberal ideology eventually failed, he wrote, to make meaningful distinctions between tyranny and freedom; it could find no democracy pure enough to deserve its devotion. Given this ambiguity, pacifism, which is a form of perfectionism, feels free to impose its own ethic over both law and custom. As Niebuhr wrote, the distinction between violent and nonviolent resistance was far from absolute. The differences were those of degree, for both opened up the same possibilities of restraint and indeed of coercion, "once the principle of coercion and resistance has been accepted as necessary to the social struggle . . . and pure pacifism has thus been abandoned, the differences between violence and nonviolence lose their absolute significance, although they remain important." [57] Pacifism has generally tended to be simplistic, and its sense of justice has been a relativist one. Yet, it has tended to make an absolute of nonviolence, even when that becomes nonviolent resistance. It fares no better in politics than as a religious heresy. While recognizing its own authority it takes a very hostile view of that of the state. In concentrating on force it loses sight of justice, although in political life the two are inseparable. In searching for the identity of human character it substitutes a truly dangerous idealism for reality; it has little understanding of the conflict of love and what has customarily been called sin. In political action it is always in favor of that love against "policy," as if the two could ever be alternatives. In searching for justice it has betrayed a fatal willingness to use its own forms of coercion. I have found Niebuhr convincing; the pacifist ideology of the Sixties persuades me that he has identified its source.

---

57. "The Case Against Pacifism," *Reinhold Niebuhr on Politics* (New York, 1960), pp. 139–151. Used by permission of the publisher, Charles Scribner's Sons.

# 8.

# CONSERVATIVE
# AND LIBERAL

## Liberal Conceptions: Fascism,
## Paranoia, and Pseudo-Conservatism

Sidney Hook's critical studies in democracy—*Political Power and Personal Freedom*—appeared at the beginning of this decade.[1] Among these essays are two which explain a good deal about certain intellectual habits which have since developed. In "The Psychology of the 'Fellow-Traveler'" Hook noted that it was not only convinced Communists who transformed ideas into ideologies; it was those sincere liberals who adopted a battery of suppositions. Among these:

> The enemy is never on "the left" but always on "the right"— where "left" and "right" are defined not by specific actions and programs but ultimate ideals. . . . there is no term like "Fascist-baiter." The term "Fascist" is used synonymously with "reactionary" and sometimes with "conservative."[2]

Hook did not expect these habits to modify themselves—he suggested, in fact, that with the passage of time the will to believe, un-

1. Sidney Hook, *Political Power and Personal Freedom* (New York, 1962). Used by permission of the publisher, S. G. Phillips, Inc.
2. *Ibid.*, p. 229.

fortified by knowledge, would cause their reappearance. His essay on "The Fallacies of Ritualistic Liberalism" suggests that habits like these can become absorbed into political discourse generally. The latter essay destroyed the credibility of Robert Hutchins, a figure used by Hook to demonstrate the passage of liberal beliefs into a kind of mythology. Whatever Hutchins discussed—education, Communism, civil liberties, opposition on the right—it was in such a way as to violate the esthetics of controversy and to show "an intellectual impatience or violence in imposing a position that cannot be sustained by judicious inquiry." [3]

The habits diagnosed by Hook did in fact become part of our intellectual life, much to the detriment of reason. The line between fascism and conservatism was consciously obliterated in the campaign of 1964. Barry Goldwater was the direct object but, by attachment, the entire conservative movement was rhetorically discredited. I have noted that this kind of reasoning, which tends to extend itself to every hospitable circumstance, has been of particular use to the anti-liberal left. But it began with the conveniences offered to liberals by its use vis à vis opposition on the right. Michael Harrington exemplifies those who raised the political issue to one of a more apocalyptic kind: his statement that "the defeat of Barry Goldwater is a precondition for the future of democracy in the United States" [4] typified this liberal response. He was accompanied by others. Here is George P. Elliott:

> The ingredients of Goldwaterism could of course be put together in such a way as to form a fascist totality. . . . Buckley intends no fascism, but his fearful hatred is so nearly total that his counsels might well become totalitarian with the heat turned up, as it will be if Goldwater gets into power.[5]

Here is John Hollander:

> His supporters, the Yahoos of respectability, may or may not turn

---

3. *Ibid.*, p. 340.

4. Michael Harrington, "Should the Left Support Johnson?", *New Politics* (Summer, 1964), p. 6.

5. George P. Elliott in "Some Comments on Senator Goldwater," *Partisan Review* (Fall, 1964), p. 589. © 1964 by *Partisan Review;* used by permission of *Partisan Review* and the author.

out to be the analogue of the German petit-bourgeois trash of
Hitler's rise.[6]

And Hans Morgenthau, with even more visionary pessimism, sug-
ested that the loss of Goldwater would cause the Republicans to
become a permanent minority party and therefore a threat to
democracy. To his alarm and consternation, either Goldwater's
victory or defeat would ensure the triumph of fascism.[7]

It is not only the disparity between actuality and supposition that
disturbs, but the virtual disappearance of those intellectual assumptions that have governed our political discourse. As for the facts—
the transfer of power from Goldwater Republicans to moderate
Republicans was, we know, achieved with no particular difficulty.
The election of 1966 proved resoundingly that the vision of the
fascist dispossessed was simply an old wive's tale. I am reminded
by the cultivation of these fears of the fat boy in *The Pickwick
Papers:*

"Then what can you want to do now?" said the old lady, gain-
ing courage.

"I wants to make your flesh creep," replied the boy.

Not much time need be devoted to the kind of reasoning displayed,
which is a form of innuendo, guesswork, and, to revive a phrase,
guilt by association.

A second major breakdown of political reason occurred when

---

6. John Hollander in "Some Comments on Senator Goldwater," p.
592. © 1964 by *Partisan Review;* used by permission of *Partisan Review*
and the author.

7. Hans J. Morgenthau in "Some Comments on Senator Goldwater,"
p. 594. Not every contributor to this subject agreed—see William
Taylor's rejection of the "apocalyptic vision that is being urged upon us
of an America that is about to show its Fascist colors," p. 607. See also
Ian McMahan in "Should the Left Support Johnson?", p. 12; R. H. S.
Crossman, "Radicals on the Right," *Partisan Review,* op. cit., pp. 563–
565; John P. Roche, "Menace From the Right," *The New Leader* (5
March 1962), pp. 15–18 and "Gideon of the Right," *The New Leader*
(3 August 1964), pp. 5–6.

sociology was converted into a branch of politics. Sidney Hook's "The Couch and the Bomb" [8] indicated how this was being done. At the beginning of the decade it had become accepted that those who took the hard line on foreign policy, anti-Communism or the bomb were outside the scope of any dialectic. In describing the birth of this intellectual habit Hook refers specifically to Erich Fromm: ". . . instead of grappling with the arguments and evidence of those who disagree with them—and with whom, as citizens of a free culture, they have every right to disagree—they seek to settle disputes by impugning their opponents' sanity." He refers to an essay of Fromm that originally appeared in *The New Leader* and was elaborated, horrendously, in Fromm's *May Man Prevail?* [9] This practice was diffused enough to become part of a standard *mythos*, the idea being that no one could take the hard line unless he were at the same a psychopath. This tended to infiltrate argument casually, and to become part of the structure of assumption. Just how far this practice went was indicated by Leon Lipson in a *Commentary* article in 1960.[10] In reviewing "The American Crisis" by David Riesman and Michael Maccoby, Lipson noted that its argument was confined to the manufacture of antitheses: there was an undefined form of sympathetic judgment opposed to the more sinister "polished rationality"; there was the hypothesis that American cold warriors were obsessed with fears about their masculinity; there was the claim that the anti-Communists "enjoy thinking about war for war's sake." When Herman Kahn ceased to be the natural object of such attitudes it proved quite simple to apply them to the position of conservatism itself.

The argument matured, so to speak, with the decade. As Lipson had suggested, the sanity of the antagonist was queried in ways which ranged from accusations of inherent blood-lust to those of sexual infamy. There is an example of the first in Dalton Trumbo's attack in *The Nation* on "the mountain dwellers, the Scythians, men with hard eyes and emaciated spirits and terrible hungers,

8. Sidney Hook, "The Couch and the Bomb," *The New Leader* (24 April 1961), pp. 6–9. Used by permission.

9. Erich Fromm, *May Man Prevail?* (Garden City, 1961), pp. 3–30.

10. Leon Lipson, "The Cold War," *Commentary* (October 1960), pp. 340–342.

bigots, phophesiers, killers, night-prowlers. . . ." [11] Super-evidently they are dwellers in Dallas, nightmares from the American past come to kill the dream of the modern. There is the conviction of David Riesman and Nathan Glazer in *The Radical Right* that "the fear of homosexuality" energizes the conservative imagination.[12] If we are to follow Daniel Bell, the anti-Communism of the right is compulsive and compensatory. It proceeds from internal fears connected to the loss of masculinity, the threat of loss of social status, and so on. It is in essence repressive and schizoid—a massive recourse to social destructiveness in order to resolve personal doubts.[13] If we are to follow David Riesman, the right finds its metier in "scapegoat" politics, and is to be understood as a vehicle of psycho-social frenzy like that which animated Frenchmen in Algeria and Japanese militarists before Pearl Harbor.[14] *The Radical Right* is probably the major expression of the myth, and the saddest indication we have of the conversion of sociology to politics. The entire baggage of the Adorno theory is once again unpacked for the purpose of proving that dialogue with the right is not necessary. There is not much effort to grapple with the fact that the "authoritarian personality" idea is now widely suspected, and Richard Hofstadter is able to repeat complacently that "violence, anarchic impulses, and chaotic destructiveness in the unconscious sphere" drive conservatives to convert their internal rage into political expressiveness.[15]

11. Dalton Trumbo, "Honor Bright And All That Jazz," *The Nation* (20 September 1965), p. 189.

12. David Riesman and Nathan Glazer, "The Intellectuals and the Discontented Classes—1955," *The Radical Right*, Daniel Bell, ed. (Garden City, 1963), p. 98. © 1963 by Daniel Bell; used by permission.

13. Daniel Bell, "The Dispossessed—1962," *The Radical Right*, pp. 1–38; "The National Style and the Radical Right," *Partisan Review* (Fall, 1962), pp. 519–534.

14. David Riesman, "The Intellectuals and the Discontented Classes: Some Further Reflections—1962," *The Radical Right*, p. 120.

15. Richard Hofstadter, "The Pseudo-Conservative Revolt—1955," *The Radical Right*, p. 64. In a note (p. 79) Hofstadter expresses reservations about the methods and conclusions of *The Authoritarian Personality*, although he says "I have drawn heavily upon this enlightening study." Used by permission of the author.

The point should be made that certain terms are misleading. Although it is the "radical right" that is under observation the entire conservative movement is implied. For example, Bell's essay on the Birch Society relates that contemptible (and highly unconservative) group to the inherent fears and beliefs of "the right as a whole." He connects the *National Review*, which has published several detailed repudiations of the Birchers, to the supposed psychic needs of the lunatic fringe.[16] Riesman establishes that the radical right is small and crazy anyhow—but somehow, magically, able to impose its views on conservatives elsewhere.[17] Hofstadter, in *The Paranoid Style in American Politics*, treats the radical right as a collection of demented Populists, but repeatedly suggests that the entire right-wing movement has been captured by them.[18] The right as a whole is the understood object of attack—the world of parochial conservatism. Indeed, when one adds up the contingent figures suspected by the political sociologists as amenable to conservative paranoia—oil men, fundamentalists, technicians, lower-middle class, the military, ex-radicals, discontented intellectuals, new wealth on the rise, old wealth on the decline, isolationists, anti-New Dealers, sour Protestants and uneasy Catholics, withered Anglo-Saxons and aggressively mobile immigrants, Populists and anti-Semites, racists and imperialists—it can be seen that the argu-

16. Daniel Bell, "The Dispossessed—1962," pp. 2, 7–8.

17. David Riesman, *Abundance For What?* (Garden City, 1964), p. 11. This is a contradiction often repeated. See Richard Hofstadter, "Goldwater and Pseudo-Conservative Politics," *The Paranoid Style in American Politics* (New York, 1965), pp. 138–141. Hofstadter's sense of the power, "zeal and gifts for organization" of the right ought to be compared with the insights of Robert Novak in *The Agony of the GOP* (New York, 1965), pp. 465–466. The ineptitude of the Republican right is convincingly described by Novak, and makes it appear as if the vision of an all-powerful rightist mafia is itself—shall we say?—paranoid.

18. In *The Paranoid Style in American Politics* Hofstadter repeatedly includes "the contemporary right wing," "contemporary right-wing thought," "the modern right-wing case," "contemporary right-wing movements [involving] ex-Communists," "highbrow, lowbrow, and middlebrow paranoids" (pp. 23–36).

ment has burst its form. This is virtually everybody on the American scene. Are they all psychopaths and authoritarians?

The theory of pseudo-conservatism is bipolar. Figures in this group are seen to be suffering from "status politics" or "the politics of cultural despair." That is to say, their psychic needs determine the aggressiveness of their position. And, it is suggested, pseudo-conservatism embraces a whole series of discreditable positions which have *naturally* attached themselves to the movement. I list below certain assumptions and responses to them that should moderate our reception of the hypothesis:

During the past fifteen years or so, the authoritarians have moved on from anti-Negroism and anti-Semitism to anti-Achesonianism, anti-intellectualism, anti-nonconformism. . . .

Richard Hofstadter, "The Pseudo-Conservative Revolt—1955" [19]

It is impossible to draw any conclusions about a relationship between anti-Semitism and propensity to support or oppose McCarthy. The available evidence clearly does not sustain the thesis that McCarthy received disproportionate support from anti-Semitism.

Seymour Martin Lipset, "Three Decades of the Radical Right—1962" [20]

---

19. *The Radical Right*, p. 76. One of the great mysteries of this kind of sociology is that it can so conveniently find anti-Semitism dispensable. It thinks nothing of calling a man an anti-Semite, and then discovering, as he is molded into a political type, that he "drops" anti-Semitism for a new kind of hatred. When Hofstadter writes in *The Paranoid Style* that "McCarthy abruptly dropped the old right-wing appeal to anti-Semitism" (p. 69) he implies that this could simply be done by *fiat*. But what we know of anti-Semitism convinces us that it is not a *position* but an aspect of permanence. It is not "dropped" nor is it "picked up," but remains characteristic. A good deal of convenience is offered, however, to those who feel that anti-Semitism and conservatism *should* go together. I note that even in the John Birch Society, in mid-1967, Revilo Oliver was attacked and then dismissed because of anti-Semitic remarks.

20. *The Radical Right*, p. 347.

21. Irving Howe, "William Buckley and the Price of Kicks," *Dissent* (January–February, 1966), p. 92. Used by permission.

The recent New York City elections should put an end to this nonsense. For the Buckley who emerged from this election was, in Mike Harrington's kindly words, "an urbane front man for the most primitive and vicious emotions in the land." This Buckley learned how easily a demagogue can inflame racist sentiments in his followers without having himself to use racist language.

Irving Howe, "William Buckley and the Price of Kicks" [21]

The ill-feeling that exists between the races in New York is due in part to a legacy of discrimination and injustice committed by the dominant ethnic groups. The white people owe a debt to the Negro people against whom we have discriminated for generations. That debt we rightly struggle to discharge in various ways, some of them wiser than others.

William Buckley, "Statement . . . Announcing His Candidacy For Mayor of New York, June 24, 1965" [22]

Although America has been for much of its history a belligerent and expansionist country, it has not been a Militaristic one, and up until the present it has resisted military control of political policy.

David Riesman and Michael Maccoby, "The American Crisis" [23]

The profession has never been fixated on a feudal myth, so that its attachment to the symbols of conservatism are compatible with flexible orientations toward domestic, economic, social, and political issues. . . . The direct involvement of the military in partisan politics has been too limited to be significant.

Morris Janowitz, *The Professional Soldier* [24]

There is a terrible simplification at work in the first column. These attitudes *en bloc* persist with no noticeable relationship to facts. As for the first pairing, it might be noted that Lipset's essay on the culturally dispossessed shows in great detail that McCarthy-

22. William Buckley, "Statement . . . Announcing His Candidacy For Mayor of New York, June 24, 1965," *National Review* (13 July 1965), p. 587.

23. David Riesman and Michael Maccoby, "The American Crisis," *Abundance For What?*, p. 28.

24. Morris Janowitz, *The Professional Soldier* (New York, 1960), pp. 254–255, 392.

ism and its derivates had no connection with anti-Semitism.[25] Yet
the momentum of Hofstadter's progress carries him from racism
through anti-Semitism to anti-intellectualism, because the progress
is theoretically pleasing. It *accounts* for qualities in American life
that liberals, to their credit, find intolerable. But it does not account
for the fact that these qualities are baffling in their refusal to be
united, and for the fact that they cannot be married to politics. As
for the second pairing, it might be noted that the Buckley-*National
Review* group has on many occasions expressed itself on the matter
of Negro and conservative relationships, and at no time has it taken
a position remotely like that discovered by Howe. If Buckley's own
statements do not suffice, the comprehensive chapter on Negroes in
Jeffrey Hart's *The American Dissent* makes plain where the conservative stands.[26] It is the mode of Negro politics which offends
conservatives, not the idea of Negro freedom. Conservatives treat
the Negro "problem" as part of a larger problem involving the
rights of property, privacy, equality, and community. If they
come to the wrong decisions it is neither for lack of conscience
nor rationality. As one of the *National Review* writers put it, the
wrong done to the Negro is "so unmanageably large a debt" that it
defies our ability to compensate it.[27]

As for the third pairing, the suspicion of the military is by now
ingrained in liberal thought; it is a convenient *bloc*—like small-town
Republicans, denominational Christians, members of the Rand
Corporation—upon which to project ideologies. The will to believe that the right controls the military and that the military con-

25. "The fact remains that the I.N.R.A. results do produce a result
that reverses any assumptions about a positive relationship between
McCarthyism and anti-Semitism. . . . The lack of a positive relationship between McCarthyism and anti-Semitism may reflect a more
general absence of any relationship between ethnic prejudice and
McCarthy support." Lipset, "Three Decades of the Radical Right—
1962," p. 345.

26. Jeffrey Hart, "The Negro Problem," *The American Dissent*
(Garden City, 1966), pp. 107–125. From *The American Dissent* by
Jeffrey Hart. Copyright © 1966 by Jeffrey Hart. Reprinted by permis-
sion of Doubleday & Company, Inc.

27. Quoted, *op. cit.*, pp. 111–112.

trols us, like the conviction that the right "really" controls that part of America which is not safely urban, is itself a mental habit of disquieting ancestry.

Running through all these ascriptions is the Adorno mentality, the heritage of a theory which for two decades has been increasingly dissipated by the cold light of inquiry. There may be an authoritarian personality—but as Edwin Barker has summarized, it makes precious few distinctions between systems, and is diffused throughout the political spectrum.[28] There is only slightly less authoritarianism on the left than on the right. There is intolerance on both sides, and agression, and the expected failure to separate effects from causes, issues from ideologies. If anything, "the authoritarian leftists appear to be more selective in their intolerance, e.g., they tend to censor only rightists." It is not a substantial base upon which to build a theory of political sociology.

Pseudo-conservatism is a concept of doubtful legitimacy. The fatal flaw is that it assigns political valencies to habitual social processes. If we take some specific example, say a realtor who refuses to rent to Negroes, we can come up with either an aberrant extremist whose ideology is racism—or a man whose business practice is highly normative on the American scene. He may even be a liberal—he is certainly at times a Jew. If we take a man of Central European extraction who has supported Goldwater we come up with either a case of status politics—or a man who participates in the immigrant passion for the politics of exclusion. The man to consult is his ward-heeler, not his psychiatrist. If we take the virulent anti-Communism of a midwestern farmer we can come up with either fears of social impotence—or the natural reaction of an ignoramus to the Cold War. What is most noticeable in books like Hofstadter's *The Paranoid Style in American Politics* and collections like *The Radical Right* is that they operate in a vacuum. There are no case histories, no studies of the complex individual, no examination of intellectual development that is *concrete*. There is only the construction of hypothetical social types. The method is simply a series of immense leaps from suspicion to certainty. It may be well to observe one other thing about a certain attitude toward history.

28. Edwin N. Barker, "Authoritarianism of the Political Right, Center, and Left," *Journal of Social Issues* (April, 1963), pp. 63–73.

it is not enough to be reminded that America has a long and brutal tradition of Know-Nothingism, Populism, Super-Patriotism and moralism. The job is to connect these to movements of the present, not simply to surmise that this kind of "history" generates present opinion. Every one with some illusion of the wholeness of history should be required to read C. Vann Woodward's essay on the Negro and the Progressives.[29] The racism of our reformers proves the discontinuity of "history"—if we were to take the shameful alliance of Progressivism and Jim Crow as making historically inevitable the present opinions of liberalism we should express a kind of logical mania. Everything would be right except our conclusions. From Wilson to the New Deal, from the Jim Crow Socialist locals to the connivance of the A. F. of L., there was evidently, the worst kind of attitude about and treatment of Negroes. But history is often discontinuous, for which we ought to be grateful. The perfervid attempts of liberals to prove that conservatism is really pseudo-conservatism is really McCarthyism is really fundamentalism are self-evidently captivated by the unity of history. But there is none, at least not in that sense. We ought to remind ourselves now and then that fascism was a movement of two generations ago in Germany, France, and Italy. It was about blackshirts and concentration camps, not the fluoridation of the Pasadena reservoir. We ought to acknowledge that people take political positions for reasons other than their sexual disorientation. And we ought to stop guessing—in the total absence of evidence—that the emotional epidemics of the past have determined the identity of contemporary politics.

## Conservative Conceptions: Gnosticism, Rationalism, and Secularism

As we see it stated in *Protracted Conflict* [30] the West is a discrete cultural system now faced with its own antithesis. The U.S. and the U.S.S.R. are "two alien systems" whose only possible

29. C. Vann Woodward, "Flight From History: The Heritage of the Negro," *The Nation* (20 September 1965), pp. 142–146.

30. Robert Strausz-Hupé, William R. Kintner, James E. Dougherty, and Alvin J. Cottrell, *Protracted Conflict* (New York, 1963).

relationship can be that of antagonism over the domination of the globe. In the view of conservatives like Brent Bozell and Eric Voegelin the antithesis faced by the West has been self-generated. Communist millenarianism is perceived as a form of Western utopianism, and may indeed be traced back to the wrong side of the Enlightenment. In Frederick Wilhelmsen's phrase, there is a "common ancestor" of both Communism and liberalism.[31] In the writing of Brent Bozell the connection is made explicit:

> Liberalism is anchored to the ancient heresy of gnosticism with its belief that the salvation of man and of society can be accomplished on this earth; and . . . gnosticism, in its moderate, Liberal expression is at the end of the rope. The Liberals' hope of perfecting man through the agency of man is collapsing, in part, because Liberals recognize that all of the Western experiments in this kind of thing, reaching back to the heady days of the Enlightenment, have tragically foundered; but more important, because Liberals are coming to understand, even if darkly, that the logic of their analysis and ambition points them down the road they cannot follow: that the gnostic dream of an earthly paradise can be realized (as Khrushchev knows), not by changing society, *but by changing man*, by transmutative surgery on the soul. *It follows that if gnosticism is ever to triumph it will triumph in the Communist form.*[32]

It is not an especially startling view—Mannheim wrote of the persistence of chiliasm in the spirit of reform; Santayana wrote of liberalism that "it relies on the force of numbers; it foretells irresistible material revolutions: and it dreams of the euphoria of a universal material health"; and Norman Cohn has written of the connection between totalitarianism and the will to perfection.[33] There are, however, some built-in difficulties in Bozell's view. The first is that liberal doctrine has been taken at its most extreme and

---

31. Quoted by Jeffrey Hart in *The American Dissent*, p. 62. I have relied greatly on this helpful book.

32. Quoted, *op. cit.*, p. 59.

33. Karl Mannheim, *Ideology and Utopia* (London, 1954), p. 203; George Santayana, "Americanism," *The Idler and His Works* (New York, 1957), p. 48; Norman Cohn, *The Pursuit of the Millennium* (New York, 1961), pp. 307–319.

been confused with liberal sociology. Since the second World War liberalism has acted as if it were inherently revisionist; when we examine specific cases like that of the "moderate" integrationist we can see that absolute social change is not implied. Liberalism has been as much influenced by Orwell, at this stage, as by Rousseau.

The whole point of the rejection of liberalism by the new left is that liberalism has been perceived, by those who ought to know, as insufficiently gnostic. The American spectrum is now not divided between Right and Left, but between conservatism, liberalism, and the left extremity. In every dialectic this makes itself clear. Writers have split into gnostics and less heretical types. Negro intellectuals have gone the way of either Robert Williams or Bayard Rustin; socialists have gone the way of either Staughton Lynd or Michael Harrington. As for students—they have either gone the way of Mario Savio, or back to their work. On the whole, liberals have become famously attached to middle-class status. In politics it is in fact the "absolute" liberal who is characteristically out of power, or who bows to the will of the conservative electorate when in power. On occasions, of course, doctrinaire liberalism can be poisonously evident; one thinks of *The New York Review of Books* and *The Nation*, and the kind of ethics they display. As Kenneth Minogue has written in *The Liberal Mind*, "while it is itself a balanced and cautious doctrine, it is nonetheless a prolific generator of fanaticisms. . . . they can introduce into political life an element of savage ferocity." [34] Generally, and I find hopefully, this ideological ferocity has given way to the kind of attitude attacked by C. Wright Mills when he wrote of liberalism's "conservative mood." [35] He found it banal that liberalism should have ceased its movement toward eternity, and called this the moral fright of the established. It was the fate of doctrine that eventually angered him, and alienated him from liberal rhetoric. The New Deal, he wrote, turned liberalism into a set of administrative routines. After the war, liberals were so busy celebrating their freedoms that they declined to use them. He summed up the matter by

34. Kenneth R. Minogue, *The Liberal Mind* (New York, 1963), p. 66.

35. C. Wright Mills, *The Power Elite* (New York, 1956), pp. 325–342.

stating that "America is a conservative country without any conservative ideology." In this he is in substantial agreement with Richard Chase, whose *Democratic Vista* reasons compellingly on the subject. According to Chase, "the inherited quality of American cultural life depends on a discontinuity between conservative feeling and liberal ideas." [36] Chase discerns the limits of liberalism:

> The real life of our culture is in the perennially unresolved contradiction between our conservative feelings and our radical ideas. The life of our emotions, our fantasies, our literature, our daily manners and morals—this shared cultural life is not at home on a middle ground whereon radical and conservative ideas have been dialectically engaged and a compromise achieved. The vital conflict, the energizing dialectic of American life, is the opposition of idea to instinct and impulse, and not the opposition of idea to idea.[37]

This accounts, at least to some extent, for the inherently revisionist nature of American liberalism. It is quite wrong to attack liberalism as a doctrine when, after all, it is also a sociology, a mode of social life with limitations.

A second objection to the idea of gnostic liberalism is that it is too selective. It surveys the thoughts of such intellectually bankrupt figures as Eleanor Roosevelt and Max Lerner, and does not cope with habitual liberal practice. An example: Evidently, as a consequence of the New York City elections of 1966 it could be seen that the electorate was composed of weak-minded liberals. Evidently, after John Lindsay's proposal for a police review board was defeated, it could be seen that the electorate was composed of sadistic reactionaries. The study of doctrine, we remind ourselves, is in itself rarely sufficient. One is reminded, in addition, of Norman Cohn's *Pursuit of the Millennium*, in which it is shown that chiliasm, although a Christian heresy, is not confined to the habits of liberalism and the practices of Communism. The mode of "endowing social conflicts and aspirations with a transcendental significance—in fact with all the mystery and majesty of the final, eschatological drama" is habitually modern. The diffusion of the gnostic wish has been so wide, I believe, that it is impossible at this point to

36. Richard Chase, *The Democratic Vista* (New York, 1958), p. 124.
37. *Ibid.*, p. 126.

separate out one element of modernity and pin the tail on the donkey. One might even argue that the liberal future is no more of a myth than the conservative past.

The conservative critique of liberal rationalism stands on firmer ground—and is substantiated both by liberal self-criticism and self-praise. The present conservatism is "anthropological" [38] and distinguishes between traditionalism as an idea and as a set of social facts. There is a distinction made between the conservatism of doctrine and the conservatism of habit. The former is familiar to us; it derives from Burke and his descendants and is essentially constitutional. Its force in America has often been dissipated by its political carriers, who have not been able to translate their principles into action. It has had to disburden itself of allies who are the cultural equivalent of the Doukhobors. The politics of those allies it has retained have both weakened and strengthened the cause: Barry Goldwater enabled conservatism to organize itself within a major party, but the improbability of his demands discredited conservative realism. Ideas that would ordinarily have been accepted as legitimate—like that of fiscal responsibility—were exaggerated out of existence. We know the conservatism of doctrine, in short, as a set of principles which has had difficulty operating in the face of cultural indifference, and which, in the last presidential election, suffered from the attentions of its candidate. The conservatism of habit has not often been analyzed. Like its complement, it derives from Burke, but it is not in the theoretical range. It is, as Burke stated in the *First Letter on a Regicide Peace*, a matter of sympathies. "Mere locality," he wrote, "does not constitute a body politic." And, he said, "Nation is a moral essence, not a geographical arrangement." He was thinking neither of the virtues of regionalism, romanticism, nor parochialism: the *Reflections on the Revolution in France* are at their most sophisticated when the subject is "our manners, our civilization, and all the good things which are connected with manners and with civilization." The sympathies of this form of conservatism have been familial, communal and religious. These sympathies have not been well articulated (except in fiction) due to our atmosphere of

---

38. *The American Dissent*, p. 189.

pluralism, and perhaps to the inexpressive conditions of their nurture. They have been suppressed by the technology and mobility of the new Western culture—and by the spirit of "rationalism" which Michael Oakeshott sees to be operating in modernity. But they have certainly been recognized; even Chase, a visible liberal, using the Burkean language of "our daily manners and morals—this shared cultural life."

Intellectuals on the right have become increasingly conscious of the conservatism of habit. Michael Oakeshott writes of the attachment to what is familiar as if it constituted a form of political training: "Coming to be at home in this commonplace world qualifies us (as no knowledge of 'political science' can ever qualify us), if we are so inclined and have nothing better to think about, to engage in what the man of conservative disposition understands to be political activity." [39] Richard Weaver writes of the moral authority of the given world: "there is a way in which 'the authority of fact' carries a meaning that we can accept. It merely requires that we see 'fact' as signifying what the theological philosophers meant by the word 'substance.' Now, the denial of substance is one of the greatest heresies, and this is where much contemporary radicalism appears in an essentially sinful aspect. The constant warfare which it wages against anything that has *status* in the world, or against all the individual, particular, unique existences of the world which do not fit into a rationalistic pattern, is but a mask for the denial of substance." [40] Weaver overstates, and introduces the idea of sin where it will not fit. But, if only on the metaphorical plane, he is expressing a truth to which conservatism subscribes.

Jeffrey Hart's *The American Dissent* examines the habits, assumptions and imperatives of the new conservatism in a more intelligent way than any of its predecessors. What Hart calls anthropological conservatism is his response to dialectic, that is, attachment to a particular culture and the will to perpetuate it. He argues that the

---

39. Michael Oakeshott, *Rationalism In Politics* (New York, 1962), p. 196.

40. Richard Weaver, *Life Without Prejudice And Other Essays* (Chicago, 1965), p. 142. Used by permission of the publisher, Henry Regnery Company.

official egalitarianism of our society has operated in spite of quasi-independent groups with their own manners, morals, and customs. These individual and particular existences may or may not have contributed to social progress, but they have been essential to the sense of individual identity. In taking this position he is not far from those liberal sociologists who, like Nathan Glazer, have written thoughtfully on ethnic self-consciousness. In one book, *Beyond the Melting Pot*, and in several notable essays [41] Glazer defined pluralism as a limitation of governmental power. It meant voluntary associations in social life, education, and even economic activity. All of these enhanced the life of those groups who insisted on making such activities private. Hart concludes, as does Glazer, that from the point of view of minorities these activities will seem exclusive and discriminatory. They will seem so especially from the point of view of an excluded majority. It should be recalled that Glazer's conclusions are critical, implicitly and explicitly, of the doctrines of progress and equality. The reception of his work has been, on the left, notably ungracious.

In his summary of Wilmoore Kendall's thought, Hart notes that there are two conceptions of the social body now dominant in our political thought. One is that of particular groups whose traditions and assumptions resist the operation of purely rational pressure. The other is that of the "open society," a body theoretically receptive to any initiative and proposal. This conception is fundamentally liberal; it makes provision for the modification of all our practices as if they were responsive only to the pressures of immediacy and plausibility. An example might be the matter of censorship, wherein liberals characteristically opt for total freedom and conservatives tend to impose moral and religious sanctions. The first view would have it that we should not deny freedom to any thought; the second, that freedom should be governed by the particular attitudes of the moral consensus. In this matter, Hart and Kendall affirm, the "actual consensus society we inherit" itself constitutes a value-system.

Kendall writes of "an orthodoxy—a set of fundamental beliefs" that resists the unlimited demands of the open society. Weaver uses the term "regime" to describe something "much more than

---

41. See notes 5, 6, 7, p. 12.

the sum of the government and the laws." And Hart writes of a set of "beliefs, traditions, customs, habits, and observances" which validate, when direct legal process does not, such things as prayer in the schools, hostility to the idea of freedom for Communists, sympathy for the rights of property as opposed to the "rights" of man.[42] This is not intended to be dogmatic:

> We should be very careful not to imagine that such conservatives as Kendall and Weaver are in favor of the suppression of all dissent. The argument really focuses on the liberal *principle* of the "open society" as found in the work, say, of Karl Popper: the alternatives are not, Kendall reminds us, the open society and the closed society, but the quite fictitious open society of liberal fancy and the actual consensus society we inherit, operating on what the framers called "the deliberate sense of the community." [43]

Hart adds that these assumptions are empirically discoverable. He draws an amusing mock-biography, which carries the individual from childhood through the university, and which shows the disparity between life as it is lived and, in this liberal society, how it is taught. There will be a sceptical reaction, he suggests, when the young man of the middle class discovers the distance between what is said—or perhaps not said—in his own home and the larger ideas of freedom to which a liberal interpretation of his civics course leads. He will find that family and community operate in their own ways, on assumptions that seem not at all related to political equality. He will sense that the very identity of family and community is inseparable from those attitudes, and that this particular kind of identity resists such notions as unlimited equality, progress, even freedom.

At school, the student may note that the equality of nations is faithfully taught; at home or in the library he will evolve ideas about nationality which correspond to realities of development, behavior, and even of relative degrees of civilization. Should he be historically minded, he may well find it puzzling to compare the liberal interpretation of African nationalism in 1960 with the evident facts about the African nations of 1968. He may find, as

---

42. *The American Dissent*, pp. 204–205.
43. *Ibid.*, p. 206.

Hart dryly puts it, "that, in point of fact, there is more historical evidence for some traditional beliefs—the resurrection of Christ, say—than there is for such liberal certitudes as progress and human goodness." In short, there will be a continued disparity between our sole intellectual tradition of liberalism and the habitual responses, not to say the facts of life, which engage him.

The received order of things bulks large in conservative thought, and its defenders view modern rationalism as a threat to that order. They have been anticipated, a case in point being Reinhold Niebuhr's attack on "The Soft Utopians." [44] Niebuhr's Christian perspective allowed him to see the failure of "redemptive history"— the phrase he used for liberal confidence in the power of reason. He isolated six articles to illustrate this confidence: (1) Ignorance is the cause of injustice and will infallibly yield to the power of education. (2) Civilization is becoming, inevitably, more moral. (3) Social justice is determined not by individual character but by the nature of systems. (4) Appeals to goodwill must be efficacious —and if they are not, there must be more of them. (5) Happiness is a consequence of the triumph of goodness over vice. (6) Wars are caused only by stupidity and are maintained only by those who fail to recognize this fact. Niebuhr's summation is excoriating:

> Liberalism is in short a kind of blindness to which those are particularly subject who imagine that their intelligence or the ineluctable processes of history have emancipated them from all the stupidities of the past. It is a blindness which does not see the perennial difference between human actions and aspirations, the perennial source of conflict between life and life, the inevitable tragedy of human existence, the irreducible irrationality of human behavior, and the tortuous character of human history.[44]

The political forms of "redemptive history" have received penetrating analysis in the work of Kenneth Minogue and Michael Oakeshott. The former states that "for liberals 'the present' means not only everything that is happening now; it also carries a further meaning that the present is only what *ought* to be happening now. . . . Time, like everything else in this social world, is simultane-

---

44. *Reinhold Niebuhr On Politics* (New York, 1960), p. 15.

ously a fact and an aspiration." [45] To accord with this, politics becomes viewed not simply as form of the possible but as a "technical" activity unrelated to anything but power. It must, Minogue insists, become coercive if "rational" progress is not being made within the state. Indeed, such politics are implicitly totalitarian since opposition to rationality must inevitably arise from immoral self-interest or class interest. If not totalitarian, Minogue suggests, they are at least a prelude to that condition. Since a cause must be sought for every social disjunction, and since that cause, in practice, is so often discovered to be environmental, liberalism attacks the sources of its own identity:

> In a hierarchical social system those at the bottom of the hierarchy will be victimized by those above. The road to freedom therefore lies in the destruction of all hierarchies and the arrival of a society which is, in a certain sense, equal. Yet in the modern world, the steady erosion of traditional hierarchies has not produced States which are noticeably freer than those of the past. On the contrary, it has produced a 'dehumanized mass' subject to manipulation. . . .[46]

Oakeshott has stated that "moral ideas are a sediment; they have significance only so long as they are suspended in a religious or social tradition, so long as they belong to a religious or a social life." [47] He is particularly impressive when, as in his famous essay "Rationalism in Politics," he dissects the errors imposed on politics by the doctrine of the mind. He argues that, purely in empirical terms, all the rationalist can do is replace one project in which he has failed by another in which he hopes to succeed—contemporary politics, in fact, unbound by any given principle, seemed at the time of the essay (1947) and must in fact seem now to be precisely of this order. In spite of the best will in the world the rationalist structures of public welfare seem not to be *curative.* Yet, as the family and community disintegrate nothing takes their place; there is only a proliferation of public agencies which substitute a material, legalistic, and eventually financial authority for one of quite

---

45. *The Liberal Mind,* p. 3.
46. *Ibid.,* p. 13.
47. *Rationalism In Politics,* p. 36.

another kind. Rationalism in politics leads to an endless succession of projects; in education it leads to the worship of mere technique; in morals it leads to behaviorism. As to the last, Oakeshott is particularly telling; he views rationalist behavior, correctly, I think, as highly discontinuous. He argues that the whole field of moral education has been emptied of substantive authority, and that morals themselves become "technique" subject to the same vagaries of fate as any other category. In default of proof of the opposite —which we well know our culture cannot now supply—this must be accepted as a fact.

Like Niebuhr, the conservative Stanley Parry argues that liberalism relies on rationalism, but that this mode is insufficiently coherent as an explanation of life's complexity.[48] It is a closed system of speculation which begins with a rejection of the world of being, unattractive as that being may appear, and ends in a form of *hubris*. He urges that the intellectual process is metaphysical, and that it must be open to transcendence because that is a way of experiencing the world. With this argument the conservative attack on rationalism blends into a related attack on secularism. In relation to this, Frank Meyer wrote that "liberals . . . are still living on inherited moral capital."[49] He meant, I assume, that history and moral tradition, while having no particular claims on liberal habits of mind, nevertheless have supplied liberals with whatever values—and habits of exercising those values—they now possess. It is implicit that these are religious values. An important statement on the relevance of "traditional" or "conventional" (these are certainly synonomous with "religious" and "Judeo-Christian") morals is that of Minogue:

> Liberalism, for example, is antipathetic to the unreflective adherence to traditional moral rules, and has therefore attempted to rationalize those rules by constructing a generalized policy adapted to the character of natural man. In this policy, most of the conventional moral rules reappear as items of technical advice. This teleological view of the moral life appears only to affect the struc-

48. Stanley Parry, C.S.C., "Reason and the Restoration of Tradition," in *What is Conservatism*, Frank Meyer, ed. (New York, 1964), pp. 107–129.

49. Quoted in *The American Dissent*, p. 76.

ture of morality; in fact it also affects the content. For it turns moral agents into calculators of consequences, opening up possibilities of individual variation which cannot appear where morality is taken to be conformity to a code.[50]

As for the permanence of moral rules, Catholics like William Buckley, Jews like Will Herberg, and Protestants like Jeffrey Hart are united in their sense that there can be no such thing under liberal secularism. Herberg writes that "a society, and the state through which it is organized politically, remain 'legitimate,' 'righteous,' and 'lawful' *only insofar as they recognize a higher majesty beyond themselves,* limiting and judging their pretensions." [51]

This is immensely difficult to resolve, and indeed the conservative movement had its own *cause célèbre* when Max Eastman, an unbeliever, left the *National Review* because he believed that morals and religion were separable. This is no place to tackle an issue that requires volumes. But one does not have to be a natural-law conservative to see that the present movement identifies its interests with those of the churches, with all the consequent benefits and dangers. It is of great interest that conservatives appeal to an argument generally attractive to liberalism—that the majority of a people within a republic ought to have their beliefs sanctioned. In the case of morals, they argue, we ought to face the implications of the overwhelming practice of Christian belief. Whether the matter under discussion is prayer in the schools or the actual teaching of religion, they believe that it is futile and baffling to pretend that Christianity is a cultural exemption. It is, indeed, native to the culture, inbred in our view of man, hospitable to our politics, and of necessity in itself a good.

I think that it is an unproven case that liberalism is an *operational* form of gnosticism. As for its being an aspect of rationalism, that has been accepted by some liberals not as an accusation but a kind of praise. The secularist argument is, from my point of view, yet to be resolved. I have not mentioned, among these limited conceptions that conservatives hold about liberals, some of the less

50. *The Liberal Mind,* p. 75.
51. Quoted in *The American Dissent,* p. 64.

defensible myths. One tires rapidly of enigmatic pronouncements on liberal decadence. One tires, even more rapidly, of praise of the bucolic virtues, and bathetic admiration for All Those Swell People Who Thought Right. There is a kind of conservative sentimentality which is the equivalent of liberal tender-mindedness. Perhaps, as liberals grow less hysterical about conservatives, conservatives will tend to become less redundant in the belief that to be liberal is to indulge in a kind of heresy.

# Intellectuals
# and the Cold War

The extremes of American opinion on the Cold War seem incapable of synthesis. The Cold War is a process; its inevitable futurity forces argument to be conditional—and therefore to follow the tracks of doctrine and ideology. Some conservatives have evolved a theory of the Suicide of the West (the phrase is James Burnham's) which accounts for the Cold War in terms of our decreasing wish to assert the values of our civilization—and our increasing wish for the gratification of total dependence upon the authority of tyranny. This is another form of sociology as politics, and it should be subject to the same suspicions as the resurrected Adorno theory which also converts beliefs into pathologies. Some liberals, among them Erich Fromm, have evolved a theory that there really is no Cold War. China and Russia are really benevolent powers whose energies are directed toward peaceful industrial expansion; if we only remove all provocations by exiting gracefully from Europe and Asia their inner benevolence will have a chance to display itself. And some radicals—one thinks of those associated with *Studies on the Left*—simply believe that the Cold War is a product of our ruthless capitalistic expansion. All these theories have been notably baffled by events: the fall of Sukarno in Indonesia, the conversion of Castro from saviour to dictator, the change in China from the Hundred Flowers period to the civil wars of 1967 have shown that history has many cunning corridors. That realization has contributed a good deal to the present state of mind.

Even when it comes to interpreting the past there is no interplay of agreement. For the conservative, the last two decades have witnessed the decline of the West. Burnham's *Suicide of the West* opens with a vision of the map of the world as it used to be contrasted to what it now is, physical evidence, in those areas marked red, of the shrinkage of Western power. Our foreign policy is one of "continuing disintegration and eventual defeat." [52] and events like Suez, Berlin, and Budapest are simply inductive demonstrations of this. The liberal looks at the same events and sees them differently: the Soviet Union now appears to him to have abandoned its belligerent posture of the fifties; the various crises in Europe, Africa and Asia have been resolved favorably for the West; the fact of polycentrism has disputed communist ideology; the precipitate Soviet retreat from Cuba and Berlin seems to have acknowledged both the power of our arms and the success of our policies. In short, the liberal views our tactics as close to the limits of political possibility.[53] It is plain that these issues cannot be thought of as simply tactical. The conservative views the blockade of Cuba as insufficient and the liberal views it as a kind of strategic absolute; the former finds neutralism to be a withering of Western ties and the latter sees in it the decline of Communist influence. Underlying these matters of policy is the question of what the West is, and what it deserves to be.

The conservative position is Christian and Augustinian; because of this it falls into two parts. There is an icy passage in *Cold Friday* in which Chambers makes clear his doubt as to whether the West *ought* to survive. If the liberal West is simply the chrysalis of the Communist West, the question can not be the survival of values but only their attenuation and extinction. As he views it, the Cold War is that part of the last two centuries of revolutionary rationalism that we are able to perceive. We have brought upon ourselves the fate of the City of Man. The other Augustinian viewpoint has been stated by Frederick Wilhelmsen in "Towards a Theology of

---

52. James Burnham, *Suicide of the West* (New York, 1964), pp. 251–277.

53. Oscar Gass, "The World Politics of Responsibility," *Commentary* (December, 1965), p. 86.

Survival." [54] While this is also a providential theory it holds out the alternative of discovering our fate through action. It offers a view of the West fundamentally Christian; its central analogy, in fact, is that the Cold War is simply the latest in the eternal conflicts between civilization and barbarism. It participates in the greater conflict of good and evil.

Wilhelmsen's essay takes up three points: the nature of history, the nature of coexistence, the identity of the enemy. For the first, we have not been entrusted with the destiny of history but only "with the duty of making it." We may fail, and that failure may have been written into creation, but we cannot proceed on the basis that *we* know it to be inevitable. This translates itself into a politics of resistance, and recommends itself to all those who believe that the Cold War exemplifies the inevitable movement of "History" towards a foregone conclusion. The second point is concerned with the politics of despair which Wilhelmsen sees to be operating not only in Bertrand Russell's counsels of surrender but essentially within the idea of coexistence. Coexistence, he states, translates itself into the slow, moderate retreat of the West from its responsibilities. It is based on "an intellectuality purged of hope" which makes possible the gradual accession to all of the demands of the Communist powers. The third point identifies both the aim of conservative politics and the nature of the enemy:

> [Politics are] in the service of something deeper than themselves: the preservation and the enhancement of civilization *and therefore the ultimate destruction of civilization's enemy.*

The concept of the West elicits only contempt from another group of thinkers, principally those on the radical side. For them the political traditions we have are hateful and irrational. The idea of representative democracy is compared unfavorably to participatory, direct or plebiscitory democracy. The culture heroes of the radical left are men whom the moderate left has contemptuously discarded—the tyrants of Cuba, China, Indonesia, and Ghana. It is no surprise to find that the West is for the extreme left only the *ancien régime*. It is somewhat of a surprise, however, to find on the

54. Frederick D. Wilhelmsen, "Towards a Theology of Survival," *National Review* (12 January 1965), pp. 17–19.

moderate left a more subtle and equivocal version of this mood. In the *Partisan Review* symposium "The Cold War and the West" [55] there was a considerable negative response to those questions which centered on the meaning of the West and the length to which we ought to go to defend it. Mr. C. P. Snow, about whom it is sometimes difficult to write dispassionately, stated that the West and East more or less equalled each other; indeed, in another and more famous statement he made it plain that a man could live as conveniently under Communism as under democracy. Perhaps he was referring to Sinyavsky. At any rate, he suggested that the West was more or less fortuitous, a product of industrialism, and perhaps a by-product at that. Mary McCarthy was rather more explicit. She found the West not identifiable as "a political or spiritual whole" and stated that it cohered simply as our standard of living elevated into a principle. The West was a form of capitalism and as such was hardly worth defending. If it came to a defeat, men might attain a degree of nobility by engaging in political agitation under our conquerors, who would presumably permit that sort of thing. Norman Podhoretz preferred a utopian future to a decadent present and suggested (although he did not personally favor it) that surrender might be preferable to the risk of nuclear engagement. He called for a study like that of Herman Kahn, but on the probabilities of surrender rather than defense, i.e., how many would be shot, deported, or imprisoned in slave camps. His query as to "how long might it take for the Russians and/or Chinese to become 'Americanized'?" should doubtless be treated with the respect it deserves.

It is plain that the sum of these opinions is a sense that the West does not differentiate us and exerts no special demands upon us. Nor do its imperatives bear on the choice of life and death. A different sense of those imperatives was adduced by Sidney Hook in the *Commentary* symposium "Western Values and Total War." [56]

---

55. "The Cold War and The West," *Partisan Review* (Winter, 1962), pp. 9–89.

56. Sidney Hook in "Western Values and Total War," *Commentary* (October, 1961), pp. 277–304. Used by permission of the author.

As I read the history of Western culture it seems to me that survival at all costs is not among the values of the West. It was Aristotle who said that it is not life as such, or under any conditions, that is of value, but the good life. The free man is one who in certain situations refuses to accept life if it means spiritual degradation. The man who declares that survival at all costs is the end of existence is morally dead, because he's prepared to sacrifice all other values which give life its meaning.

Throughout the symposium, which he thoroughly dominated, Hook argued against H. Stuart Hughes, his chief opponent, that some wars—the Cold War among them—were worth fighting. Hughes was the perfect opponent, temperamentally and intellectually. He summed up all those attitudes on the left—quasi-pacifism, suspicion of the United States, appeasement—hospitable to the renunciation of our role in the global balance of power. His suggestion that after surrender we practice passive resistance and underground activity was met by Hook with the incredulity it deserved: the fate of resistance within the totalitarian state is a subject too well and painfully known to become the toy of moral conversation. It was much better, Hook pointed out, to be neither red nor dead—especially since surrender would surely result in our becoming both. Willingness to fight, he suggested, was the best possible guarantee of not having to fight. Hook's rampage through his opposition is best summed up in a short burst of dialogue between himself and Hughes. The distinction he makes is central to the response of liberalism to the war in Vietnam:

> Hughes: I'm delighted to find myself in agreement with Mr. Hook on one thing. I also regard myself as a socialist, and I think our view of the good society is almost identical.
> Hook: No, I'm afraid not.
> Hughes: We both believe in a democratic socialist society.
> Hook: No, you are prepared to surrender the world to the Communists.

The many liberals supporting the war in Vietnam are precisely not going to surrender the world to the Communists. They are strikingly differentiated from those liberal intellectuals who are against the war. John P. Roche, a former president of the ADA, wrote in *The New Leader* in 1965 that "ever since the pace of hostilities in Vietnam accelerated, and particularly since the Administration's decision to bomb North Vietnam, there has been a certain element of hysteria in liberal circles." [57] He correctly identified the key argument against the war, i.e., that our Vietnam involvement was supposedly immoral. The political prayer meetings of the left have concentrated on this theme—although, as Roche points out, "there is nothing more immoral about bombing staging areas in North Vietnam than there is in North Vietnamese support for Vietcong terrorists in the South (who have murdered from 20 to 30 thousand village officials in the past six years)." Roche found himself in the same position as Jacob Javits, who stated in 1966 that he was "obviously at variance with some part of the liberal community" [58] because of his stand on the Vietnam war. The position for which both Roche and Javits spoke—and they are men whom no one would have any particular trouble in defining as liberal—is a conservative one. It is, to be sure, not as thoroughgoing as the position stated in *National Review*, which argues for a much greater escalation of the Asian war, and for more direct action (such as bombing the Chinese nuclear reactors). But on some important grounds the moderate liberal and conservative positions coincide.

Both positions are interventionist. Both view the Vietnamese war as an extension of the Cold War and, in particular, as part of the unacknowledged war we have been conducting against the influence of China. Both are oriented toward global strategy. This strategy has been stated in lucid and compressed form by Oscar Gass in "The World Politics of Responsibility": [59] It begins with the assumption that limited war, of which Vietnam is a clear example, actually makes more remote the chances of nuclear war since it shows both our will to resist and the power of our nonnuclear deterrence. It argues that there is, in fact a *moral* argument to be made for our presence in Vietnam—"The take-over by Ho Chi-minh's men in Saigon would probably make the Nazi occupation of Vienna and Prague look like a picnic." It observes

57. John P. Roche, "The Liberals and Vietnam," *The New Leader* (26 April 1965), p. 16.
58. Jacob Javits, quoted in *Time* (4 February 1966), p. 25.
59. "The World Politics of Responsibility," pp. 88–89.

that Vietnam is part of a strategic design involving all the nations of Southeast Asia, ranging from Laos, which is indifferent to the West, to Australia, which is part of it. Finally, both positions are implicitly hostile to the role of the United Nations; Gass, writing in *Commentary*, going so far as to say that "it is, I think, at least fifteen years since any informed and reflective person has believed that the United Nations could be the principal channel of a responsible American participation in world politics."

The anti-war left has been thoroughly bewildered by such opinions and by its own isolation. Its response has taken two forms, the public action of demonstration, teach-in, and "emigration" from the larger community; the rhetorical action of a paper war of manifestoes, articles, letters to the editor and *feuilletons*. It is, I think, quite plain why the anti-war left has become isolated and ineffectual. It is difficult to act when the institutions of the nation are directed toward consummation of the war; it is very hard to fight an economy. The inchoate response of public opinion is politically of greater importance than the attempts of intellectuals to frame a position. The similarity between conservative and pro-war liberal has been an embarrassment. The consequences of the radical turn from nonintervention to apologetics for the Viet Cong have been severe.[60] Simply in terms of modes, the failure of the anti-war left to counter the strategic arguments of its opponents has been instrumental in its failure to exert opinion. Finally, the appeals to morality of both sides have resulted in acceptance of the idea that morality is positively served by acting against Communism. This has been true not only of the general public but of the much prized academic audience.

The cultural position of the anti-war left has been widely interpreted (particularly by those within it) as a paradigm of the situation of the intellectual. Indeed, the haste with which the Vietnam war was domesticated has been unseemly. In "Vietnam: The Bar Mitzvah of American Intellectuals" [61] the war was seen as an

---

60. See Michael Harrington, "NLF Support Not Legitimate Peace Work," *New America* (25 November 1965), pp. 1, 7.

61. "Vietnam: The Bar Mitzvah of American Intellectuals," editorial in *New University Thought* (Summer, 1965), pp. 2–4.

opportunity for intellectuals to achieve that *public* power long denied them. It was the initiative of mass action which attracted; through the teach-in and demonstration the American intellectual could finally affect those policies formulated without his consent. With this as a base, the intellectual could then assume his real role as advisor of elected government: a combination of visionary democrat and philosopher-king. The theme has been replayed whenever the anti-war left has connected Vietnam with its *own* cultural predicament: one writer foresees "a national mobilization of university teachers and students" [62]; a second finds that the teach-in is a "fresh model of democratic social criticism [which] constitutes a symbolic threat to those whose power rests on an irrational base." [63] Purely as a domestic intellectual experience, the war in Vietnam furnished intellectuals with an image both self-conscious and self-regarding. Here is a statement from *The Correspondent* on the status of the anti-war left intellectual:

> But perhaps most important was the germ of an idea which permitted the concerned professional to envision himself as the conqueror, not of government, but rather of his own sense of impotence. This dimly formed vision of self, more than anything else, perhaps links the professor garbed as guerilla warrior with the professor debating in a marathon teach-in. [64]

The combined force of the escalation in Vietnam and the collapse of the teach-in has served to emphasize the impotence observed. The process of the teach-in itself was soon found to be disappointing—and at times degrading. It called for a parity with students which even faculty radicals were reluctant to assume. Its methodology was weak; its emotions strong; and soon the shout and the slogan became its principal armament. When confronted by the factualness of its opposition it seemed to be only a more

---

62. Kenneth E. Boulding, "What the First 'Teach-In' Taught Us," *Dissent* (January–February, 1966), p. 10.

63. Peter Lathrop, "Teach-Ins: New Force or Isolated Phenomenon?," *Studies on the Left* (Fall, 1965), p. 43.

64. Marc Pilisuk, "The First Teach-In: An Insight Into Professional Activism," *The Correspondent* (Spring–Summer, 1965), p. 6. Used by permission of the author.

recent form of revivalism. As a mode it soon the lost the power of novelty and shared the fate of demonstrations of the earlier Sixties. But perhaps the fate of the teach-in was most inexorably the product of its object. It was well known by the opposition and widely admitted by its proponents to be a mode of radicalizing the campus. Its real object was the nature of university politics, and its real concern was to redistribute the power of the campus. As such it was bound to separate itself from the issue of the war and become attached to the larger question of power for intellectuals. Irving Kristol, in a recent *Encounter* piece,[65] observed that the teach-in had become a *dialogue des sourds*. Its modes—protest, harangues against the power structure, folk-singing—foreclosed any question of public influence. I would add that it has become the opposite of a *public* movement; it seems eventually to be a circular process in which particular sympathies are cultivated and particular ideologies celebrated. It lost all power of public influence when it translated itself into the exhibition of the grievances of a special class.

In the rhetorical war those liberals against our Vietnam commitment have had to range farther and farther for their justification. They have been caught by the very nature of their position on the social spectrum, conservatives have a body of strategic doctrine from which to draw and radicals operate from their confidence in the conspiracy against humanity which is the inner policy of fascist America. Those against the Vietnam war are singularly disarmed. They have neither doctrine nor a battery of facts, and their response has been fitful, inconsistent and, incoherent. Even their most respectable figures, like Hans Morgenthau, have been led into great errors of conception. He is betrayed into the last infirmity of liberal mind when he leaves the hard ground of politics for the quagmire of Frommian pathology: "We are here in the presence of an issue not of foreign policy or military strategy, but of psychopathology." [66] Psychology appears at moments of con-

---

65. Irving Kristol, "Teaching In, Speaking Out," *Encounter* (August, 1965), pp. 65–70.

66. Hans J. Morgenthau, "Vietnam: Shadow And Substance," *The New York Review of Books* (16 September 1965), p. 4. Copyright © 1965, The New York Review, used by permission.

venience; and to be able to dust off the war as a "defense mechanism" of the national ego is to triumph over the irritating complexity of the material world. In a like way Morgenthau's acceptance of the "genocide" theory of our involvement brings the solvent of hypothesis to the substance of reality.

At its worst, the anti-war left has completely left the field of reason and indulged itself in the satisfactions of hysteria. The *Partisan Review* symposium of 1967 "What's Happening to America?" [67] was founded on the premise that the whole country—not to speak of all of Western culture—was an historical abortion. Susan Sontag's hate-filled diatribe against the white race, like her praise of those "inarticulate" and "demasculinized" students whose very being expressed contempt for their origins, revealed fairly clearly that the war serves only as a fulcrum for the estranged left. Insofar as actual values are concerned she sees the restructuring of human character itself as our one proper cultural aim. It is our existence and not our actions to which she objects. Her diffuse hatred of this nation, like that of other contributors, has very little to do with the war in Vietnam. That war is a bad one, like most wars. It may not be the right war. But it is certainly the war we are now in. To make it the occasion for the hysterics of the left intelligentsia is to play with an issue that deserves a much better fate. Inexorably the left intellectuals have severed the fact of this war from both strategy and morality. They are satisfied to see this war as final proof of our universal decadence, and they long for the close of the curtain upon our fate, either the *deus ex machina* of an aroused and demonic China to end our dominance, or our own subsidence into the saving ecstasies of unconsciousness. It is a long way from the Geneva treaty of 1954. It is a long way from anywhere.

It is noteworthy that there has been a respectable counter-argument to the thesis of the war's immorality. In "Peace, Morality and Vietnam" [68] Zbigniew Brzezinski wrote that the whole point of the war was to establish a détente. He was typical of a large

---

67. "What's Happening to America?", *Partisan Review* (Winter, 1967), pp. 13–63.

68. Zbigniew Brzezinski, "Peace, Morality And Vietnam," *The New Leader* (12 April 1965), pp. 8–9.

number of writers associated with *The New Leader* who found the conduct of the war harrowing—but who judged its objects to be both strategically and morally defensible. While acknowledging the destructiveness of the Vietnamese War they were mindful of the far greater human damage that would occur after a Communist victory. These writers remind us that civilian deaths are frequent and tragic, but that they are not an American object. They contrast these deaths with the *policy* of terror of North Vietnam, which has resulted in the death of many thousands for purely ideological reasons. Specifically, they compare the operations of Communist terror in the past with future probabilities; [69] they diagnose the connection between Communist propaganda and our own protest; [70] they note the "emotional and intellectual investments" of the left in our defeat.[71] This is not to say that all moderate liberals are for the war—a great number of people, particularly in the academy, exercise their right to dissent. Many of them have produced arguments of weight against our involvement in the war. They have unquestionably sharpened our reflections on the war. But they have been generally outpointed by their counterparts. It is when the left opposition turns itself into a chorus of moralism that the most powerful differences of intellectual capacity appear. When we look at something like the *Partisan Review* symposium "On Vietnam" [72] the reduction of most responses to cries of imperialism, the reduction of strategies to a simple demand for our unqualified departure, make fairly clear the present diffusion of political mentality. It is certainly no crime to be against the war—there are many who have made distinguished claims for their position. But, in some ways worse than a crime, it is an embarrassment to pretend that the Cold War bears out only those ideas to be found in the works of Rudyard Kipling.

---

69. Stanley Rothman, "More on Vietnam," *The New Leader* (7 June 1965), pp. 34–35.

70. Leo Cherne, "Responsibility And the Critic," *The New Leader* (16 January 1967), pp. 9–13.

71. Murray Baron, "Morgenthau," *The New Leader, op. cit.*, p. 35.

72. "On Vietnam," *Partisan Review* (Fall, 1965), pp. 620–656.

# 9.

# THE WRITER

## Prophets and Functionaries

The most influential school of criticism in this country has been
Arnoldian, Marxian, and Freudian. Its claim of "deep intellectual
seriousness" [1] has made writers conscious, perhaps excessively, of
the need to relate their work to social realities. At its best, in the
earlier work of Lionel Trilling, this kind of criticism was immensely valuable. In sympathy with the criticism of F. R. Leavis
it imposed upon literature the idea of responsibility—always, of
course, with the proviso that the concept of a liberal culture was
served. As the verve which sustained this school disintegrated, it
became less and less capable of determining the status of either
writers or their work. It had always been rather weak on aesthetic
matters in any case, preferring to account for literature in terms
of modern political life, and remaining singularly closed to the

---

1. Norman Podhoretz, "The Know-Nothing Bohemians," *Doings
and Undoings* (New York, 1964), p. 147.

possibility that some forms of art resisted that comparison. Unhappily, this school of criticism flourished in a time of artistic sterility. Since the main issue was always the cultural status of literature the matter of a work being any good tended to be secondary. Cultural criticism had the effect of raising some very bad authors to a kind of eminence solely because of their seriousness. There were other things that accounted for the intellectual decline of this school, among them its famously ingrown consciousness. There was its "myopic sympathy for Freud's but not Calvin's image of man's limitations." [2] Yet, as regards sexual analysis the preferences imposed by cultural criticism involved a certain distortion—even a Genet or Reage would come to be viewed as being socially therapeutic. As for Mailer and Baldwin, they were easily mistaken for realists and moralists. No matter how finally self-concerned such writers were they became admired to the extent that their work explained evil in social terms.

Typically, this school was intensely concerned with the present. Among its triumphs were the interpretations it offered of writers like Kafka and Orwell and the sympathies it engendered toward the sociology of writing. It was notably weak historically, and abandoned to the study of the academy most literature before the nineteenth century. Its bias toward "the seriousness that . . . gave the intellectual life of the 30s its special force" [3] made this school pre-eminent so far as understanding the life-cycle of writers on the left. As George P. Elliott wrote, this had its exaggerated side:

> One of the *Partisans* once wrote that nobody who had not been a Communist and then left the Party could pretend to understand modern America. Boy, did I ever feel left out of the swim! I was never even a Schachtmanite. [4]

Cultural criticism, the idiom of the functionaries, was fairly hopeless for other writers, and addressed Eliot, Ransom, Proust, Pound

---

2. Paul Levine, "American Bards and Liberal Reviewers," *Hudson Review* (Spring, 1962), p. 95.

3. Norman Podhoretz, "The Young Generation," *Doings and Undoings*, p. 106.

4. George P. Elliott, "Who is *We?*", *A Piece of Lettuce* (New York, 1964), p. 209.

and others with a kind of schizophrenia. It never succeeded in coming to terms with the religion of Eliot, the southern traditionalism of Faulkner, or the historicism of Pound. These things it reduced to "myth." Although profoundly interested by Jewish writing the functionaries were ineffectual in addressing themselves to Judaism. This was a pity, because many of them were Jewish. Although proud of the attempt to come to terms with their Jewishness they reduced the Jewish novel to a vehicle of liberal alienation. Its protagonist, Hamlet-like, served to condense into his person the political and psychological uncertainties of modern intellectuals. Finally, the functionaries said nothing of importance on Christianity, which seems at least a strategic error for the literary critic.

The obsolescence of this school arrived quietly but inevitably. Trilling had written that sociology made the traditional novel inauthentic, since realities were presented in a more authoritative way. This was true, but it did not indicate that cultural criticism was much more vulnerable to sociology than was fiction. We have, of course, never gone to the novel for facts, although we have certainly been encouraged to go to cultural critics in pursuit of it. The claim of the functionaries to sociological enlightenment appeared quite illegitimate when compared to the work of Riesman or Glazer. For one thing, its attitude toward the mass was unhelpful. It was sociological about intellectuals, and about a highly restricted form of intellectual at that. If the object of examination was a Jewish liberal who had once been a Communist, never a religious believer, and generally a Freudian moralist, this criticism would serve. There was some difficulty in comprehending sociology in its wider implications. Finally, there was the ontological difficulty; this school could never hope to be much better than its material. The high hopes it held for Bellow, Mailer, Baldwin, and others were dashed by the failure of these writers to become great. Eventually its energies became adapted to unpromising objects: Norman Podhoretz writing about seriousness in profoundly impotent novelists; Stephen Marcus trying to extract meaning from the subject of pornography; Diana Trilling writing tediously of Marilyn Monroe. But perhaps the last cause was that the functionaries did not understand the prophets. They attempted to rationalize the status of writer and to explain prose style as a function of liberal intellectual life. The form was too delicate for the substance.

For better or worse the writer of the Sixties is quite illiberal. His hostility to liberalism is enormous, for he has no use for either psychological or political sublimation. The character of a modern writer (the subject is Mailer) is drawn by Christopher Lasch:

> The confusion of power and art, the effort to liberate the social and psychological "underground" by means of political action, the fevered pursuit of experience, the conception of life as an experiment, the intellectual's identification of himself with the outcasts of society. . . .[5]

But this is not ineffably radical. The writer of the Sixties has assumed—among other guises—the vatic sensibility. Prophecy and destruction animate his mind, and he requires nothing to justify them.

In some ways the prophet is like Whitman, although a great deal of energy has mistakenly gone into the effort to prove that a writer like Mailer is recreating the barbaric strength and primitivism we associate with Whitman. But there is a fundamental divergence. In 1871 Whitman wrote that the new writers should be sacerdotal, implying that the role of writing was the civilizing of the continent. It should, he said, be "fit to cope with our occasions, lands, permeating the whole mass of American mentality, taste, belief, breathing into it a new life, giving it decision, affecting politics. . . ." There is a great difference between the sacerdotal and the prophetic, a difference as great as that between the priest and the dweller in the wilderness. The ferocious antagonism between the Beats and the functionaries is proof of this—the classical attacks on the former are those of Norman Podhoretz, Diana Trilling, and Louis Simpson.[6] But it is not the Beats alone (they are

---

5. Christopher Lasch, *The New Radicalism in America* (New York, 1965), p. 347.

6. Diana Trilling, "The Other Night at Columbia," *Claremont Essays* (New York, 1964), pp. 153–173; used by permission of the publisher, Harcourt, Brace & World, Inc. Norman Podhoretz, "The Know-Nothing Bohemians," *Doings and Undoings*, pp. 143–158. Louis Simpson, "On Being A Poet in America," *The Noble Savage*, V (1962), p. 24 ff.

with the exception of Ginsberg not good enough writers to force criticism to grapple with their work) who enforce the new sensibility, although they did a lot to make it possible. The prophets are writers like Baldwin, Mailer, Burroughs—all those who reject the essentially liberal orientation of the functionaries. A good statement of their position is that of John Fowles: "I feel I have three main politico-social obligations. First, to be an atheist. Second, not to belong to any political party. Third, not to belong to any bloc, organization, group, clique or school whatever." [7] The prophets are not liberal because they are not social.

The primary object of the prophets is the self. They share an interest in the sexuality of perversion for several reasons. Like Ginsberg, they may be rational about their homosexuality. Like Mailer, whose literary fondness for sodomy matches the appetite of his readers to witness it, they pit the asocial Reich against the civilizing Freud. Like Burroughs, they assert the condition of ecstasy over that of reason. Their politics are of course fascinating. Almost universally the prophets share a passionate admiration for Fidel Castro—the big poems and literary declarations come from Mailer, Jones, Ferlinghetti.[8] The functionaries are, to their credit, intelligently anti-Communist. The prophets cultivate enthusiasms for dictatorships of the left, and try, whenever possible, to obliterate the distinctions between East and West. Most important of all, the idea of liberal culture profoundly displeases them—when they hear the word "culture" they reach for their pens.

For some of the prophets it is necessary to go back to Carlyle and envision the writer as hero. William Burroughs serves that purpose as seen by one of his biographers, who acknowledges that he is performing a variant of hagiography.[9] Burroughs is seen as

---

7. John Fowles, "I Write Therefore I Am," *Evergreen Review* (August–September, 1964), p. 17.

8. Lawrence Ferlinghetti, "One Thousand Fearful Words for Fidel Castro," *Evergreen Review* (May–June, 1961), pp. 59 ff.; Norman Mailer, "Letter to Castro," *The Presidential Papers* (New York, 1963), pp. 67–75; LeRoi Jones, "Cuba Libre," *Home* (New York, 1966), pp. 11–62.

9. Alan Ansen, "Anyone Who Can Pick Up A Frying Pan Owns Death," *Big Table*, I (1959), pp. 32–43. Used by permission of the author.

the paradigm of the modern hero, the man who first kills and then performs a miracle. His great accomplishment has been to kill himself as an agent of the culture, to have wiped out his assets and cut the psychic ties to the community of normalcy. What matters is that Burroughs has recreated himself into an instrument of artistic potency. As Alan Ansen has put it:

> How many addicts one knows incapable of more than a sob or a monosyllable, how many queers who seem to have no place in life except the perfume counter at Woolworth's or the economy price whorehouse. To use drugs without losing consciousness or articulateness, to love boys without turning into a mindless drab is a form of heroism.[10]

Better than anyone else, Lionel Trilling has understood this kind of heroism. His essay on pleasure refers itself to the "insult offered to the prevailing morality or habit of life" by violence, disgust and perversion.[11] Yet Trilling is powerless to do anything with this insight. He can only remark that those who would destroy the habits and values of bourgeois society would be no less hostile to the most benevolent socialist society on earth. The following is the antithesis of the statement on Burroughs that I have quoted; it will be seen that no synthesis at all is likely:

> There is developing—conceivably at the behest of literature!—an ideal of the experience of those psychic energies which are linked with unpleasure and which are directed toward self-definition and self-affirmation. Such an ideal makes a demand upon society for its satisfaction: it is a political fact. It surely asks for gratification of a sort which is not within the purview of ordinary democratic progressivism.

The point is precisely that democratic progressivism or liberalism, whichever term is preferred, has no tangencies with the writings of prophets. Trilling's indignation must itself be qualified; his essay on Freud praises those biological instincts which resist culture while

---

10. *Ibid.*, p. 37.

11. Lionel Trilling, "The Fate of Pleasure," *Beyond Culture* (New York, 1965), pp. 57–87. From *Beyond Culture* by Lionel Trilling; copyright © 1963 by Lionel Trilling; reprinted by permission of The Viking Press, Inc.

his essay on culture attacks those instincts which refuse to shape themselves to acceptable political forms.

The life of Burroughs shows the operation of forces not culturally utilizable. His biographer, Alan Ansen, is measurably less intelligent than Trilling, but when he says that we live perpetually with heaven and hell he acknowledges something to which Trilling is resistant. The question is not religious—neither Ansen, Burroughs, nor Trilling being remarkable in that respect—but really political. What is connoted is the anger of the writer at the conditions of life, his hatred for social constrictions, his defiant grasp of the death instinct or unpleasure even as he is admonished that he must respect life. The functionary would make the pathology of the writer innocent. It boils down to whether the energies and perversions of writers like Burroughs can be saddled with appropriate political forms. Trilling thinks that ought to be the case; he evidently dreads the inherent fascism of artistic pathology. Norman O. Brown hopes it will be the case: "a little more Eros would make conscious the unconscious harmony between 'dialectical' dreamers of all kinds—psychoanalysts, political idealists, mystics, poets, philosophers—and abate the sterile and ignorant polemics." [12] Facts, of course, have proven otherwise. The added ingredient of Eros is singularly present in Burroughs and Mailer but it abominates political form and does anything but create harmony.

Norman O. Brown's interpretation of Henry Miller seems to me seriously mistaken. He takes Miller as the archetype of the prophet —and sees in him the Utopian, civilizing force of Eros. But when Miller says that this cultural era is past he means that all of it, including its liberal standards, should be dispensed with. He does not speak of power as being amenable to political shaping; in his terms man will not form it but "radiate" it.[13] And he does not, as Trilling sees it, conceive of the self apart from culture so much as he sees it against culture. The prophets have taken him willingly as their God, but the religion in which he figures is antagonistic to the liberal response, antagonistic finally to reason itself. Per-

---

12. Norman O. Brown, *Life Against Death* (Middletown, Conn., 1959), p. 322.
13. *Ibid.*, p. 305.

haps the classical image of the prophet is Paul Bowles' description
of Burroughs in Tangier:

> At the Hotel Muniriya he had a Reich orgone box in which he used
> to sit doubled up, smoking kif. I believe he made it himself. He had
> a little stove in his room over which he cooked his own hashish
> candy, of which he was very proud, and which he distributed to
> anyone who was interested.[14]

This particular image has many structural counterparts. One thinks
of the integrity (of a sort) with which the mutual masturbation of
Ginsberg and Orlovsky is propagated as a kind of literary proof of
their divinity. The vortex of life in which the prophet subsists cannot be reduced to culture. Orgone boxes, kif, ideological homosexuality—these cannot be liberalized and reduced to the bodily
sanity of the pleasure principle. Burroughs is not the ultimate figure
of the deviate as hero; for that we have to go the "Elsie" of Hubert
Huncke: junkie, artist, and hermaphrodite.[15]

The prophet, at least in his guise of homosexual and junkie, is
in the world of ecstasy. It is as far as may be imagined from a social
communion, and the politics which derive from this condition are
as unthinkable to the liberal as to the conservative mind. Burroughs'
hilarious "In Quest of Yage" makes Norman O. Brown sound like
Mathew Arnold:

> Maybe I could capture an Auca boy. I have precise instructions for
> Auca raiding. It's quite simple. You cover both exits of Auca house
> and shoot everybody you don't wanna fuck.[16]

I dislike spoiling any joke, but surely there is at least the germ of a
political attitude here?

Norman Mailer exists in relation to the functionaries much as
H. L. Mencken did to their forebears, he is the antithesis they have
called into being. When, around 1960, he seemed to inject some
new energy into the realm of culture it became necessary to view

---

14. Paul Bowles, "Burroughs in Tangier," *Big Table*, I (1959), p. 43.
Used by permission of the author.

15. Hubert Huncke, "Elsie," *Kulchur*, III (1960), p. 44 ff.

16. William Burroughs, "In Quest of Yage," *Big Table*, I (1959),
p. 60.

him as a test case. F. W. Dupee found that Mailer was attempting to work a way out of the present creative stalemate.[17] Like Norman Podhoretz [18] he sought to understand Mailer as one of our own, that is, difficult, perverse, anti-moral, but necessarily involved in penetrating the evils of Eisenhower's America. The effort of the functionaries at this time was to place Mailer as a moralist *malgré lui*. He was searching for the moral authority so conspicuously absent in the Fifties; in this sense he was carrying the political vision of liberal criticism to its natural conclusion. As Diana Trilling saw it, his purely political function was to make us aware of our own dilemma:

> We accepted the premise of a civilization intolerable to itself; we concurred in the negation of moral values on which we had established our enlightened political ideals. . . . If Mailer's dual wish—to preserve us from the malign forces of political reaction but also to give civilization another push toward the extinction to which it seems inexorably drawn—leads him into moral and political self-contradiction, he is not alone in this dilemma. It is the dilemma of anyone of high political seriousness.[19]

Thus far Mailer could be a representative figure, a mind more daring than the liberal in its attachment to the Id, and more ready than even the functionaries to claim that art had its politics. The Mailer of the later Sixties was to force a response of quite another order.

George Steiner wrote uneasily in 1961 that Mailer's socialism was a queer brew.[20] Altogether too personal, lyrical, charismatic. His seriousness was beginning to come into question because the sexual and political energies of his work seemed to repel rationalization. The publication of *The Presidential Papers* sealed Mailer's fate; in that book it was plain that politics had become "romantic," with all of the dread connotations aroused by that term. A long and very acute essay by Richard Gilman in *The New Republic*

17. F. W. Dupee, "The American Norman Mailer," *Commentary* (February, 1960), pp. 128–132.

18. Podhoretz, *op. cit.*, pp. 179–204.

19. *Claremont Essays*, p. 194.

20. George Steiner, "Naked But Not Dead," *Encounter* (December, 1961), p. 67 ff.

summed up the case of the functionaries. Mailer's individualism had become freakish. His gospel of the orgasm was the opposite of utopian, for it brought to bear not the enhancement of Eros but the violence, sadism and *heroism* that liberal Freudians found it impossible to accept. I might add that Mailer's much-attended short story "The Time of Her Time" was beginning to be seen for what it was, a parable of contempt for liberal culture. One gathers that the heroine of that story—Jewish, intellectual, neurotic—fulfilled a representative role and adopted an allegorical posture that was altogether too informative. At any rate, orgasm was no longer therapy in Mailer, but political parable. The quintessential disappointment of the functionaries, to return to Gilman, has in his essay its summation:

> What he is asking from politics in these essays, diatribes and calls to order, is what it cannot give. . . . There is a perennial and necessary tension between the protective and material function of politics and the transcendent and liberating function of art; and it is a tension that Mailer, like all romantics, cannot bear, so that he seeks to dissolve it. And doing this leads him to his most dangerous formulations, including the notion that "existential politics is rooted in the concept of the hero." No, it could not be more wrong: totalitarian politics, mystical politics, the politics of immolation and disastrous ambition are rooted in that concept.[21]

After this (and it seems to me to be quite correct) it remained only for Mailer to be read out of the party in the *Partisan*. Elizabeth Hardwick's review of *An American Dream* in the *New York Review of Books* was unarguable. Her perception of the badness of the novel was accompanied by that of its worship of power.[22] The politics toward which *An American Dream* strives is decidedly not that of democratic progressivism.

The opposition to Mailer has filtered into the new left, where it is a point of faith that writing and politics inhabit the same skin. In *Studies on the Left* the two Mailers were summed up.

21. Richard Gilman, "Why Mailer Wants To Be President," *The New Republic* (8 February 1964), p. 23. Reprinted by permission of *The New Republic*, © 1964, Harrison-Blaine of New Jersey, Inc.

22. Elizabeth Hardwick, "Bad Boy," *Partisan Review* (Spring, 1965), pp. 291–294.

There was the man who spoke for Castro, civil rights, outcasts—and who attacked the cultures that could produce a J. Edgar Hoover.[23] This Mailer was profoundly right about the culture and his violence could be understood as a moral passion. But the other Mailer could not be acceptable to the left, if only because that passion was not capable of political sublimation. The resemblance of his Kennedy to Liston and his Stevenson to Floyd Patterson was something of a bone in the throat. The aesthetic quality of Liston's body and that of Kennedy's personality impeded the ideological sense. That he writes about the defeated idealism of Stevenson is bad enough, if true enough—it finds its metaphor in Patterson the born loser and liberal's liberal. What is unforgivable is Mailer's conviction that the future belongs to those who have power. The hipster as symbol of the outcast was much more presentable than as symbol of the politician. In making art responsive to life Mailer has exaggerated the demands of the reigning criticism. The crevice beneath the surface of cultural criticism—its vulnerability to what is humanly excessive—has been exposed with intentionally black humor. Mailer's mystery and heroism, his profoundly anti-social ethic, have been seen not as the vehicles of fiction but as values. It is no wonder that the reappraisals of Mailer that emanate from the functionaries are as disappointed with his sense as with his style.

## Revolutionaries

There are some quarters in which Norman Mailer could pass for an Augustinian moralist. Of the new ideologies available to writers there is neo-Reichianism, which resists even the forms of heroism Mailer finds politically appropriate. There is the ideology of ecstasy, combining Boehme with Marx. The "true sane madness" of peyote, for example, dissolves both time and space as it attunes the user to that reality which lies behind our cultural appearances.[24]

23. Lawrence Goldman, "The Political Vision of Norman Mailer," *Studies on the Left*, IV (1964), pp. 129–141.

24. Michael McClure, "Drug Notes," *Evergreen Review* (July-August, 1962), p. 103 ff.

It integrates the user with the universe—as he is a writer it gives him access to objective reality while refining his lost sense of rapture and revery. Its political uses are no less important, for the junkie as hero may "see the truth where it is and . . . fail to see it where it is not." [25] Obviously few things are more dangerous to the liberal custodians of culture. In fact, the great hostilities that are generated are those between the functionaries and the revolutionaries. Along with fascists, Stalinists, academics, capitalists and columnists is "that unique figure of atrophied balls and authoritarian yearning, the American Liberal." [26]

The conflict is at its most visible in contrasting statements by Philip Rieff and Paul Goodman, both of whom have established reputations on the respective Freudian and Reichian moralities they defend.[27] Rieff, writing in *Commentary*, offers a canon of the works of Reich satisfying to the establishment. *Character Analysis* is tolerated and even used, but such books as *Listen, Little Man* and *The Function of the Orgasm* are relegated, with the system of Orgonomy they represent, to an order of science comprising the squared circle, perpetual motion, and the theory of phlogiston. Goodman and those others who speak for the Reichian artist refuse to allow that the later books are illegitimate; simply in the realm of myth and possibility they embolden the act of writing. Rieff had written of *Listen, Little Man* that it was the production of an egomaniac. He notes (correctly, I think) the overwhelming tone of redemption which Reich finds peculiarly appropriate to himself. Goodman is reduced to analogy; he finds the work of Reich Dostoevskian and goes on at some length about his moral frenzy and "inwardly oppressed strong soul." These are concepts as applicable to Reich or Dostoevsky as they are to *Mein Kampf*. The point of course is that Reich's later work is taken seriously by the revolutionaries; Goodman finds his theories on cancer plausible and others accept them as demonstrable.

On the issue of sexual experiment liberals and revolutionaries

25. Paul Bowles, "Kif—Prologue and Compendium of Terms," *Kulchur*, III (1960), pp. 35–40. Used by permission of the author.

26. Marc Schleiffer, "Editorial," *Kulchur*, II (1960), p. 18.

27. Philip Rieff, "The World of Wilhelm Reich," *Commentary*, (September, 1964), pp. 50–58; Paul Goodman, "The Fate of Dr. Reich's Books," *Kulchur*, II (1960), pp. 19–23.

cannot even begin a dialogue. Goodman writes with asperity of *The New Republic* and its cancellation of a review of *The Sexual Revolution*. In his view sexual experience for adolescents will remove the tensions inherent in their—and our—life. As Rieff more dubiously sees it, the aim of this freedom is to divest parents of moral authority. A political vision is subcutaneously within a sexual vision. The opposition extends itself—Goodman's appeal for sexual freedom for adolescents is not without merit, when we consider the general adolescent mess in the United States. Yet even his program has boundaries—those writers on the outer fringes of the revolutionary movement propose as a more saving form of freedom that sexual relations occur within the family itself. This will "resolve" the Oedipus complex and at once invigorate both art and politics.

The politics of sexuality engages Rieff, and his long, intelligent piece in *Commentary* is concerned with Reich's union of absolute sexual freedom with a new form of political expressiveness: "the instincts and the proletariat must triumph together, or not at all." Reich had no more use for the left than the right, in classical terms of definition. The revolution was denied in Russia when it failed to attain the moral, sexual level. It was betrayed in America by liberalism, which accepted the idea of the superego as a political equivalent. Perhaps the fundamental rebellion of Reich was against the crippling process of thought itself. It is in thought, after all, that repression begins—a conception which makes the work of the revolutionaries much more lucid. Burroughs' method of composition, for example, consisting of random pages being stapled together, is a Reichian gesture. The strictures of the functionaries ought to be understood as deriving not only from ideas of what is novelistic; their attacks on the Beats, their punishment of Mailer and their ambivalence toward the Reichian artist depend on the idea of propriety. It is not illogical, especially if we consider the hesitant remarks of Diana Trilling on the uncertainty of liberal culture as to how far we may subscribe to the *social* cathexis of the id.[28]

---

28. "Where do we, where shall we, where can we derive our moral sanctions—from a failing tradition or from the wild free impulses of our racial infancy, from the Ego or the Id?" *Claremont Essays*, p. 195.

The functionaries, quite rightly, are stuck with their sanctions. They find the family indispensable. They have aesthetic difficulties over the idea of pure instinct. Their social framework is communal and their politics are rational. Most interesting of all, they reject grand systems of religion—when Rieff notes that Reichian psychotherapy implies a system of cosmological beliefs he sums up the crowning objection of cultural criticism. That cosmology, for the revolutionary, is nothing less than the end of his creation.

The revolutionaries are at their most ideological on the subject of novelistic politics. Freudo-Marxism, the term used by Rieff to describe the politics involved, operates to the point of transparency in Burroughs' Yage episodes. Burroughs in quest of Yage is the revolutionary in quest of the perfect, primitive sensory experience. For some decades now the hero has been searching for the perfect orgasm: Miller in Paris, Mailer in New York, Burroughs in the jungles of Peru. The Yage search has overtones of the Holy Grail. What Burroughs finds instead is a form of psychological colonialism—western rationalism has reached even into the jungles to transform the pristine homosexual act into a political comedy: "I thought I was getting that innocent back woods ass, but the kid had been to bed with six American oil men, a Swedish Botanist, a Dutch Ethnographer, a Capuchin father known locally as the Mother Superior, a Bolivian Trotskyite on the lam, and jointly fucked by the Cocoa Commission and Point Four." [29] Spengler couldn't be more inclusive.

The odyssey is fated, there are no more golden young men, even in the forests of Peru. The Canal Zone is the home of a special class, with its own low-frequency civil-service brain wave. There is nothing there but catatonic public functionaries and fat American wives gorging candy. The Reichian phrase "character armor" appears at strategic intervals, usually when Burroughs is trying to get across the difference between primitive virtue and civilized madness. After a rhapsody on the polymorphous homosexuality of Peruvians he contrasts this human potentiality with the power of repression: "He has been blocked from expression by the Spanish and the Catholic Church. What we need is a new Bolivar who

---

29. William Burroughs, "In Quest of Yage," pp. 44–64.

will really get the job done." [30] Burroughs stands in relation to that Bolivar somewhat as Mailer does to John F. Kennedy. As he blunders through the backwoods territories of South America, persistently searching for the final narcotic and the primeval masculine embrace, he acts out a political and mythical role. On the one hand the fisher king; on the other, the Reichian hero. At the heart of the Yage episode is the visit to Colombia, which Burroughs sees as the junkyard of western civilization. He does his job well, and uses the reductionist mode as intelligently as Conrad does in *Heart of Darkness*. Human relations—"catatonic," "ugly," "cancerous," "sterile," "frozen"—are both existential and political. After a view of the judges and customs officers, the whores and one-dollar boys, the tourists and especially the politicos, the predictions of Reich seem to be objectively proved. All that character-armoring, with its consequences of disease and repression, is a view of the state through the wrong end of the telescope. There is an Elizabethan word for it, no longer in use: microcosmography.

The politics of ecstasy are accurately described by Paul Bowles in a kind of Cook's tour of drugs.[31] Bowles writes with some lovingness of the dissolution of Judeo-Christian society by the Third World, those cultures which will have absorbed enough of the West to immunize themselves to it. The drug cultures have ingrained in them two principles entirely inhospitable to liberalism: the attachment to pleasure apart from sanctions, and the root isolation of the individual from matters of dialectic. His description has elements of fact and of myth, and will be seen to furnish the revolutionaries with a special political motivation:

> The last strongholds of cultures fashioned around the use of substances other than alcohol are being flushed out. In Africa particularly, the dagga, the ganja, the bangui, the kif, as well as the dawamesk, the sammit, the majoun and the hashish, are all on their way to the bonfires of progressivism. They just don't go with pretending to be European. The young fanatics of the four corners of the continent are furiously aware of this.[32]

---

30. William Burroughs, "In Search of Yage," *Kulchur*, III (1960), pp. 7–18.
31. Bowles, "Kif," *op. cit.*
32. *Ibid.*, p. 36.

The totalitarian impulse—connected here to that democratic "progressivism" which is central to the thought of Trilling—is repelled by the politics of ecstasy. In the essay on Burroughs by Donatella Manganotti the politics of drugs and homosexuality is given a cosmic interpretation.[33] In fact, she perceives the works as a theodicy. The wanderings of Burroughs through the Amazon basin are quite literally a quest for the Grail, in overt form a quest for "civilization, society, and progress." Indeed, the role of Burroughs is Platonic, and *Naked Lunch* is the avatar of *The Republic*.[34] The mechanism of the vision is yage itself, a drug which has to be taken with other people, which involves a conception of relationship. Its end is the defeat of reality as we know it—the repressive, totalitarian relationships imposed by the liberal state. And its power, the *primum mobile* of this cosmology? That resides in its deity, the guru William Burroughs. He is linked to the gods and the oracles of the Greeks, and it is in terms of this essentially religious revelation that Burroughs' revolution is to be understood. The ends it serves will perhaps be contrasted with the forces it generates; when this is all justified on the grounds that it liberated Allen Ginsberg's anxious soul we may tend to find it both trivial and presumptuous.

The apocalypse of the revolutionaries is probably in *FUCK YOU / a magazine of the ARTS*. Quotation for the next few pages is bound to be difficult. The sub-title is *Total Assault on the Culture* and it is true enough. Part of *FUCK YOU* is concerned with obscure sexual postures. Many of its pages are devoted to the perversions, which are graphically and lovingly described. Perhaps of more importance are the cultural oppositions. One side consists of the Goon Squads, J. Edgar Hoover, middle-class liberals, and censorship; on the other are Ed Sanders, Lenny Bruce, Mailer, Ginsberg, and other freedom fighters on the side of Reich and truth. The strength—and whatever greatness may be attributed—of this publication resides in its logically brutal adaptation of liberal protest. It is all here, the position paper, the petition signed by those eminent in the intellectual world, the sympathy toward dissent

33. Donatella Manganotti, "The Final Fix," *Kulchur* (Autumn, 1964), pp. 76–87.
34. *Ibid.*, p. 82.

and deviation. There is the correct attitude toward police brutality and authority in general, the emphasis on rights of the individual; even the sanctions involving the cause of art. But it is all for real, "If you smoke pot, suck cock, shoot junk, march in the street, or talk dirty, know what the legal ground rules are, & protect yourself in advance." [35] Nothing is sacred, not even the demonstration for civil rights.

Conceivably of more interest is the matter of Reichian politics. The writers who staff *FUCK YOU* have two statements on the democracy of sexuality:

> There has been great discussion of the *New Freedom in the Arts*. The facts are that the old line totalitarian fuckhaters, those who shudder at the thought of a guiltless freak-cock grooved into a moist cunt or trembling mouth, but love it when a bazooka blasts off the head of a gook in South Vietnam, *ARE STILL IN POWER!*

> We shall not be free until we can fuck in the streets or anywhere under the Rays of Ra, until all gentle AC-DC gobble cadets can suck cock, grope or bugger in total leisure anywhere, until we can smoke our hashish, or snort the energetic freak powders under our own judgement all over the universe!

Both are authentically, exaggeratedly liberal. Pacifism and freedom—and every other conceivable subject amenable to the logic of liberalism—are carried to a kind of ultimate. The right to welfare is adapted to the right of absolute sexual satisfaction; the machines will work and we will make love in gorgeous deviancy. That Aristophanes tackled (and probably solved) the issue some millennia ago affects neither the program nor the joke.

There is an entire vocabulary lifted from the canon of radical resistance to cultural oppression: "nonviolent guerilla warfare," "resistance for peace," "love," "direct confrontation." The central figure is the writer; his central work, carrying to a conclusion the vision of the functionaries, is the direct exertion of art upon culture. Responsibility is accepted as the burden of the literate mind. Surely nothing could be more complete in the way of communication than this strategy for deviants—phone work, manu-

---

35. Allen Ginsberg, in *FUCK YOU*, VII (September, 1964), p. 2.

script preparation, letter writing, note taking, press releases, public campaigns, and so forth.[36] The mind retentive of the experiences of the Thirties will find this intolerably familiar. Those who place their faith in civil rights will see themselves in a mirror of distortion. And those who define the role of art in the terms offered by the functionaries will find that imitation is the tribute paid by seriousness to seriousness.

The contributors to *FUCK YOU* are aware that pornography has no social dimension. The only way to endow it with meaning is to make it political. Hence the parody only half-seriously exaggerated: "Fuck for Peace!" and slogans of a kind intended to be politically abrasive. The culmination? perhaps that is the "Fuck-in," the sit-in carried to its logical conclusion. If the historian in me speaks, I would say that I find this morally offensive. But I see the point of the joke.

*FUCK YOU* is only the visible part of the iceberg. From there we go downhill to such publications as *Intercourse*, also a cultural manual. It is of course perfectly serious and dedicated to the concept of sexual freedom that the more advanced elements of the mass media nervously approve, as it were, *in absentia*. That this publication is both mindless and nauseating seems less important than that it is serious; perhaps most telling of all is its list of directors, all of whom are prominent in the establishment of the sexual left. Here poets, authors of marriage manuals, and the clerks of genitality practice the strategy of ideological copulation.

The writers on the new sexual left are awesomely political. The second issue of *Intercourse* undertakes to defend us from the guardian priests and politicians who would abuse the unconscious; "*they know*, that if you control the sexual erotic strivings of the individual, you thereby control the *individual*." [37] The two world orders it perceives are those of power and love. There are those who are for the bomb—with its "rather obvious phallic significance" —and those who would substitute for it the psychological benefits of incest. Should the family abandon its unreasonable attachments to guilt and permit the Oedipus complex to be "resolved" through

---

36. "Editorial," *ibid*., pp. 3, 4.

37. William Wantling, "Suicide: a partial statement," *Intercourse* (1965), p. 6.

sexual action we are promised that "hatred, crime, wars, slaughter and the insane seeking of power . . . would slowly die out."

It would be redundant to deplore the moral and scientific views exhibited, and would only furnish the occasion for the ingenuity of contemptuousness. The politics of this proposition alone have sufficient interest. Whether visionaries or strategists, those in the sexual freedom movement combine their strength with that of a more familiar progressivism: with pacifism, civil liberties, and especially with those elements which define and honor themselves insofar as they oppose the radical right. As regards the last, the enemies of sexual freedom are identified with those of political freedom. The militarists, corporationists, and politicians of the right are seen as sexual cripples who compensate for their deficiencies by the joys of power. On the right the "unresolved" Oedipus complex leads to the condition of anti-genitality; hence the root of Birchian politics lies in the middle-class family itself. The analogies which emerge are unsurprising. Power replaces love, the megaton blast replaces orgasm, censorship sublimates impotence, hostility to total sexuality embodies hostility to the principle of life.

Although there are the martyrs of occasion (in this issue Mr. Walter Jenkins) the standing hero is Wilhelm Reich. Over all his brooding presence makes itself felt by a moralizing power. The seriousness of *Intercourse* is a consequence of its avoiding what obsesses most casual pornography, i.e., raw carnal pleasure, such aesthetics as accrue to deviancy. But the betrayal of pornography is the triumph of ideology. In some ways the tone of *Intercourse* is ecclesiastical. There are listed the appropriate modes of sexual congress; the means of producing abortions; bibliographies of works on sexual freedom. There are interchanges of letters among the elect. There is even a British section, which like *The New Yorker* or *Partisan Review*, gives the reader access to the best of what is being thought and censored abroad. Over all is an oppressively ethical atmosphere, a coercive and admonitory sense that we must all go out and fuck for peace. The *kairos* of the movement is expressed by one of its contributors, the writer Tuli Kupferberg, ". . . together with the future sexual revolution which is simmering . . . there is a great social revolution preparing. . . . What glory when these burst forth together in some great Spring of Desire"[38] Even the functionaries would be awed by this dedication of art to life. Pornography, once the last resort of those disqualified from social life, has been converted into a kind of world federalism.

## Saviors

Uneasy lies the head that wears a crown. The Jewish writer's kingdom seems increasingly to be that of the Groves of Nemi. The issues are these: who will be most authentically social, and most symbolically Jewish? There are essentially two views on the issues: one, represented by the functionaries, takes them seriously. The other, represented by Leslie Fiedler, takes them comically. But both agree that the role of the Jewish writer today encompasses more than the practice of the novelist's trade.

It had been expected since the Thirties that the Jewish writer would concern himself with the social facts of the emigration. His milieu would be Brownsville or Williamsburg. His characters would derive from the world of the poor and self-conscious. The disappearing strength of religion would be replaced by the sensibility of radicalism. In the passage from *Jews Without Money* to *Herzog* things changed a good deal, but they also remained the same. The problem of modernness underlay the secular Jewish novel. The Jewish novelist as interpreter of the modern and therefore as agonist of identity became commonplace, indeed institutional. But the antipathies between the Jewish writer and Jewish culture remained. The modes of irony and comedy were not satisfactory in dealing with this antipathy; for one thing, it was too close to the bone; in any case the novel resists complete sublimation. Apart from any *social* experience (the reality imposed by the Second World War on the nature of being Jewish) a new way of looking at Jewish fiction was being examined. This is nowhere so well examined as in Norman Podhoretz' "Jewish Culture and the Intellectuals."

38. Tuli Kupferberg, "Death & Love," *Kulchur*, III (1960), pp. 29–32.

The Jewish intellectual, once he went to Columbia and sub-
scribed to the *Partisan Review*, belonged to the Republic of Letters.
If there was room for Kafka and Proust in this Republic there was
none for Judah Halevi and Sholom Aleichem. Podhoretz found
himself in a wildly improbable situation. As a Columbia under-
graduate absorbed in the conversation of great ideas he was committed to the essential unity of culture; as a student at Jewish
Theological Seminary he was forcibly committed to the greatness
of Yiddish writing. The essay is a very good and very funny account of the dialectic of being modern. In the daytime Podhoretz
tried to account for Jewish literature in the terms of Blake, Lawrence, and Flaubert. At night he tried to bring the standards of
criticism to bear on Bialik, Halevi, and Ibn Gabirol. He produced
in the first instance surprise and in the second outrage; his circle
at Columbia viewing with astonishment the claim of Jewish literature to any standing at all, and his Seminary class responding to
the secularity of criticism with the blood of the six million. The
matter was unresolved: "very little of this has anything to do with
that part of me which reads English, French, and Russian fiction,
and everything to do with that part of me which still broods on the
mystery of my own Jewishness." [39]
The most extreme form of the problem was stated by Seymour
Krim, whose rebellious essays against the critical intelligentsia are
footnotes to the suffocation of literature by criticism.[40] Krim is
eccentric to the joint where this stops being an intellectual benefit,
but he is keenly aware of the fate of fiction when it begins to be
instrumental. Podhoretz has written something which we may
take to be the antithesis of Krim's idea. "For me literature is not an
end in itself . . . I look upon it as a mode of public discourse
that either illuminates or fails to illuminate the common ground
on which we live." The novel, having no final importance of its
own, becomes for Podhoretz a vehicle of cultural insights; what
matters are the attitudes exposed by writing. Armed with a tremendous animus against the functionaries, Krim tells his own in-

39. *Doings and Undoings, op. cit.*, pp. 112–125.
40. Seymour Krim, *Views of a Nearsighted Cannoneer* (New York,
1961). See John McCormick, "The Confessions of Jean Jacques Krim,"
*The Noble Savage*, IV (1961), p. 6 ff.

tellectual biography. He found himself in a milieu in which the Jewish writer, supposedly fertilized by his exposure to radicalism, took upon himself the comprehension of the entire printed universe. Yet it was not an act tending to enlarge freedom, since it was unthinkable to leave the ideational line:

> It was truly immoral to the whole act of writing. *Commentary*, taking its cues from the universities and the various respectable academic and/or ex-radical pros like Richard Chase, the Trillings, William Phillips, Leslie Fiedler, Dwight Macdonald, became a suburb of *PR* in literary evaluation and both magazines were sewed up with *reactionary* what-will-T.S. Eliot-or-Martin Buber-think timidity.[41]

The movement, centering around *Partisan Review*, was inbred, "overcerebral, Europeanish, sterilely citified, pretentiously alienated." It was the product of "a monstrously inflated period wherein it thought it had to synthesize literature and politics and avant garde art of every kind, with its writers insanely trying to outdo each other in Spenglerian inclusiveness of vision." Perhaps the central fact of Krim's experience was the war between aspiration and shame:

> Most of my friends and I were Jewish; we were also literary; the combination of the Jewish intellectual tradition and the sensibility needed to be a writer created in my circle the most potent and incredible intellectual-literary ambitions I have ever seen. Within themselves, just as people, my friends were often tortured and unappeasably bitter about being the offspring of this unhappily unique-ingrown-screwed-up breed.

That this is not wholly true is evident, but it is a good corrective to those who view the Jewish writer as naturally disposed to the purveyance of cultural philosophy. Just as the Negro writer has been assumed to be "naturally" concerned with telling how it is to be a Negro (Ralph Ellison is a glorious exception) the Jewish writer has "naturally" come to be seen as the vehicle of a specific cultural view. Alfred Kazin has called him a connoisseur of the new chaos.[42] In an age of the apocalypse he has furnished the

41. Krim, *op. cit.*, p. 15.
42. Alfred Kazin, "The Jew as Modern Writer," *Commentary* (April, 1966), p. 41.

complex, overborne intellect demanded by our needs and tastes. It has been suggested that this role is not displeasing to publishers. Leslie Fiedler believes that the Jewish writer himself accepts it—the best are amused, the second best embarrassed, the worst "atrociously pleased." [43] His *Waiting For the End* is about the Jewish figure (both the novelist and the character he creates) who has something special going for him in Jewishness. To participate in it by birth, conversion, or through literary strategy is to participate in the kind of thing often called alienation—the Gentile Jew is the new equivalent of the White Negro. One of the good things about Fiedler is his range; he goes over this new pseudomorphosis from its intellectual to its commercial forms, from Kafka to Uncle Tom Golden. We began with a culture in which the Jew was an outsider—how much so, we have only to read the less attractive remarks of Henry James to find out. We have now a culture in which the Alienated Jewish Intellectual Novel is as much a genre as are the ode and the epic. Jewishness is now many things: a sign of suffering, virtue, and estrangement; a sign of superior sensibility; a commodity. It's not as good as being a Negro, but it sells books. Fiedler's investigation into the special status of the Jewish novelist overturns many rocks, and offers many reasons, although I don't think all of them are convincing.

We cover briefly the vicarious shame over Germany, the polite new phenomenon of philo-Semitism, the general canonization of minorities. There is the mystique of Jewishness—although in operating on this Fiedler works rather too hard at manufacturing myths. It turns out that the Jewish patriarch is seen as Abraham, the wielder of the knife of sacrifice and—could it have been otherwise?—castration. The full picture is that of "the nightmare of the Jew's alluring daughter flanked by the castrating father." That is a pretty *professional* nightmare, the kind of thing that makes the analyst secure in his vocation. But he is taking his own pulse. Fiedler is more to the point when he talks about two other things, the meaning of secular Jewishness and the special place of vulgarity in modern life. On the first he should be quoted:

---

43. Leslie Fiedler, *Waiting For The End* (New York, 1964), pp. 9–103.

Through their Jewish writers, Americans, after the Second World War, were able to establish a new kind of link with Europe in place of the old paleface connection—a link not with the Europe of decaying castles and the Archbishop of Canterbury, nor with that of the Provençal poets and Dante and John Donne, nor with that of the French *symbolistes* and the deadly polite *Action Francaise*—for these are all Christian Europes; but with the post-Christian Europe of Marx and Freud, which is to say, of secularized Judaism, as well as the Europe of surrealism and existentialism. Kafka, neo-Chasidism —a Europe which at once abhors and yearns for the vacuum left by the death of its Christian god.

Through the overstatement some things do become plain. The Jewish writer is expected to legitimize through the process of his fiction and the exertions of his personality the present cultural condition. If the novel is indeed to be instrumental, and if our lives are chaos, then the novel will illuminate that chaos by participating in it. I am not sure that Fiedler approves of this to the extent that Podhoretz so obviously does, but it ought to be clear that this asks the novel to be a parasite of sensibility, a kind of adjunct of "the culture" which follows the fortunes of its host.

The functionaries persist in admiring the fallacy. Kazin writes solemnly that the Jewish writers now represent to us the unreality of our present lives and our anxiety. There are at least two answers to this. The first is, *ad hominem,* that I have no sense of my own unreality or anxiety. The second is that this unreality, anxiety, alienation, is carefully cultivated in our literary world. We ought to go back to Richard Chase's intelligent remark that estrangement makes those who have it rather comfortable. It is either a literary pose, a personal neurosis, or a financial arrangement, with absolutely no meaning when translated into cultural or political terms. My own sense of it is that it substitutes for talent.

In two essays Lionel Trilling has tried to make clear how much of a strategy alienation is.[44] The idea that the avant garde writer is the alienated man he finds to have both authority and sanctitude. But it does not have legitimacy, if we mean by that a responsibility to fact which it is the fate of every concept to undergo. Trilling

---

44. Lionel Trilling, "On the Teaching of Modern Literature" and "The Two Environments," *Beyond Culture,* pp. 3–30, 209–233.

writes with intelligent appreciation of Saul Bellow's response to the iconic argument that "modern society is frightful, brutal, hostile to whatever is pure in the human spirit, a waste land and a horror." That, Mr. Trilling says, is not so much an argument as it is a totem. If the novel is to respond to cultural life it will have to do that in all its complexity—the writer cannot elevate himself into greatness on the prestige of his attitudes. How ready we are, he remarks, to undertake "the socialization of the anti-social, or the acculturation of the anti-cultural, or the legitimization of the subversive." How ready we are to look into the abyss as tourists.

The Jewish writer has become an apostle of modernity to the extent that he takes upon himself our guilt and anxiety. Because of this he has become more and more of a caricature. As the ideas become more fixed the novels become worse—in the case of Mailer they evanesce into the unstructured cries of how bad it all is. Benjamin De Mott's essay on the cultural bandwagon [45] notes how easy it is for the novelist to become attuned to public sympathies, and how fatal for his craft. There seems to me to be another kind of error involved, and since it bears on the operation of social forces it is a very important error. A student asked Leslie Fiedler, "do we have to become Gentile Jews before we can become White Negroes?" In the light of the whole White Negro mess, with its scrambled Reichian genitality and its fake union of feeling and form, this is bad enough. All that has seeped down to *Playboy* and the *Evergreen*, where it belongs anyhow. It is even worse from another point of view. Once the Jewish novelist has been permitted to become the demiurge of modernity he fulfills a new mythical role. In bad novel after bad novel, in one terrible term paper after another, the idea liquefies and congeals: The Jew is the agent of a new cultural fertility. Through his loving kindness and sexual adroitness, through his insight and guilt, he somehow atones for us all. He is Seymour Glass and Holden, S. Levin and Asa Leventhal. When he beds a woman in a novel it is comical but redemptive. When he suffers a blow to his ego we are all participating in the shame of being human. And when he cuts the anchor and turns himself on, the greatness of his orgies and the perfection of

45. Benjamin De Mott, "Jewish Writers in America: A Place in the Establishment," *Commentary* (February, 1961), pp. 127–134.

his feeling show us all where we ought to be going. For my part I hate to see the Jew become a swinger so soon after he has finished being a climber. The really bad thing, though, about turning the Jew into a symbol of better sex and spirit and sensation was outlined some time ago by Hannah Arendt. In a luminous essay on "The Jews and Society" [46] she said this about the new mania depicted by Proust, the social cultivation of the sexual invert and the cultural invert: "In both cases, society was far from being prompted by a revision of prejudices. They did not doubt that homosexuals were 'criminals' or that Jews were 'traitors'; they only revised their attitude toward crime and treason." I don't think anything remains to be said.

---

46. Hannah Arendt, *The Origins of Totalitarianism* (New York, 1958), p. 80 ff.

# 10.

# *THE WRITING*

## *Totems*

It is impossible to doubt the satisfaction with which terms like "predicament" and "alienation" are deployed. Groaning with seriousness, the critic sanctifies a rite in which those writers comfortable beyond excess entertain themselves with Doubt. To account for modern fiction the critic first accounts for the modern world, "the alienation of the self . . . the dominant political trend of the age . . . the antagonism between instinct and civilization . . . the absolute nudity of the self in a world devoid of preconceived values." [1] Once they have become habitual such phrases exert the power of axioms. Their adequacy for the historical situation is rarely tested, as rarely as their adequacy for fiction and drama.

The historicism which fascinates itself by contemplating our

---

1. Ihab Hassan, *Radical Innocence* (Princeton, 1961), p. 20.

"predicament" assumes that all men take such ideas seriously. It might be suggested that even in the universities, where there is the most vigorous propagation of the syndrome, neither faculty nor students live the life of their ideas. The faculty contemplate their careers and the students live essentially in the natural condition, preoccupied with their emotions, status, and bodies. No one in mass culture knows that he is in mass culture. Intellectuals of a certain kind suspect it, and differentiate themselves in advance—into a more exclusive form of mass sensibility. The striated view that men and societies live by decades can only seem ridiculous when compared to experience; the idea that we cumulatively failed in the Twenties; strove magnificently in the Thirties; were baptized by the Forties; suffered our indignities quietly in the Fifties is simply the imposition of the experience of an incredibly removed minority upon the character of modern life. The best indication of this is the exasperation of the clerks of seriousness with the present generation, an attitude based on nothing more than the unwillingness to recognize that the experiencing of history is really subjective. This last is perhaps the real "predicament" of writing. Although mankind, as is habitual, lives a-historically and peaceably with its own particular, temporal presence, writing involves the simultaneous comparison of values. The tone of modern life, no different from that of any historical period, is furnished by its confrontations with the natural exigencies of being; the tone of modern writing, critical and creative, is more nearly ideological. The writing is not concerned with natural experience unless, as in the case of sexuality, it can become instrumental; it has found a habitual pattern whereby our experience can be invested with those romantic advantages that accrue to psychological failure. The lesson of the nineteenth-century novels has been quite lost, and modern fiction continues to assert that to be in history confers a unique and tragic meaning on human feeling. The point of *War and Peace*—or of *Invisible Man*—is quite otherwise, for the infinite capacity of human character can not even be named in cultural terms.

The insistent formality of modern writing is the best indication of its principles. Its great mode is reduction: the telescoping of character and sensibility into categories rigorously dependent on politics. As far as character is concerned it is now possible, un-happily, to rationalize all of fiction in advance—the rebel, the initiate, the sufferer, the alienated exhaust the possibilities of character. Marcus Klein puts it nicely:

> These are not bad days for fiction, but it is noisy in the literary marketplace. Unless your special noise is that you are a Jew, a Negro, a junkie, a physicist, a homosexual, a prophet of holocaust, a prisoner, a Penrod run away from home and gone on a romp toward Dharma, a bulgy and guilt-laden American, or a spectacular and streamlined coward, it is not so easy to get a hearing.[2]

The readers of Dickens were at least uncertain as to the fate of Little Nell, but we are too well informed on the fate of character in fiction. We know what will happen because ideas, unlike men, are finite and predictable—and once we have made men into ideas there can be no astonishment at their "predicament." It will be understood that when I talk about what "happens" I do not mean the intricate choreography of the novel—the unexpected perver-sions and peripeties. The fellatio undergone by Rabbit, the sodomy celebrated by Rojack, the pederasty confirmed by Vivaldo are part of the mechanics of biology. In terms of what humanly "hap-pens" *Mansfield Park* is a much more revealing—and far more *dangerous*—book than *The Story of O*.

In one casebook after another, in one exhibition of intellectual vulgarity after another, we are reminded that modern writing is formally divided into categories. The age from seventeen to twenty-one is to be satisfied with Holden Caulfield as its representative figure; its fathers recognize that in Herzog they receive their own apotheosis. The underground is even more limited, for the stock types are fewer. The once private vision of erotic withdrawal has given way to a new one, and the underground hero, carried off by the police "waving genitals and manuscripts," [3] can possess only a

---

2. Marcus Klein, "Quiet Voice in the Marketplace," *The New Leader* (6 March 1961), p. 27 ff. Reprinted with permission from New Leader issue of 6 March 1961. Copyright by American Labor Confer-ence on International Affairs, Inc.

3. Allen Ginsberg, "Howl," *Writers in Revolt*, Terry Southern,

single set of attitudes. They have been pretty well listed by George P. Elliott:

> "The world is vile. I am vile. Sex is life.
> "I am a great man at sex. I am a great writer. Sex is reality.
> "I write to change the world. Even if I did change it, it would still be vile. Sex is vile.
> "Who am I?
> "Vote for me." [4]

As Philip Roth has written,[5] there is a built-in embarrassment of the imagination for the modern writer. He has his hands full trying to understand or even make credible the American reality. The culture daily tosses up figures that are the envy of any novelist: Charles Van Doren, Roy Cohn, Sherman Adams, Dwight David Eisenhower. Or Mario Savio, Ronald Reagan, Bobby Kennedy, and Lurlene Wallace. The standard response of the writer is to place himself in the reader's line of vision—to claim, as variously as Salinger or Mailer, that the selfhood of the artist is the burden of the work. The book becomes meta-fictional; it conveys the attitude of the author far more directly than literature has ever permitted itself to do. It does not require fictional credence but it does demand that the events allow principally an interpretation of the author's politics, or sex habits, or cosmology. In that sense *An American Dream* is a vehicle for Mailer's Reichianism; *Another Country* is *Corydon* set to music; and *Naked Lunch*, far from being the *ultima thule* of the underground, seems to resemble most closely *Uncle Tom's Cabin*. As spectacles of artistic daring they fall somewhat short of Botticelli's madonnas, whose faces incorporate a feeling and an experience intensely at variance with the limits of seriousness.

Those critics not imposed upon by the new fiction and the drama or rote protest have been pitiless. There is De Mott on Salinger,[6]

Richard Seaver, and Alexander Trocchi, eds. (New York, 1965), p. 22.

4. George P. Elliott, *A Piece of Lettuce* (New York, 1964), p. 46.

5. Philip Roth, "Writing American Fiction," *Commentary* (March, 1961), pp. 223–233.

6. Benjamin De Mott, "Dirty Words?", *Hudson Review* (Spring, 1965), pp. 31–44.

Phillips on anti-literature,[7] Brustein on the gaping profundity of Arthur Miller.[8] Perhaps most incisive is Harold Rosenberg: "History has blessed us with a cult that takes everything seriously, which could indeed be called a 'cult of seriousness.' I mean the literary intellectuals. This cult has chosen as its fabulous profession to keep hunting the Zeitgeist in order to submit to its command." [9] Hunting the *Zeitgeist* has its fictional equivalent in William Eastlake's dialogue of the Zia and the Navajo. The Zia, a Conradian convert to civilization, expounds that "God is a unicorn. The only problem is exploding populations and dwindling resources. I know I speak too much of Beethoven but Beethoven, my friends, is a universe." He is the Seymour Glass of the Pueblos. The Navajo, who has been there before, replies, "I don't know whether the Zia got this kind of talk at Utah Aggie but don't forget he had been to Salt Lake and Denver too." [10]

If there is in fact a predicament it centers on the nature of tragedy. More and more insistently tragedy is being defined not as what you do but what happens to you. In order to accommodate a sensibility of failure it has been bowdlerized—that is, I think, the correct term for a literature which offers answers to unresolvable questions. It seems no coincidence that the historical event of Eichmann and the literary event of *The Deputy* raised the one true note of doubt in this decade; having encountered evil on its own terms we were reluctant to conceive them. The intellectual scandals surrounding these events were the certain indication of their authenticity.

---

7. William Phillips, "Notes on the New Style," *The Nation: 100th Anniversary Issue* (20 September 1965), pp. 232–236.
(8 February 1964), pp. 26–30.

8. Robert Brustein, "Arthur Miller's Mea Culpa," *The New Republic* (8 February 1964), pp. 26–30.

9. Harold Rosenberg, "Death in the Wilderness," *The Tradition of the New* (New York, 1961), pp. 241–258.

10. William Eastlake, "What Nice Hands Held," *The Kenyon Review* (Spring, 1960), p. 194 ff. Used by permission. Life imitates art; here is Hubert Selby's own interpretation of *Last Exit to Brooklyn:* "I'm trying," Selby says, "to overwhelm the reader with truth, like Beethoven." From Webster Schott's review in *The Nation,* reprinted as an advertisement in *The New York Review of Books* (31 December 1964).

Raymond Williams has written finely of liberal tragedy—the attempt to account for evil in social terms.[11] In its beginnings it told how man was destroyed by the greatness of his capacities, but it has dwindled into retailing the themes of victimization:

> The conviction of guilt, and of necessary retribution, is as strong as ever it was when imposed by an external design. And this is the heart of liberal tragedy, for we have moved from the heroic position of the individual liberator, the aspiring self against society, to a tragic position of the self against the self. Guilt, that is to say, has become internal and personal. . . . Liberalism, in its heroic phase, is beginning to pass into its twentieth century breakdown: the self-enclosed, guilty, isolated world; the time of man his own victim.

The act of liberation becomes narrowly historical and political, culminating in the socialist drama of Arthur Miller, in which social contradictions make the human dilemma. The differentiated self disappears, and we all become part of a movement. Eventually the theme of victimization *becomes* tragedy, although of an unsatisfying kind. It gives rise to a stock figure: the "heroic liberator opposed and destroyed by a false society: the liberal martyr." In the work of Ibsen the liberal hero fights against the social life. He finds a world full of compromise and hypocrisy; in it the great struggle is to locate himself. As the drama has attenuated from Ibsen to Miller the liberal hero attains a political eminence. He begins to translate suspicion of society into anger at the "collective persecution" of its components. Far from measuring his character and fate by actions he comes to believe that he suffers for what he is and naturally desires. Merely to live in society (which is by definition evil) is to become its victim. At that point we are in the Sixties.

What Williams sees as the "collective persecution" of society (which stands in the same relationship to modernity as the matter of God's existence did to the milieu of Voltaire) Harold Rosenberg

---

11. Raymond Williams, "From Hero to Victim: Ibsen, Miller and the Development of Liberal Tragedy," *Studies on the Left*, IV (1964), pp. 83–97. Used by permission.

identifies as the "material weight of society." [12] Under this load we all become outlaws—but, as Rosenberg warns, it is easy to get quite sick of outlaws. The literature of the outcast is the cheapest form of intoxication now available.

Perhaps the salient form of liberal tragedy is the Jewish novel, in which the comedy of human action takes its parodic character from the tragic circumstances of exterior life. Since that life is by definition inhospitable to the liberal, humanitarian impulses, the protagonist functions as a hero of sensibility. This is best viewed in Bernard Malamud's *A New Life*.[13] There is first of all and most recognizable a diffuse sense of guilt. The hero, it goes without saying, is Jewish, neurotic, victimized. As a substitute for heroic action there is heroic pity. There is a rigorous structuring of values around liberal politics. And there is an obsession with redemptive genitality which takes the place of what we once would have called religion.

*A New Life* is in fact not without religion—but that is split into two parts. The dogmatic part is political and the existential part vitalistic. The book begins with S. Levin's arrival at Cascadia College from the East; he takes the chairman's wife as his mistress (perhaps a new classical form of wish-fulfillment for the academic audience) and violates the torpid placidity of the college by his urgent, undefined vision of truth. He has been preceded by Leo Duffy, a mad, bad Irishman who is in a sense the book's hero, and is certainly the object of love for Levin's pregnant soul. Levin has suffered, which is good; he is a reformed alcoholic. He is Jewish, and from New York, which is even better, for these are the indications of his superior sensibility and experience. Best of all, he believes in love and in academic freedom. He is one of the many figures of the Christ-*cum*-Quixote of our time, whose ineffectiveness is a form of grace. He stands for the mind redeemed by love in

12. Harold Rosenberg, "Notes From the Ground Up," *The Noble Savage*, I (1960), pp. 50–59. See James Baldwin's apostrophe to history in *Seeds of Liberation*, Paul Goodman, ed. (1964): "The framework in which we operate weighs on us too heavily to be borne and is about to kill us."

13. Bernard Malamud, *A New Life* (New York, 1961).

the body redeemed by potency. The drunken lilt of his mistress, "I married a man with no seeds at all," defines the situation he redeems, for like Lady Chatterley, she is tied to a husband sterile in the ambiguous sense intended.

The synthetic primitivism of love in *A New Life* is becoming habitual to the present—Levin and Pauline meet in a glade primeval and uncontrollably sink to the earth. The entire affair suggests something which is part of dehydrated liberal tragedy: that a certain warmbloodedness and emotional fervor are the full measure of human possibility. Throughout the book the commentator delights in those who are "warm," which would not be objectionable if warmth were not also interpreted in moral and political terms:

> Levin's freshmen, when he met them, were eighteen and warm. . . . very few he knew were committed to ideas or respected intellectualism. They showed almost no interest in the humanities and arts. . . . They overvalued "useful" knowledge and confused vocational training with humanistic education. They consistently applied standards of technical efficiency to the values and purposes of life; so did too many of their professors. Even their fears were unimaginative. . . . They had not earned their innocence.

Evidently to be "committed to ideas" is better than merely having rational ideas; it is the act that matters, the emotion as representation of truth. The vitalistic ideal is that of the natural opposed to the useful, the humanities and arts opposed to purposes which are examined. The doctrine of warmth connects Malamud to Heller and Donleavy; it is the singular virtue in a world that permits no other kind. Noticeably, the students have not had the definitive experience of earning their innocence; they have committed the error of having been born after the Thirties, the modern Renaissance.

The infatuation which Levin the redeemer has for Duffy, the baptist who preceded him, is pitched upon the identification of pure expressiveness with the highest good. Here is the resemblance once more to Heller and Donleavy—and to Mailer and Baldwin. Duffy's potency is metaphorical also: his drinking, his arguing, his madness and his political radicalism all serve to commend him. "Leo was the oddball's oddball, he hit the wall with his head." His excellence lies in the fact that he is at odds with his civilization.

Levin himself is much concerned with "life" and very much opposed to "things." But his complex of beliefs is predictable. He is
for "creativeness" in English composition and against grammar;
he is for a "liberal position" and against the terror conducted by
all the Philistines against all the Intellectuals:

> Add to a backlog of personal insecurity his portion of the fear that
> presently overwhelmed America. The country was frightened silly
> of Alger Hiss and Whittaker Chambers, Communist spies and Con-
> gressional committees, flying saucers and fellow travelers, their
> friends and associates, and those who asked them for a match or the
> time of day. Intellectuals, scientists, teachers were investigated by
> numerous committees and if found to be good Americans were
> asked to sign loyalty oaths. Democracy was defended by cripples
> who crippled it. At Cascadia College the American fear manifested
> itself, paradoxically, in what was missing; ideas, serious criticism, a
> liberal position.

The book is self-evidently a mirror of the times, but a rather
special one. The whole apparatus is here: individual against society,
reality against foreign policy, genital liberalism against repressive
conservatism. The uses of implication are various. In the most
evasive style Hiss is equated with Chambers and "Congressional
committees" diffuses a veil of unlikehood over "Communists";
fellow travelers are as probable as flying saucers, and the ultimate
stigmata of the destruction of democracy is the loyalty oath. The
word "serious" has run through this discussion—as used in the quotation I take it to mean a variety of things: predominately, a generalized hostility to and detachment from American civilization.
But how "serious" can a book be which talks incessantly of the
"humanities" and "arts," of "ideas" and of "intellect," and which
never progresses beyond these platitudes? It is rather like Mailer
writing of love.

What S. Levin stands for in this book is also redemption by intellect—but what he offers to the sterile academicism of Cascadia
is the sterile liberalism of *The New York Post*. He stands eventually only for "academic freedom," for the "visionary ideal" which
is only a function of his personality. With some fashionable lat-
terday Emersonianism and Thoreauism the theme is present:
"Whoever would be a man must be a nonconformist." When S.

Levin standing at a urinal and listening through the wall, dimly, to this utterance sighs "Amen," the contribution of his thought has been defined. He believes in nonconformity without ever discovering that the idea is inapplicable when divorced from its religious origins and ineffectual when made to serve as an end in itself. The book is full of small allegiances to great ideas, yet it is shamefully barren of their elucidation.

I have taken Malamud's *A New Life* as representative of the fiction of totemism and I think Jonathan Baumbach's *The Landscape of Nightmare* can stand for the criticism which makes that fiction possible.[14] This book attempts to show that there is an underlying myth of victimization in American fiction—and to validate the fiction because of that myth. There is a great and uncontrolled proliferation of demi-critical terms: "birth," "initiation," "martyrdom" and "primal" experience. There is a stultifying array of fashionable terms having to do with our "predicament": "guilt," "identity," "innocence," "redemption." This terminology, which is largely derivative, is accompanied by a superficial sense of what American culture is, and by an ethical psychology thinly drawn from Erich Fromm.

Baumbach writes of Jewish novelists that "what *is* relevant is the similarity of their moral preoccupations, the concentration on the burden and ambivalence of assuming personal responsibility in a world which accommodates evil." This kind of profundity does not a novel make. When Baumbach invokes the word "Dostoevskian" to explain Bernard Malamud, when he tries to sell us the idea that "victimizer and victim" are the essential roles of our life, we know that he has made two rather large mistakes; he is looking at life through the eyes of the middle-brow critic—and he is assuming that the function of the novel is to reflect a seriously limited view of the culture which sustains it.

In each of the novelists taken up by *The Landscape of Nightmare* (they are by no means exclusively Jewish—only existentially so) Baumbach claims to see a particular myth that gives his work its character. The myth is attuned to the critical milieu. Robert Penn Warren, for example, is generalized to the point where none

---

14. Jonathan Baumbach, *The Landscape of Nightmare* (New York, 1965).

of his fictional characters seem to have any specific relevance, "All of Warren's main characters experience at one time or another the loss of innocence and are characterized in terms of their accommodation to their Fall." The immediate situation is not dealt with; *All the King's Men*, which I take to be our political novel par excellence, is never approached on the level of political meaning. What we are given instead is a kind of psychology that has become all too familiar to readers of middle-brow criticism:

> Since Duncan Trice, who is considerably older than Cass, initiates him into vice, he is, in effect, the father of Cass's adultery with Annabelle. What Cass has learned from Duncan he had put into practice with Duncan's wife. Therefore, Cass's crime, Warren suggests, is implicitly incestuous, for if Duncan, the man whose death he affects, is his "substitute" father, Annabelle as his wife is a sort of symbolic mother.

An examination of this may be in order; not only to find what lies behind its Draconic logic, but to see why this *kind* of guilt should be pumped into the story. That it is all assertion and worse is plain—the passage operates from the verbs "is" and "suggests" and from the disarming phrases "therefore" and "in effect" with no sustaining argument. What matters is that the mundane is linked to the unutterable. The action of the novel derives a Higher Importance if it can be related to the Oedipus complex. It is more relevant, evidently, if it can reflect upon those matters of paternity, identity, and selfhood which are the existential realities of the moment. And it attains its most important dimension of meaning insofar as it can be made to express that sense of psychological—and cultural—failure which is central to totemism.

Baumbach's habit of invoking Dostoevsky is the kind of ploy we have come to expect from those enchanted by profundity. Not only is Malamud a Dostoevskian writer, but Salinger as well: "Holden is Prince Mishkin as a sophisticated New York adolescent." One might as well say that Holden is an adolescent form of Dante Alighieri. Granted that Salinger invites a response to "innocence" and "guilt"—yet it seems obsessive to call Stradlater, Holden's roommate, "one of Holden's destructive fathers." Not only this boy but another is a "destructive father" because they are of the world—and "two years old [*sic*] than Holden." In order to

be totemic Baumbach forgets what it is to be tribal: it is so necessary to his critical position to find symbolic paternity and rejection at the core of the modern experience that he ignores things
that may be rationally explained on some other basis. The two
destructive "fathers," Stradlater and Ackley, may be seen in some
other relationship, as siblings; or simply as competitors from the
peer group. They may even be seen as individuals, although this
may sound like a deliberate provocation.

In short, *The Landscape of Nightmare* is one of the most academic books which it is possible to conceive. It has faithfully
adapted all the second-rate ideas taught at third-rate universities.
It brings into play a response that is now standard. The endless
reminders that American novelists of the last decade are *somehow*
Dostoevskian is an indication of a strategy and a poverty of mind.
It is a strategy insofar as it tries to endow their work with profundity; it is a clue to the nature of totemism insofar as it permits
nothing to exist on its own terms. Styron, also a "Dostoevskian,"
is pushed and molded until he too becomes what he ought to be.
His characters are replete with Heaven and Hell, Loss and Innocence, Guilt and Meaning. Even so limited a thing as crossing a
river emerges as something Other: "the ferry ride that separates
Port Warwick from the mainland is employed symbolically to
suggest the classic voyage across the river Styx." Having said this,
what has been gained? Is it a *serious* voyage—or is it perhaps a
crossing like that of *The Frogs?* Does the novel mean any more
when we find that it can be mythologized? On the contrary, it
means a good deal less. The reason for this is that you cannot talk
about innocence and guilt on the purely literary level. All of the
symbols of theology have been ransacked, but its systematic attack
on their meaning is never explored. The ludicrous thing about
totemic criticism is that it takes these concepts, which are of a
subtle and complicated nature, and swallows them whole. It accepts neither their infinite variations nor the imperatives they
assert. That, I think, accounts for the *entertainment* of both fiction
and criticism; large ideas are being used promiscuously and without any consequences to those who wield them.

It has for the most part been Jewish critics who have responded
to the literary propagation of totemism. They have been most

jaundiced in the case of the totemic figure who is Jewish. Robert
Alter has written of the Jew bearing love throughout (literary)
America exactly as the sultry and exotic Latin bore the power of
evil through the novels of the last century.[15] Harvey Swados has
pointed to the tension of psychological dialectic in the Jewish
novel, the writer's self-hatred and despair transparently visible
through the "human superiority" of the figure he constructs.[16]
Stanley Edgar Hyman has pinned down the nature of Salinger's
Big Religious Package: the ruinous love of the insufferable Glass
family for its own essence.[17] Salinger has of course brought out
the worst and best of the critics—a short lambasting to rival those
of Hyman and Benjamin De Mott is supplied by Isa Kapp in *The
New Republic*.[18] All resent the evasiveness of Salinger toward
ideals and moral concepts, his purgatorial depiction of a world
which has failed to be intelligible to adolescents. Perhaps the most
pointed, as it is the most angry, of comments is that of Jane Hayman on the White Jew who believes in the power of love and the
holiness of weakness:

> Sexual love, love of the little guy, and mother love are equally
> important. . . . In every case, love of weakness in general—com-
> passion—is the thing that counts. . . . Such a plethora of feeling
> might almost be Franciscan except for the fact that the modern cor-
> relative of the saint's inner light is a rich, morbid self-hatred. . . .
> The cult of compassion is in fact a cult of failure.[19]

The subjects of this love are generally involved in pain; it seems
that to avoid Reich is to commit oneself to Fromm. The pantheon
of the miserable—dwarfs, cripples, homosexuals, whores, addicts,
and especially adolescents—fills out the work of those now in the
center ring. This work has penetrated the culture at large; from

15. Robert Alter, "Sentimentalizing the Jews," *Commentary* (September, 1965), pp. 71–75.

16. Harvey Swados, *A Radical's America* (New York, 1961), p. 155.

17. Stanley Edgar Hyman, "J. D. Salinger's House of Glass," *The
New Leader* (21 January 1963), pp. 22–23.

18. Isa Kapp, "Salinger's Easy Victory," *The New Republic* (8 January 1962), pp. 27–28.

19. Jane Hayman, "The White Jew," *Dissent* (Spring, 1961), pp. 191–
196. Used by permission.

Albee to Warhol the crime of self-hatred is punished by acts of self-love.

The score card of critics must include Richard Kostelanetz' angry "Militant Minorities," [20] the mordantly intelligent "Jewish Writer in America" by Karl Shapiro,[21] and, inevitably, Leslie Fiedler's "Zion as Main Street." [22] The first of these views the manufacture of Jewish culture heroes as part of a program. Kostelanetz begins by surveying the Southern writers, and notes that their progress toward worldly success and influence has set the tone for imitation by the professionally Jewish. There was the core of critics and propagandists; the common ideology (Marxian liberalism); the valuation of social experience and the consequent testing of literature against it; the hierarchy of reputations; and, finally, the irresistible temptation to grasp for major status, once christened "the-Saul-Bellow-shall-be-our-Greatest-Writer-or-bust movement." Kostelanetz is extremely perceptive on the sensors of the movement: the inflation of minor reputations as a form of compensation; the capture of sympathetic Gentile authorities on literature; the distortion of argument, as in the attacks on Hannah Arendt by those committed to "group innocence."

It would be redundant to state the indignation of Karl Shapiro; although it should be said that his essay on "psychologically Juda-istic" literature is worth much more attention than it has received. At the other extreme, Leslie Fiedler is equally important. After the facile images and allegories, after the amateur psychoanalysis, Fiedler has really much more to say in his unserious way than those who wrap themselves in the toga of culture. Triumphantly, reversing the idea of "seriousness," he has turned to culture itself for an explanation: the political radicalism of the Thirties endured its senility in the campaigns of Adlai Stevenson: the great sexual revolution turned into a "vaguely Freudian broadmindedness toward masturbation in the very young and casual copulation in the some-

---

20. Richard Kostelanetz, "Militant Minorities," *The Hudson Review* (Autumn, 1965), pp. 472–478.

21. Karl Shapiro, "The Jewish Writer in America," *In Defense of Ignorance* (New York, 1960), pp. 205–217.

22. Leslie A. Fiedler, "Zion as Main Street," *Waiting For the End* (New York, 1964), pp. 65–88.

what older." The universalizing of Jewishness—the presence of the mock-camp-imitation-crypto-Jewish protagonist—enabled liberal dissent to make its last stand in fiction. Perhaps the final word on that issue belongs to George Santayana, a man most unsympathetic to the aesthetics, morals, and politics involved, "We are still in the liberal world, not at all alarmed by a moral chaos, if only a mechanical industrial order, firmly advancing beneath, renders that moral chaos harmless and entertaining.[23] He was speaking (not especially intelligently) of the writers of two generations ago; those who, like Gide and Lawrence, were to furnish modernity with a new set of values. If he was wrong about them he was right about something else. The only reason that the novel of fake guilt and fake love has a chance to succeed is that the reality it excludes permits that success indifferently. Is it too much to suggest that the great secret, the best-kept secret, of the decade is that literature doesn't mean anything to anyone? The great reality is that mechanical order firmly advancing beneath. Santayana, of course, was wrong about one more thing—it is not moral chaos which becomes harmless and diverting. It is, I think, the moral pretension.

\* \* \*

The idea of Negritude, which has satisfied and confused the avant garde squares of the Sixties, is really divided between two forms. The first of these involves the emotions popularized thirty years ago by Langston Hughes. Hughes and Countee Cullen wrote then about the romance of African descent; in a graphic line of the latter ("My conversion came high-priced") there was a sense that civilization had damaged something more important and more natural than it could ever know.[24] The term "Negritude," first used by Léopold Senghor, had two implications. It could mean recognition of black identity, and a corresponding pride in that

---

23. George Santayana, "Americanism," *The Idler and His Works* (New York, 1957), p. 40.

24. I am indebted to St. Clair Drake's essay on Negritude and pan-Africanism; in *Soon, One Morning*, Herbert Hill, ed. (New York, 1963), pp. 78–105.

identity—or it could be a mystery of ever-more centripetal musing on African Personality. It was used culturally at once; Senghor himself theorizing that Negritude was a nonmechanical, symbolic and sexual way of regarding life. After writing about the Negro sense of "communion . . . myth-making . . . rhythm," Senghor went so far as to say that the Negro spirit belonged to a special nervous and glandular human system. This, St. Clair Drake noted, put him in perilous association with those who emphasize such differences for more interested reasons.[25]

This conception of Negritude is specifically African. It regards Africa as the spiritual homeland, and its great men tend to be politicians. It has sentimental liabilities, some of which were attacked by Ezekiel Mphahlele in *Encounter*.[26] After exhibiting some poetry by Senghor and Aimé Césaire, the kind often encountered on public monuments, Mphahlele found an equal amount of sense in the brutal self-consciousness of Roy Campbell—and a good deal more sense in the writing of I. A. Richards. Mphahlele's impatience with Negritude of the cultural variety is not unique, as he himself notes:

> The Negro artist must resolve for himself and others the problem of reconciling their desire for integration with their refusal to forego their cultural identity. . . . James Baldwin, for instance, has, after many years of self-imposed exile in France, come to recognize both the inherently alien nature of his American experience and his commitment to help the Negro people in the United States. The late Richard Wright came to very wild and irritating conclusions about Ghanaians when he came to Africa and failed to put himself across. Ralph Ellison simply felt no emotional attachment to Africa. Lorraine Hansberry, like Langston Hughes, feels only a humanitarian sympathy with Africa.

Like Ellison, Mphahlele has no use for mythology; the business of the writer is only to write. It is in one sense a footnote to history; something like Allen Ginsberg's praise of Pound because good anti-semitic poetry is hard to write.

25. *Ibid.*, pp. 86–89.
26. Ezekiel Mphahlele, "The Cult of Négritude," *Encounter* (March, 1961), pp. 50–52. Used with permission.

Perhaps the best comment on the reaction of Negro intellectuals to Negritude is a short story by Rush Greenlee, "To Lie Down in Negritude." [27] It is both realism and parable: the story of a university group called The Descendants of African Slaves. The rather too-symbolic heroine is a mulatto whose *virtu* has been attenuated by her bloodlines. The group regularly meet to discuss their alienation from America, after which the heroine is soundly satisfied by the hero, a visiting African diplomat. His psychic integrity is impressive; he is entirely Black, with no sense of the loss of the self, and with inhibitions that are tribal rather than existential. Perhaps his greatest talent is his willingness to use power—personal, political and sexual—without guilt. Among the dehydrated American Negroes he looms as a figure mythical in his capacities. The interesting thing is that he has a politician's contempt for Negro ideology.

The second form of Negritude was for all intents and purposes discovered by Norman Mailer. There are so many good accounts of the hipster or White Negro that lengthy discussion here would be redundant. On the symbolic Negro, Mailer's own definition is as good as anything else: "urban adventurers who drifted out at night looking for action with a black man's code to fit their facts." [28] Their rages and desires were born to be expressed, and in this they are the only fully human animals recognized by Mailer. The shreds of philosophy adhere to this idea of Negritude: worship of the orgasm according to Reich; an imposition of Being according to Sartre; even the unsuspected presence of Marx to account for the "extreme contradictions" of the society which creates the character of its agonist.

Lesser literary minds have drawn on Mailer's reserve; and energy, orgone, sex, body, blood and *prana* have become bywords of rebellion against our anti-sexual country. The military metaphor invites extrapolation: in Mailer's terms an actual "time of violence" will and must occur. In a sense the literature of this kind of Negritude anticipates the day of the Lord: LeRoi Jones's *Slave*

27. Rush Greenlee, "To Lie Down in Negritude," *Kulchur*, XV (Autumn, 1964), p. 57 ff.
28. Norman Mailer, "The White Negro," *Advertisements For Myself* (New York, 1959), pp. 337-358. Used with permission.

has the hipster on the barricades; Mailer's own "Time of Her Time" is a tactical approach (in its own way a triumph of the reductive) on the *corpus* of liberalism. The tone of this kind of writing, as exemplified by Genet, Baldwin, Jones and their imitators, is anti-liberal. That is its special strength and weakness. Between its politics and its primitivism it wrenches liberal responses violently. The strategy—to carry liberal sympathies beyond the point of liberal sanctions—is fairly visible. Yet those with an average literary memory will not be stunned by this form of Negritude— how far is it from Vachel Lindsay's *Congo* to James Baldwin's doctrine of life forces? And how long has it been since the immoralist became a public figure?

*The Blacks* has endowed symbolic Negritude with a certain *cachet*. It was, interestingly, the point of contention between Lorraine Hansberry and Norman Mailer; the former arguing for its essential falsity, psychological and racial; the latter only too pleased to find in it dialectical ammunition.[29] Mailer's piece in *The Presidential Papers* has an expansionist quality; he includes the orgasm (that existential moment beyond the power of the state to affect); the totalitarian conditions of liberal existence; the failure of the middle class to come to terms with instinct. There is a good account of the relationship of liberal audience to ritual drama, a subject of great fascination that has been taken up also by Robert Brustein [30] and Susan Sontag.[31] The energies of primitivism—"Let Negroes negrify themselves. Let them persist to the point of madness in what they're condemned to be, in their ebony, in their odor, in their yellow eyes, in their cannibal tastes"—would not be acceptable without a suitable form. As seen by Brustein in *The Theatre of Revolt* [32] the philosophy of Negritude endows the tastes of Genet with social meaning. As a form of psychodrama

29. Norman Mailer, "A Review of Jean Genet's *The Blacks*," *The Presidential Papers* (New York, 1963), pp. 199–212.

30. Robert Brustein, "Everybody's Protest Play," *The New Republic* (16 May 1964), pp. 35–37.

31. Susan Sontag, "Going to Theater, Etc.," *Partisan Review* (Summer, 1964), pp. 389–399.

32. Robert Brustein, *The Theatre of Revolt* (Boston, 1964), pp. 389–395.

*The Blacks* permits and therefore exorcises the secret wishes of its audience. As a demi-philosophical statement it reveals Genet's "anarchistic desire for total liberation." In short, it is a political parable as well as a nightmare.

The drama and fiction of Negritude have assiduously followed Genet—although *The Toilet* stands in the same relationship to *The Blacks* as *The Battle of the Frogs and Mice* to the *Iliad*. This drama and fiction have built-in political components. The superior essences of its heroes (who combine the primitive desires of Genet with the primitive wisdom of Voltaire's *naïfs*) sustain themselves in battle against the repressive power of the state. That power is seen in two forms. There is the vast, Spenglerian agglomeration of church, FBI, university, and corporation; and there is the power of liberalism. Baldwin, Jones, and Mailer, among others, are particularly anatomical on the subject of Negro and Jewish bourgeoisie.

Yet the idea of a battle supplies only half the truth, for the relationship of Negritude to liberal life is also one of salvation. It is salvation of the old kind, full of the strainings of intense belief, suffused with a kind of love. The point indeed of the drama of Negritude is that its agonist is a religious figure. Robert Coles lists the ideological shapes of character in the world of fiction at large, and points out that they serve an illustrative function—they are not so much individuals as they are representatives of the Negro struggle, the alienated mind, the repressed instinct. They have solutions to offer. For example, Baldwin "is determined to offer a general truth out of the sphere of his own life, and has a grandiose remedy for our social ills. For Baldwin—a sharp critic of America's vulgar piety—it is love, love, love." [33] Most critics of *Another Country* have been embarrassed by the details of homosexual love, and have chalked up these messy episodes to the private life of Baldwin—somewhat as Milton's feelings about women came through in *Paradise Lost*. The irony in this case is that the flaming prose of these moments (by far the most involved writing in the book) are probably not personal but ideological. Baldwin's famous rejection of Christianity has made these encounters indispensable.

---

33. Robert Coles, "Baldwin's Burden," *Partisan Review* (Summer, 1964), pp. 409–416.

What remains is a familiar, dogmatic view of love: "I have always felt a human being could only be saved by another human being. . . . One must say Yes to life and embrace it wherever it is found." [34] This attacks us at our most guilty point, self-evidently. It is made fairly clear by Norman Podhoretz why the audience is susceptible. The *mélange* of black and white, homosexual and heterosexual is a metaphor of love's identity; it strives not only for the psychological freedom of which we are so proud but for the idea of equality itself. The great and perhaps sole values are those centering on the individual and "love." As Podhoretz notes, there is nothing surprising about this, "it is, after all, only a form of the standard liberal attitude toward life." [35] There is, of course, a significant exception—Baldwin makes a dogma out of a value and a program out an inclination. He takes "these liberal pieties literally" for the first time in recent history. Having said this, Podhoretz himself goes somewhat hesitantly to the end of a limb. The "moral sickness" of American life consists in its refusal to tolerate homosexual love, which in turn destroys the capacity for any other kind of love. This is hopelessly fashionable, and one of the more feeble responses to *The Symposium* that we are likely to read. It ignores a fairly well-known fact that homosexual love is not altogether a contract between consenting adults, but is a process of conversion. In blunt terms, homosexuality too often operates by the seduction of those unable to comprehend its meaning, frequently children. Any sociologist remotely familiar with case histories will quickly drop his illusions as to the ideology of homosexual *freedom*. It is in fact a coercion of those unable to make distinctions. There is one other matter, but I am hesitant to mention it when it is so obvious: There is, after all, the possibility that homosexual love, like heterosexual love, may be a form of lust. In that case the ideological benefits of "sexual articulation" of feeling are extraneous. This is somewhat far afield, but the totemic

34. These lines from *Nothing Personal* by James Baldwin and Richard Avedon (New York, 1964) are quoted by Robert Brustein, "Everybody Knows My Name," *The New York Review of Books* (17 December 1964), pp. 10–11.

35. Norman Podhoretz, "In Defense of James Baldwin," *Doings and Undoings* (New York, 1964), pp. 244–250.

structure of Negritude-love-selfhood-salvation requires, occasionally, that it be confronted with facts.

It was remarked by Susan Sontag, apropos of *Blues for Mister Charlie*, that the Negro has become the mask of virtue in American theatre. The old liberalism, whose archetypal figure was the Jew, has been replaced by a more authentic victim. Although the Negro now dramatized is essentially anti-liberal, the fiction that projects him is sustained by liberal sensibility. It makes for a certain confusion:

> In the theatre, as among educated Americans generally, liberalism has suffered an ambiguous rout. . . . In *Blues for Mister Charlie*, Broadway liberalism has been vanquished by Broadway racism. Liberalism preached politics, that is, solutions. Racism regards politics as superficial (and seeks some deeper level); it emphasizes what is unalterable. Across a virtually impassable gulf, the new mask of "the Negro," manly, toughened, but ever vulnerable, faces his antipode, another new mask, "the white" (sub-genus: "the white liberal")—who is pasty-faced, graceless, lying, sexually dull, murderous.[36]

As Miss Sontag notes, what is being demonstrated is not simply the guilt of whites but their inferiority as human beings. This means their sexual inferiority.

Racism and sexism are the dynamics of the play. The late Richard Henry is—as has been widely observed—a savior in terms of both conceptions. The agit-prop quality of his language is emphatic. In facing Lyle, the redneck who ultimately murders him, he launches into an unmotivated lecture on the sexual superiority of Negroes to Caucasians. It is gratuitous in every sense but one: as ventriloquism of Negritude. His death scene ends with the assertion that white women prefer Negroes; it is punctuated by the reminder that the relationship of white man to black man is that of symbolic castration. The mind boggles not at the revolutionary quality of the insights but at their sense of utility. The white liberal sense of guilt is served by the act of death; the moral virtues of sexual energy are given the same mythological status as in Erich Fromm's textbooks on love; evil is accounted for in the satisfying

---

36. Susan Sontag, "Going to Theater, Etc.," *op. cit.*

terms of the American South; the situation attains "reality" as it blurs over into the public realm of civil rights. It is probably the single most conformist piece of creative writing of the decade.

By the middle of the Sixties the Negro served as *objet-trouvé* of the Broadway intellectuals. He was in *The Toilet, Slave, Dutchman, Blues for Mister Charlie, Sydney Brustein, The Owl and the Pussycat, Slow Dance on the Killing Ground, Raisin in the Sun,* and *Golden Boy.* In more than one he was Fidel Castro in blackface.[37] The plays and prologues of LeRoi Jones insist on this; it is not only that they address themselves to Crazy Horse, Patrice Lumumba, and "black dada nihilismus" but that they are sustained by the metaphor of revolution. Jones's principal meta-theatrical statement is in fact "The Revolutionary Theatre." [38] Clay, in *Dutchman,* his alter ego Ray in *The Toilet,* and his avenger Walker in *Slave* are all taking part in a larger drama: The Destruction of America. The conception is operatic, "wiggly Liberals dying under blasts of concrete. For sound effects, wild screams of joy, from all the peoples of the world." Between every line of the plays we are intended to hear those blasts and screams, and to absorb the hatreds for which they stand. Yet, these hatreds must be justified once we have accepted the guilt for them.

The multiple intentions of Jones defeat themselves. Stanley Kauffmann has written that Jones is in "The Tradition of the Fake" [39]—he condemns his times only to live off them. The *fact* of revolution cannot tolerate the distance between his *modus vivendi* and his *modus scribendi.* But there is another and more important thing to be said. The concept of Negritude cannot contain the meanings for which it is the metaphor. It cannot at the same time stand for Reichian sexuality and a spiritual if de-Christianized love. It cannot sing "the holiness of life" even as its rhetoric ("hate," "crack their faces open," "filth," "brains are splattered over the seats") revokes that condition. And it cannot, given the

---

37. I have used the phraseology of Mathew Andrews, "Theatre," *Kulchur* (Spring, 1965), pp. 79–81.

38. LeRoi Jones, "the revolutionary theatre," *Home* (New York, 1966), pp. 210–215.

39. Stanley Kauffmann, "LeRoi Jones and the Tradition of the Fake," *Dissent* (Spring, 1965), pp. 207–212. Used by permission.

vulnerability of the human mind to logic, indefinitely continue both to satisfy and degrade its liberal audience. One set of emotions must sooner or later prevail; if that is not already the case. The departure of Jones from the intellectual life of the decade is a kind of burlesque of the decline of Hemingway and Mailer: Before we were aware of it Jones was playing himself in the pages of *Esquire*. He is traditionally American in the sense that the artist has become an entertainer.

Two important essays in the early Sixties proved the possibility of an alternative; they were written by Ralph Ellison in response to the assumption that the business of the Negro writer is to tell how it is to be Negro.[40] Their immediate occasion was Irving Howe's "Black Boys and Native Sons," [41] a piece which argued that the fundamental truths of the Negro condition had been stated by Richard Wright—and betrayed by Baldwin and Ellison. The responses of Ellison argued that Negritude was too narrow a concept for the writer, and in a fine display of reasoning these essays firmly divided the worlds of the writer and the functionary. Howe's essay was a form of orthodoxy: The literature of the Negro movement was justified to the extent that a real social issue and real feelings were explored. As he saw it, Wright had made it impossible ever again to hide the animosities between black and white; in short, as a Marxist critic Howe was satisfied by the quality of representativeness in the novels of Negro anger. To an extent the position is useful and the praise of Wright merited. But Ellison points out that Wright can not be identified as either the true voice of feeling or as the undisputed patriarch of his tribe. It is not solely the business of the Negro writer to reveal the *racial* hatreds within him; yet the determinedly cultural mentality of Howe allowed of no other object.

If a novel is a weapon in the war of ideas it may also be more—

---

40. Ralph Ellison, "The World and the Jug," *The New Leader* (9 December 1963), pp. 22–26, and "A Rejoinder," *op. cit.* (3 February 1964), pp. 15–22. Reprinted with permission from New Leader issues of 9 December 1963 and 3 February 1964. Copyright by American Labor Conference on International Affairs, Inc.

41. Irving Howe, "Black Boys and Native Sons," *Dissent* (Autumn, 1963), pp. 353–368. Used by permission.

it may be, as Ellison suggests, a celebration of human life, something independent, ritualistic, ceremonial at the core. Howe's "Northern white liberal version of the white Southern myth" prevented him from realizing this; and it prevented him from seeing that even in Macon County, Alabama, the forces that operated to shape the consciousness of Ellison were Marx, Freud, Eliot, Pound, Hemingway, and Gertrude Stein.

Ellison's rejection of the totem of "Negroness" was one of the more honest gestures of the decade. He wrote with much less fanfare than his contemporaries of the *difference* between collective and individual experience; in so doing he restored to fiction those standards which prevented "all those who suffer in anonymity" from being creators. The unconditional clarity of Ellison translates Negritude from a myth of potency and victimization to a special perspective of the American experience. Ellison's account of this, too long to reproduce here, centers on the fact that this experience demands certain attitudes even as it rejects certain privileges. The claims of Negritude seem diminished and its binding force is dissolved by an intellectual act of will:

> While one can do nothing about choosing one's relatives, one can, as artist, choose one's "ancestors." Wright was, in this sense, a "relative"; Hemingway an "ancestor." Langston Hughes, whose work I knew in grade school and whom I knew before I knew Wright, was a "relative"; Eliot, whom I was to meet only many years later, and Malraux and Dostoevsky and Faulkner, were "ancestors"—if you please or don't please!

A full cycle has occurred, and it is a promising sign. The appeal to Faulkner is as ideological a statement as Mailer's allegiance to Reich or Jones's to Genet. Ellison is saying that Negritude, like some other totems of our time, is an artifact of a certain splendor, ornamentation, and power. But it is still a block of wood.

## *Tabus*

Avant-garde homosexuality is the most current form of underground literature. It is unlike the familiar styles of deviate artistry, those limited to ingenious photographs, biographies of seduction, and apologies which plod from Alcibiades to Frederick the Great. The true measure of the old style was tonnage; it poured out (and of course continues to do so) in a great flood of publication. For the most part its aim was verisimilitude; the important thing otherwise was its deliberate alienation from cultural norms. The new literary homosexuality is different in both class and kind. Some of the fundamental aims are retained; there is still a market for vicarious ecstasy and for the inherent hostility toward the mundane expressed by the art of homosexuality. One important difference is that the new writing is directed toward a new audience, the great army of middlebrows who are perpetually hovering on the brink of emancipation. It has an element of seriousness; indeed its object is to draw together the opposing worlds of instinct and culture. In order to do this it borrows weapons from psychology, and demonstrates that the homosexual act is biologically sanctioned. And it borrows weapons from politics, attempting to derive from the toleration of the liberal frame of mind some justification for homosexual freedom.

The homosexual literature of the Sixties is ideological. Its outer form is that of the novel but its inner form is that of the tract. It is based on a bipolar attitude that the proper response to the human predicament is the act of deviancy, and that the culmination of enlightenment is the explosion of outmoded sanctions. These are the major positions—they refer themselves, in the case of the former, to *Saint Genet*, and, in the case of the latter, to such a representative tract as Gore Vidal's *The City and the Pillar Revised*. There are of course contingent positions that the homosexual act is a Reichian form of salvation, that the "camp" tastes of homosexual art endow a subject with its proper irony, that the rejection of bourgeois-liberal culture is figured by this kind of avant-gardism. In spite of these motives, there is an irreducible element of romanticism, one which resists the best efforts of those critics sympathetic to the role of the underground which they take to be expounding our own guilt to us.

Vidal's book is fittingly accompanied by two essays on sexual norms.[42] It is itself of limited novelistic value; an acute review by Hilton Kramer indicates that it was rewritten (it first appeared

---

42. Gore Vidal, *The City and the Pillar Revised* (New York, 1965).

in the late Forties) in order to accommodate recent tastes for symbology.[43] The original story ended in a murder of the unwilling beloved—the present form culminates in a homosexual rape that has a cathartic effect on the hero. In the past two decades the logic of poetic justice has changed. The first ending is generic to "problem literature" while the second, influenced by the commodity market, has Baldwinized itself into respectability. Its "naturalness" enables the hero to view life with fortitude. We have moved from guilt to acceptance—although of what the later ending does not make plain. Vidal, a keen observer of the *Zeitgeist*, is able simultaneously to please the renewed interest of middlebrows in anal intercourse and to make that perversion indicative of a new cultural relativism.

The accompanying essays work rather hard to make the point that homosexual behavior is not subject to normative criticism. The essays are intellectually careless, attempting to justify "sexual candor" on the grounds of the new freedom and associating sexual conservatism with Mr. Barry Goldwater. Vidal's argument—"the idea that there is no such thing as 'normality' is at last penetrating the tribal consciousness, although the religiously inclined still regard nonprocreative sex as 'unnatural,' while the statistically inclined regard as 'normal' only what the majority does"—[44] covers everything but the real issues. Very few who object to pederasty go back to Aquinas but depend instead on cultural beliefs which the evasive term "tribal" hardly contends with. It may be regrettable, although I do not find it so, but most of us do have some belief in what is normal. As for the statistical straw man, even the Kinsey report had little effect when it contrasted practice and ethics, so that it is quite wrong to imply that what is done translates itself into what is believed. Aside from these objections, the nature of homosexual culture is never mentioned by Vidal—although it ranges from the ubiquitous idea of "camp" so well explored by Susan Sontag to the unhappy world of the drag queen portrayed by John Rechy. There is of course an irony involved. The "religiously inclined" are not entirely *outside* the homosexual culture. Indeed,

43. Hilton Kramer, "Queer Affirmations," *The New Leader* (30 August 1965), pp. 16–17.

44. Vidal, *op. cit.*, p. 249.

the mechanics of religion have been assimilated. Finally, the homosexual subculture is by its own consent not concerned with the ethical *neutrality* of the deviate act. The ideology of homosexual culture, whether on the Broadway stage or in the underground, is forcefully committed to the very differences stated by its critics. It is not unnormative but anti-normative. Which is to say that norms operate among those who defy them.

Leslie Fiedler has argued that the underground writers are "nonparticipants in the past." [45] The tradition from which they disengage "is the tradition of the human, as the West (understanding the West to extend from the United States to Russia) has defined it, humanism itself, both in its bourgeois and Marxist forms; and more especially the cult of reason." The specific ideas attacked are rationality, work, duty, and vocation. The specific institution attacked is Protestant humanism. And the specific mode attacked is consciousness. The conversion of hero to anti-hero attempted by Hemingway has been succeeded by the conversion of both to the nonhero—who is, as Fiedler suggests, nonmale. Fiedler seems to me mistaken in his confidence that the nonmale is the new psychic ideal of our times, just as he is mistaken when he identifies underground love with *pleasure*. The nonmale is in one sense Reichian, but his object is more ideological than simple genitality. He is not motivated by post-Freudian empiricism, nor by the disinterested clarity of scientific relativism. He is on the contrary in search of an experience—ornate, self-defining, passional —that is essentially religious. In one sense underground sexuality is very like the mass conversion of intellectuals to Catholicism which took place earlier in the century. It shares some of that baroque sensibility, and earnestly seeks for a kind of moral pain to accompany Reichian pleasure. In effect it has its own form of dualism. An essay by LeRoi Jones combines the romance of this attitude with a political statement that heightens the sensation. It endows the new sensibility with a kind of historical legitimacy:

> Selby's hoodlums, Rechy's homosexuals, Burroughs's addicts, Kerouac's mobile young voyeurs, my own Negroes, are literally not

45. Leslie A. Fiedler, "The New Mutants," *Partisan Review* (Fall, 1965), pp. 505–525. © 1965 by *Partisan Review;* used by permission.

included in the mainstream of American life. These characters are people whom Spengler called *Fellaheen*, people living on the ruins of a civilization. They are Americans . . . formed out of the conspicuously tragic evolution of modern American life. The last romantics of our age.[46]

As to their being romantics there can be no doubt; that is the definitive term. The cultural view which sustains this is, however, open to question. It offers the possibility, among others, that the seriousness of the functionaries (who have endowed us with this totemic belief in our decline) has once again resulted in an attitude more absolute than they are prepared to acknowledge. The hidden strength of underground writing is the philosophy or hobby of cultural disappointment.

The most visible product of the ideological underground has been James Baldwin's *Another Country*. The argument of this book is not that homosexuality is biologically normative but that it is ethically superior. It is a commonplace of criticism that the heterosexual love scenes are stilted and distant while the others are described in flaming and ecstatic prose. They are pitched on the metaphor of religion that was so much abused by Sartre in his book on Genet—for example, Baldwin's chapter "Toward Bethlehem" leaves little doubt as to the kind of response it hopes to evoke. In this chapter all of the right ideological moves succeed each other. Eric, the seducer of Vivaldo, has been established as the *penis ex machina* of the novel—Cass Silenski has named him to her cuckolded husband as the one man she knows both ethically and sexually prepotent. As a bisexual Eric fulfills the holy role once played by the hermaphrodite. As the seduction scene progresses we find succeeding each other in benign profusion all those terms—"childish," "trusting," "love," "satisfaction," "innocence" —that we have come to associate with the liberal conception of personal virtue. These words, sanctified by marriage manuals and the reigning sensibility, validated by Fromm and Marcuse, are the operative descriptions in Baldwin's account of buggery as an act of grace.

---

46. LeRoi Jones, "Introduction," *The Moderns* (New York, 1963). Used by permission of the publisher, Corinth Books, Inc.

*Consummatum est.* Vivaldo, even to "revelation," has found the holy knowledge with which to formulate his life. The translation of this religious experience to Vivaldo's relationship with Ida ("like two weary children. . . . she was stroking his innocence out of him") would seem to undercut the argument that a *psychological* norm underlies the matter. We are vulnerable in our piety before the childlike and the primitive, and *Another Country*, like *The Family of Man*, intends to elicit a response in terms of values. Its ending, with the epicene Yves striding from the airport "more high-hearted than he had ever been as a child, into that city which the people from heaven had made their home," is a rather witty parody of *Paradise Lost*. It carries the metaphor of childhood, the one sacred metaphor of liberalism, to an inexorable conclusion. If *The Fire Next Time* is in praise of genitality *Another Country* is an eulogy on the love beyond understanding. That it is specifically homosexual love gives some idea of how normative the underground really is. It is not a new form of experience developed from the Enlightenment; it is simply the old ideas applied to new relationships. It would certainly not be excessive to call it a form of orthodoxy. And indeed the homosexual subculture is full of such forms.

The reviewers have been baffled by the new tractarianism; the worst have outdone themselves trying to acquiesce in *la nouvelle vague;* the best have adopted a simplistic moral position; the uneasy herd has tried to err on the fashionable side of toleration. This does not include such *pro domo* criticism as Kerouac's reception of *Naked Lunch*, of course. I have somewhat more sympathy for John Rechy's *City of Night* than most reviewers, although Richard Gilman [47] and Alfred Chester [48] have written accurately of its flaws. Rechy's prose style is affected, yet his view of the homosexual condition is partially free of cant. He has no illusions about its thaumaturgic quality. His piece on Miss Destiny is a minor classic, although written in a prose style both romantic and hysterical. But the style is native to the subject. Chester's own collection of underground fiction, *Behold Goliath*, is unromantically

---

47. Richard Gilman, "City of Dreadful Night," *The New Republic* (14 September 1963), pp. 21–23.

48. Alfred Chester, "Fruit Salad," *The New York Review of Books*, I, 2 (1964), pp. 6–7.

attentive to the nuances of homosexual relationships. The short story "From the Phoenix to the Wild Bird" is ironically aware of the demi-religious values which are at the heart of (literary) homosexual affairs. Two lovers discuss the ethos of their relationship, and make the connection between God and evil that has become predictable since the appearance of Genet on the spiritual scene: "God wills us to break God's laws. In our black night of hatred and demons and horror, in our violation of God's laws, all the saints and angels acquiesce. God too. He doesn't merely pardon us. He loves us." It should be plain in this redaction of Blake and Dostoevsky that the last thing of interest to the apologist is the concept of moral neutrality. Vidal and the other logicians to the contrary, the homosexual subculture cares passionately about the normative. This is nowhere so well brought out as in Chester's "In Praise of Vespasian," which culminates in an act of fellatio described in this way:

> The eyes chant. The hearts carol. Undine sings. Aphrodite hums. Now, in this frozen night of joy, there are no swords between men. There are no secret jealousies, no envies, no rivalries, no rancor against the hero's choice, against him who will know the ultimate accomplishment of love. And Joaquin, beside the swaggerer, closes his eyes, drops to his knees violently as if suffering a conversion or a revelation and, throwing wide his arms to grasp him who comes to them, opens his lips upon Life Everlasting.[49]

The scene is a Parisian *pissoir;* the agents are a group of deviates therein assembled; the hero is an exotic African who bears love to those awaiting him. The *sensibility* of homosexual avant-gardism, ignored almost completely by those with Reichian or Brownian points to score, is heavily romantic. It is much closer to Wilde than to Baudelaire. The amusing thing is that those critics most susceptible to the "freedom" of underground writing do not recognize its passionate attachment to mythology.

Paul Goodman's essay on underground mores is one of the better critiques available.[50] He sees three general motives for the ex-

---

49. Alfred Chester, *Behold Goliath* (New York, 1964).
50. Paul Goodman, "Underground Writing, 1960," *Utopian Essays and Practical Proposals* (New York, 1964), pp. 222–235.

ploitation of the unutterable, the technological, which satisfies our need for "universal reporting and spectatoritis"; the fevered search for vitality; the post-liberal nihilism of the world of letters. He is very good on the fake demonism of the underground, which "serves the same function for the philosophy of the mass audience as the bathos of Tennessee Williams does for its sexuality. The poet caters to the tender pornographic side, combining lust with punishment." What is most objectionable to Goodman is the element of illusory horror—the kind of thing implied by Collingwood and Santayana when they described a culture rotten with entertainment:

> In my opinion, there is something dishonorable and exploiting, queasy-making, about hipster writing—and, similarly, much of the school of Sartre. Life strategies that are brutal necessities for folk who are in clear and present danger, and that precisely would not be written up, are toyed with by intellectuals who evoke fantasy dangers so that they can thrill to extreme situations; and indeed thereby they create unnecessary real dangers, as if life weren't hard enough.

Goodman concludes that the underground is culturally not up to nihilism. It manufactures sects and symbols, but is short on imperatives. Perhaps the most notable thing is its practice of accommodation; it is no less a part of the market economy than any other institution.

When we progress, if that is the term, from homosexual to heterosexual sodomy the identity of the market values becomes clear. To use a phrase from *The Nightclerk*, the "hybrid couplings and unusual courtships" follow a single pattern. In *An American Dream* there is the same theorizing about God and Evil which energizes the deviate experience. Here is Cherry on The Meaning Of It All: "There is no decent explanation for evil. I believe God is just doing His best to learn from what happens to us. Sometimes I think He knows less than the Devil because we're not good enough to teach Him." Like Baldwin's vocabulary of sanctification, this kind of theological name-dropping occurs when Mailer finds himself stalled by the naturalist dilemma: If the only realities are movement and sensation, then no particular importance can attach to their occurrence. Yet to make the natural into the ethical supposes a system of values. Mailer refuses to recognize the transcendent but finds himself compelled to use it. The now famous account of Rojack's bash with the German maid deserves the attentions of a pack of dons unleashed on the ghost of Lawrence; it suffices to note that the metaphysics of the underground are described with the customary faith that a dialogue in which God and the Devil are named must be profound. Aside from the acrobatics involved, the act is a form of communion with forces more important than we suspect. But for a culture raised on *Faustus* it is pretty small beer. I have mentioned that in my opinion *Mansfield Park* is a more dangerous book than *The Story of O;* the chapter in the *Confessions* of St. Augustine on robbing a pear-tree is infinitely more dangerous than Mailer's shadow-boxing with the ultimate. Eventually there is the appeal to experience; no man who has ever been in a whorehouse will take seriously the claims of sodomy to damnation. As for confusing it with salvation—to each his own.

The market in tabus has been brisk, and makes Henry Miller seem innocent. The triad of homosexual love, straight love, and drugs is at the center of Alexander Trocchi's *Cain's Book.* Among its impurities is a sex act conducted with the assistance of a one-legged lady. One wonders whether there are enough readers with that particular kink to make the write-up worthwhile, or whether it is simply a bonus. Stephen Schneck's *The Nightclerk* is a fantasy evidently stimulated by *Naked Lunch.* In addition to the rest there is the violation of a woman in the throes of a Grand Mal seizure and the abuse of a child; at its more relaxed it conveys the rape of a sleeping nun, but quickly passes on to more incendiary matters. Jack Gelber's *On Ice* displays every masturbation of its hero. Hubert Selby's *Last Exit to Brooklyn*—probably the best of the underground books—offers homosexual conversion, drag queens, benzedrine highs, and plain mob violence. In all fairness, it should be added that this book has some documentary power and stands up as a work of fiction. David Storey's *Radcliffe* has neither the power of fact nor the pleasures of fiction to recommend it—it seems to be simply *Lady Chatterley* in homosexual terms. There are, however, added attractions of bisexuality, oral rape, and so on. Sanford Friedman's *Totempole* is a Freudian fable about the one sin so problematic to Stephen Daedalus. The list is endless, but one thing is missing—there is no saturnalia in these chronicles of the liberal mind within the repressed body. With dogged seriousness these books try to account for the modern "predicament" in terms of repressed sexuality. They end up with the same validity as the lyrics of *Intercourse*, which promise that war and cancer will cease with the resolution of the Oedipus complex. The underground prefers mythology to psychology. The mode is much more religious than clinical—common to most of the work is the belief in the special, sacred meaning and transcendent value of the aberrant act. The functionaries ought to get together with the writers; they have too long been defending the underground novel on the grounds of its realism.

# 11.

# *CULTURE HEROES*

## *The Existential Hero: Power*

Liberalism has pondered the question of heroism with results unsatisfactory both to itself and its critics on the left. Its ambivalence
toward heroic action and personality is nowhere better brought
out than in Arthur Schlesinger's essays on these subjects.[1] In
common with theorists both liberal and conservative, he assumes
that political heroism has its roots in democratic practice. Schlesinger begins "On Heroic Leadership" by noting that classical democratic theory resists individual leadership. The majority, as we see
in Locke, asserts its power in some indefinable way—the un-
named process, as Schlesinger suggests, is as automatic as spontane-

---

1. Arthur Schlesinger, Jr., "On Heroic Leadership and the Dilemma
of Strong Men and Weak Peoples," *The Politics of Hope* (Boston,
1963), pp. 3–22 and "The Decline of Greatness," *op. cit.*, pp. 23–33.

ous combustion. There is very little provision in classical theory for leadership; indeed there is a built-in hostility to anything that might undermine the doctrine of equality. Yet, while classical democratic theory insists on the inherent leadership of the majority itself, the American experience as formulated by men as various as Jefferson, Jackson, and Emerson has tended toward the imposed leadership of executive power. Schlesinger approves of this highly. It relieves us (although he is not entirely forthright on the subject) of the Marxist dilemma by reintroducing individual moral choice in the shaping of history. In the purely pragmatic sense it insures the workings of the executive branch.

The limits of the liberal position become plain in Schlesinger's attack on Max Weber's idea of charisma. He argues that charismatic leadership, which is rooted in a tribal concept of community, cannot possibly apply to industrial society. It is at the root of the totalitarian experience, as we have seen in the progress of twentieth-century dictatorship. Having said this, Schlesinger acknowledges a dilemma of liberalism: With no alternative explanation of reality "the conventional political theory of democracy remained unprepared to deal with the problems of leadership. And the intellectual position of defenders of democracy was further demoralized by the Weberian analysis of authority in terms which excluded democratic leadership." The only possible way out of this is through dialectical maneuvering, and for the rest of the essay Schlesinger tries to work out some sort of compromise between leadership and responsibility. In this he is notably unsuccessful—but for an essay written in 1960 that is not of much consequence. It sufficed, at the beginning of the decade, to affirm the hope that leadership would become ever more progressive. Although Schlesinger was highly realistic in his appraisal of the Third World—"every nation has to work out forms of freedom consistent with its own culture and traditions"—he refused to relinquish the liberal hope that leadership could be absorbed into ideals of responsibility and indeed of benevolence. It was enough at this point to disapprove of charisma, and to assume that the concept of leadership would share in a general distribution of enlightenment.

The ironies involved are fairly plain. These essays were written at the beginning of a decade whose cultural tone was to be anything but enlightened. Fiction and drama, to say nothing of philosophy, were to celebrate the life of the unconscious—and were to connect political life not with the authority of reason but with that of sexuality. (Classical democratic theory evolved from the rights of property or those other "rights of man." An influential group of writers today, principally on the new left, evolves its idea of freedom from sexual relativism. Freedom is viewed as deriving from individual and unlegislatable sexual needs. The tyranny of government is not judged politically—even full electoral rights are not forms of freedom since there is no "real choice" between philosophies. Real freedom is absolute, and rests on the right of each individual to resist the will of the majority. Since the individual is principally a sexual organism, it follows that the only real form of democracy is that his needs be sufficient unto themselves). There is an added particular irony. Writing shortly before the presidency of John F. Kennedy, Schlesinger was able to state that democracy would experience far less need of charismatic leadership since that issue would come to be seen in "realistic" terms. We think not only of Schlesinger's subsequent attitudes, but of the response of the American public to the "style" (we are really going back to Weber here, if we consider the ambiguities of the term) of the President. This is to say nothing of the response to the assassination of 1963. James MacGregor Burns was conceivably more "realistic" when he wrote, in the same year that Schlesinger published his essays,

> The trouble with Kennedy is that he lacks liberalism's tragic quality. . . . I mean that so many of its finest and most passionate causes, like Spain, have been lost causes; that so many liberal heroes have had their tragic denouements. . . . If he should die tomorrow in a plane crash, he would become at once a liberal martyr, for the liberal publicists of the land would rush to construct a hero.[2]

Schlesinger's dialectical quandary—especially clear when we think of his baroque praise of FDR in *The Politics of Upheaval*—

---

2. James MacGregor Burns, "Candidate on the Eve: Liberalism Without Tears," *The New Republic* (31 October 1960), pp. 14–16. Reprinted by permission of Harrison-Blaine of New Jersey, Inc.

indicates that heroic leadership is of more importance to political experience than liberals might in theory accept. He comes perilously close to admitting this in "The Decline of Greatness" when he writes regretfully of "the epic style of those mighty figures of our recent past who seized history with both hands." The ironies become more involved when we see him reflecting that a free society cannot get along without heroes since they represent the power of freedom itself. In 1958 this needed neither refinement nor modification—everyone then knew what "freedom" meant. Its transvaluation was to occur as the new decade aged. The idea of what was heroic was to overflow its original form. The idea of freedom was to cease being political, as we understand the term, at the moment it ceased being liberal. Empowered by a sense of cultural guilt, envisioned as a form of individualism liberated from *all* cultural restraints, it was to circle deviously but irresistibly back to the charismatic. It was to introduce into our culture the imperatives of a left hostile to liberalism, and refer itself to a sense of the exhaustion of liberal culture.

The culture hero of the Sixties was in some forms political but he was certainly not democratic. As Fidel Castro or Kwame Nkrumah, as Mao Tse Tung or Patrice Lumumba, as Sukarno, Ben Bella, or Nasser, he was consciously admired as the opposite of the liberal hero. The famous distinction of the left between "form" and "essence" makes this plain. The Sixties marked the second time in this century that American culture heroes were imported from cultures with a self-evidently superior dynamism. It was hardly the authority of principle that attracted on this occasion; it was on the contrary the power of action. In fact, the important thing about the new heroism was that it could dissolve principle and completely redefine traditional motives. There is an important essay by David McReynolds which clarifies this.[3] McReynolds remarks that even pacifism is now no longer pacifistic. The much idealized Third World has come to power not by the evolution of moralities but through revolutionary violence. Its leaders, those who have captured the imagination of the left, have furnished pacifism with a new dilemma: shall it continue to accept moral

---

3. David McReynolds, "Pacifists in Battle," *New Politics* (Summer, 1965), pp. 29–35.

principle, or shall it be transformed into a mode of action? That dilemma is in the process of being resolved by changing the idea of pacifism to that of resistance, nonviolent and otherwise.

Certainly the place to start is with Castro himself—as an existential figure he is part of our own mythology. As we look through the writings of Norman Mailer, LeRoi Jones, Warren Miller, C. Wright Mills, Huberman and Sweezy, and the theorists associated with *Liberation* and *Studies on the Left* we see the construction of a figure beyond politics. An existential vocabulary is brought into play which centers on terms like "human" and "warmth," and which deals in only a quasi-metaphorical sense with potency. Dennis Wrong, in a very informative essay on "The American Left and Cuba," [4] has drawn attention to the existential radicalism which informs this view. Before the new left hardened its sympathies into ideology it was "more attracted by direct moral protest than by political analysis." It "valued action and the evidence of vitality over intellectual rigor." He refers specifically to *Studies on the Left*, and when we look at this publication it is easy to see why. In one piece, Dale Johnson's "On the Ideology of the Campus Revolution," [5] the existential vocabulary takes the place of what would once have been political distinctions. When Johnson likens the Cuban revolutionaries to the dissenters in the American student movement he discards the "motivating ideologies" of both Marxism and liberalism; what matters is the "refreshing combination of humanism and rationalism." However vaguely, it is "the better human values" which animate Fidelista and FSM. It is these values which separate the left from liberalism. When the truly democratic leader is celebrated, Wrong remarks, it is not on the grounds of "formal" political democracy, it is because he offers something more genuine, more truly connected to life as it is experienced in terms of needs and desires:

> Castro's admirers . . . [attempt] to extol "economic democracy" at the expense of "formal" political democracy, to minimize the destruction of civil rights and liberties by treating voting and parties as the sole content of Western political institutions, and, finally, to

---

4. Dennis H. Wrong, "The American Left and Cuba," *Commentary* (February 1962), pp. 93–103.

5. Dale Johnson, "On the Ideology of the Campus Revolution," *Studies on the Left*, I (1959–1962), pp. 73–75. Used by permission.

celebrate the superior "direct" democracy of the single leader, or cadre of leaders, who needs no institutional apparatus to mediate his interpretations of the will of the people.

The last phrase, with its reverberations of Weberian theory, is of particular interest. Schlesinger wrote of the ambiguous splendor of those who "seized history with both hands," but even as he uttered this it was with the qualification of the liberal mind, it was to be understood as a metaphor. The sense of the new left is more literal. Castro is the paradigm of the new culture hero, the figure who cuts the Gordian knot of history by the thrust of his personality. Whether in the writing of Mailer or in that of other apologists for power, it is evident that the substitution of the term "human" for "political" is the crucial event in a new kind of definition.

Castro himself has found the phraseology useful. In response to LeRoi Jones's questions he said, "I consider myself a humanist. A radical humanist." [6] Jones's "Cuba Libre," from which this quote is taken, is one of a new form of historical documents, the personal account of reality. It can be a very useful and legitimate kind of writing if we recall books like Shirer's narrative of Berlin before the war. But it can also be a very misleading kind of writing, because it is based on a limited kind of observation—in some cases, we recall, it satisfied the observers that Mao was really giving China a more rational social structure. In any case, Jones and others wrote of Cuba in the accents of revelation; they had seen the real thing and were preoccupied with setting down their own human response to the revolution.

The great moments in "Cuba Libre" and in Warren Miller's *90 Miles From Home* are existential moments. In this they resemble the classical work of the genre, C. Wright Mills's *Listen, Yankee*. A large and fraudulent part of the exposition is furnished by the passions of the interlocutors. Whenever anyone says anything in these accounts it is with a redeeming passion. Whenever anyone is viewed in these accounts it is with a sense that his feelings mean a good deal more than those ideas which make impossible demands of consistency on us. There is a cast of beautiful people—enthusiastic women, intellectuals from the Third World, alienated Negroes from the United States, Castro himself—who validate the revolu-

---

6. LeRoi Jones, "Cuba Libre," *Home* (New York, 1966), p. 53.

tionary experience simply by the power of their responses. On those rare occasions when ideas are visible the narrative slows down, the tone becomes hysterical, the whole performance sinks into resentful subjectivity. And if there is a special vocabulary of "warmth" and "humanity," passion and beauty for the revolution, there is an accompanying mode for the inimical culture of the West, "filth," "stupidity," "rotting of the mind," and so on. The limply aesthetic conclusion of Jones's piece—"we are an *old* people already. Even the vitality of our art is like flowers growing up through a rotting carcass"—makes fairly plain the simplified existentialism on which these insights are built.

The central problem of these pieces—one central to the decade itself—is the dilemma of the intellectual. Repeatedly, Jones talks about the *powerlessness* of the intellectual. His hatred of the West is a form of self-hatred; the crescendoes of his essay occur when he is taunted by the fully committed intellectuals of other countries into revealing that he cannot *act* in the United States, that as an individual he cannot alter the course of history. It leads to a symbolic confrontation. After observing the reluctance of one of his companions to trust men in uniform Jones makes the leap into faith by asserting that it is only our false idea of realism that causes such mistrust. He ends by expressing an exultant confidence in the machine guns surrounding Castro, by accepting the uniform as a symbol of existential reality and the gun as the power of truth itself. He reminds one of George Patton. Simply on the level of symbol we can see the quintessential difference between liberalism and the left. In 1961, at a time when the criticism of Castro was not fashionable, John Roche wrote this:

> A year or so ago when an enthusiastic friend told me we must all rally to Fidelism and bring "real socialism" to Latin America, I suggested gently that I could not see social democrats canonizing a man in love with a tommy-gun. The reply: Castro was "utterly unimportant"; it was Fidelism that counted. But Castro was and is important, and I have never known a man who treated a gun as a symbol—instead of an instrument—who was not fundamentally depraved.[7]

---

7. John Roche, "The Triumph of Primitivism," *Dissent* (Winter, 1961), pp. 16–23. Used by permission.

Politics, for the moment, aside, the new culture hero of the left is by definition not acceptable to the liberal mind. What matters is that he is an intellectual with the power of action; as Mailer put it, the link between Hemingway and himself.

With Mailer's essay on Castro we come to the great divide of the decade. Castro is celebrated as the kind of figure—the subculture surrounding him consists of Hemingway, Mailer, Mailer's Kennedy, Stephen Ward, Caryl Chessman, Jean Genet—who has broken out of the Freudian system of personality. What unites him and the others I have mentioned is their adoption as intellectuals by the left. They have all, at one time or another, been invoked as symbolic of the modern existential condition. And they have all become mirror images for intellectuals, examplars of actuality. If they are celebrated as intellectuals with the power to act they are perceived also as something more; they are significantly beyond principle and within the liberated area of human responses traditionally acknowledged to be criminal. The moral is self-evident.

Mailer's "Letter to Castro" is in the literary sense a companion piece to *The Old Man and the Sea.* There is the same fakery of language and feeling. Both author and subject are revealed in a prose that assumes the toga; a prose that labels itself "Truth," "Fact," and "Plain words" in order to pre-empt our responses. The imitation Spanish, the short, hard declarative phrases are the residue of Hemingway's style. All his exaggerations of tone and all his rhetorical masculinity are burlesqued, although the intention is to recall them.

The Castro of this piece is not a political person, although he is often addressed as a hero. Perhaps the central statement in Mailer's essay is this: *"you were aiding us, you were giving us psychic ammunition, you were aiding us in that desperate silent struggle we have been fighting with sick dead hearts against the cold insidious cancer of the power that governs us."* [8] He has been detached from Cuban politics and assimilated into an existential frame of another character. Used as a vehicle in this way Castro loses the legitimate force of his own consciousness and the meaning of his

---

8. Norman Mailer, "The Letter to Castro," *The Presidential Papers* (New York, 1963), pp. 67–75. Used by permission of the publisher, G. P. Putnam's Sons.

position. The long digression on Hemingway makes this plain—the function of Castro (one can see him, with nothing else to do in Havana) is to placate The Old Man by inviting him, the other self of all alienated American intellectuals, to come back to Cuba.

There are probably reasons for admiring Castro. None of them, without mistaking their subject, can include his tonic effect on those writers in the United States who suffered "a slow deadening. . . . exhausted our vision . . . sank into apathy." By this point, like Mailer's Kennedy, he is more thaumaturgic than symbolic. He has become a hero of libido. Mailer calls this kind of figure "The Existential Hero" but he is really a form of the Reichian Hero, "a hero central to his time, a man whose personality might suggest contradictions and mysteries which could reach into the alienated circuits of the underground." As it was put in the 1960 campaign, Sergius O'Shaugnessy born rich. When all the playing with words is done; when Eisenhower, yet once more, gets his lumps for alienating intellectuals and McCarthy is exhumed for frightening them; when the FBI and Nixon and the party bosses are gang-tackled *in absentia*, what remains is the idea of *machismo*.

In more ways than one Hemingway is the ancestor of Mailer— but it is not the best Hemingway, only the author of *For Whom the Bell Tolls* and *The Old Man and the Sea*. It is the man with the gun who lived, by a vast coincidence, in Cuba. We have seen the original of Mailer's Castro and his Kennedy before. They go back to the overdone tautness of Robert Jordan, Hemingway's only ideological hero. Surely it is not a coincidence that he too is a guerilla leader, a sexual redeemer, an intellectual with the power to act. Coincidence seems ever more doubtful when we compare Mailer's sense of the heroic past with Lionel Trilling's explanation of that past as seen by Hemingway:

> It was a country which had grown by the leap of one hero past another. . . . And when the West was filled, the expansion turned inward, became part of an agitated, overexcited, superheated dream life. . . . it was almost as if there were no peace unless one could fight well, kill well (if always with honor), love well and love many, be cool, be daring, be dashing, be wild, be wily, be resourceful, be a brave gun.[9]

9. "The Existential Hero," *ibid.*, p. 39.

What Mailer accepts in the new hero Lionel Trilling long ago rejected in the old:

> For when we think of how clear a line there is between Uncas, Chingachgook and Tamenund, the noble Indians, and El Sordo and Anselmo and the rest of the guerilla band, we see how very like Cooper's is Hemingway's romantic sense of the social and personal virtues.[10]

It is a conflict not only of liberal and radical judgment but of a superior and an inferior critical mind. The point is not the originality of the existential hero but his antiquity. His sensibility is neither new nor self-justifying. In a luminous passage Trilling makes his central point: it is not what he does, but what he is. The "essential inner dullness" of Robert Jordan is a consequence of a failure of intellect. He does not embody the tensions of the historical events in which he is located. His fate is determined by moral and political contradictions, but he does not really know them. His inadequacy—like that of Mailer's Castro and Kennedy—is that he must penetrate the complex secret but at the same time "have no wish to use it, only to *experience* it." Trilling's essay is already two decades old, but it remains the best introduction to the existential hero of the Sixties. There is an inner dullness to Mailer's heroic figures; they are all in a sense glandular productions. Equipped with the right attitudes, disburdened of the right sanctions, externally vital and sexual, they are within simply literary. Hemingway had read Freud and empowered Robert Jordan with a psychology adequate to the Thirties. Mailer has read Reich, and endows his culture heroes with a psychology to suit the Sixties. They give the impression of being more than a little criminal and sadistic; these potentialities alarm and please us, and give us a feeling that they are true to both style and life. But they are versions of the later Hemingway hero. The culture hero as guerilla, lover, and martyr is not new—he is another of the mirror images of the intellectual.

---

10. Lionel Trilling, "An American in Spain," *Ernest Hemingway: Critiques of Four Major Novels*, Carlos Baker, ed. (New York, 1961), p. 80.

# The Existential Hero: Suffering

The three books by Caryl Chessman—*Cell 2455, Death Row; Trial By Ordeal;* and *The Face of Justice*—had as their immediate purpose the demonstration of his innocence. He repeated throughout these books that "whatever else I had been or done, I hadn't committed the red-light crimes. I wasn't the red-light bandit." [11] The books had secondary intentions: to demonstrate that the death penalty was both inhumane and ineffective as a deterrent; to draw attention to the inequities of sentencing: to prove that "existence can be salvaged"; to master the art of writing itself. It is important to note that they were written for legal rather than moral vindication. Chessman refused a lesser plea that might have saved his life because he claimed to be innocent, not because his crime was, in the moral sense, a relative one. As Chessman grew in literary sophistication he realized that the affair could no longer be contained by such a literal intention:

> Here in Caryl Chessman the dark criminal legend was a perfect hate object, an ideal outlet for repressed hostility, a natural target for personal frustration and hidden guilt feelings, a splendid whipping boy, an open invitation to express violent sentiments, an opportunity to take a foursquare stand against sin and to participate, at least vicariously, in a cosmic battle between good and evil.[12]

That is one side of the issue. From another viewpoint he could be seen as a natural object of admiration, an ideal outlet for humanitarian *ressentiment,* an open invitation to express nonviolent sentiments, an opportunity to participate in the social battle between good and evil—which is to say, between left and right. When his defenders wrote that he was a "symbol of the human dilemma" [13] and that his was "a history so full of fearful symbolism" [14] it became evident that the case transcended not only the facts of the crime but of biography itself.

11. Caryl Chessman, *Trial By Ordeal* (Englewood Cliffs, 1955), p. 90.

12. Caryl Chessman, *The Face of Justice* (Englewood Cliffs, 1957), p. 35.

13. Stuart Palmer, "How Many More Chessmans?", *The Nation* (21 May 1960), pp. 439–440.

14. Elizabeth Hardwick, "The Life and Death of Caryl Chessman," *Partisan Review* (Summer, 1960), pp. 503–513.

Chessman was himself anxious to be understood as an existential figure. He was of course in the ultimate existential condition, living under the continuing immediacy of death. That he took on the guise and eventually adopted the language of the existentialists is one of the ironic happenings of modernity. Being about to die he went to the art form that instructed him how to feel about this:

> "He," says Michaux, "who wants to escape the world translates it." So, paradoxically, does he who is doomed and who wants to escape back *into* the world, the world of warmth and love and purpose. But his translations often are terrible rationalizations, offered in a language only he understands. As in a nightmare, he cries out and no one hears him. He is brave and his bravery is in vain. He runs but he must run in circles. . . . On Death Row life not only copies art, it creates a grotesque art form all its own that makes life its slave, death its master.[15]

His own writing and the best writing about him make it plain that the ideas are no less authentic for being adopted. Elizabeth Hardwick's essay says something of equal importance for *The Stranger* and for *Trial By Ordeal:* "He had to bring himself forth from the void of prison, from nothingness, from nonexistence. This condition of his nothingness, his nonexistence, makes his remarkable articulation, his tireless creation of himself as a fact, his nearly miraculous resurrection or birth—which it was we do not know—a powerfully moving human drama." [16] The whole point of his life, for intellectuals of every persuasion, was that he became literate, that he became conscious, that under the fact of death he reconstructed his character. His years on Death Row were a highly compressed version of the life of the mind.

There were, however, even in the best of writings on Chessman, variations on the existential theme that tended toward mythology. The first of these consisted of a violent attack on society, as if the true guilt for the crime rested there. Chessman had criticized the juridical procedure, not the structure of Western civilization. His social psychology was clearly of a familiar kind: "we live in a world of norms but not always in a world of normalcy." [17] He

---

15. Caryl Chessman, *Trial By Ordeal*, pp. 119–20.

16. Elizabeth Hardwick, "The Life and Death of Caryl Chessman," p. 504.

17. Caryl Chessman, *Trial By Ordeal*, p. 168.

was interested in social pathology not because it symbolized an underlying failure of our culture but because something had to be done about rehabilitating criminals. Second, the tendency among intellectuals was to treat this as another Dreyfus case. While Chessman specifically believed that he was being victimized he attributed this to the prejudice of the court and the ambitions of the prosecution. He believed that he was in one sense a scapegoat, although not because society was projecting its own guilt upon him. But this was one of the essential points of his *figura* as perceived by many intellectuals. Third, he never intimated that the crime for which he was accused was a morally relative one. Yet this, most of all, magnetized the intellectuals who declared for him.

The first step in his construction as an avatar of the modern intellectual was to arraign the common enemy, the phobic middle class. Paul Goodman did this in "The Fate of Dr. Reich's Books" [18] and his later "Comment" on Caryl Chessman.[19] In the first piece Goodman remarks that the majority of Americans—certainly of the readers of *The Catholic Worker*—were for the execution of Chessman. Goodman took this as an example of the "emotional plague" diagnosed by Reich—the existential circumstances of repression. It led Goodman to this solipsism: "the *tone* of such a majority was, to my mind, the frightening and portentous fact about that case. It means that when I walk down the street I am not safe, for these are the thoughts and feelings that seethe just beneath the surface in the majority of my fellow-citizens." It means, of course, no such thing. Out of its vast store of moralism the American public retained its faith in the death penalty—and seems not to have had designs on Goodman at all. Goodman's later piece is revelative; it explains how Catholic sexual education, which encourages masturbation and its accompanying guilt feelings, result in a tormented middle-class adult. It follows that all Catholics will be unreasonably hostile to all sexual deviancy. His Hobbsian view of Catholic attitudes—"a child defeated in his sexual expression identifies with his oppressor. . . ." —is somewhat afield from

18. Paul Goodman, "The Fate of Dr. Reich's Books," *Kulchur*, II (1960), pp. 19–23.
19. Paul Goodman, "A Comment," *Kulchur*, IV (1960), pp. 3–5.

Chessman but altogether too close to the habitual opinions of the left intellectual. The case has been lifted out of its context, placed within that of Reichian pathology, and universalized into the condition of all intellectuals alienated from all repressive majorities.

There are many intelligent things in Elizabeth Hardwick's essay, but it is built around the fallacy of the execution being a psychological sacrifice. It is prefaced by a quotation from *Fear and Trembling* which describes the falsity of the sacrifice of Isaac, visible only to the intended victim himself. The big point is the "sacrificial and symbolic nature of the case." It becomes part of the pathology of scapegoats. Viewed in this way, Chessman's crime (forcing the victim to commit fellatio) involves the Freudian process of projection: "It has been widely suggested that Chessman's execution was society's punishment of its own perverse wishes or deeds." One could argue that the twelve years of delay, public sympathy, and judicial aid by the higher courts proved the opposite—but both arguments are of course equally empty. The psychological argument is notoriously double-edged, allowing it to see ambiguities in the most literal circumstances. It may be that the public simply resisted the idea of enforced fellatio on the grounds that it was in fact a form of rape. Perhaps of more importance than the sexual offense was Chessman's intellectual offense: "His life represents our defeat. . . . The nihilism at the bottom of Chessman's fate, his brains, what the newspapers called his 'evil genius,' made him a fearful and dreadful example. His cleverness undid him." That this is very far from the facts is obvious—it was his cleverness which kept him alive in Death Row while it served as a human abbatoir for dozens of more ordinary criminals. It was his cleverness that mobilized the intellectuals, that attracted good lawyers, and, eventually, almost succeeded in a permanent stay of execution. Miss Hardwick's view is really about the fate of intelligence in America. It is altogether too easy to invoke the idea of projection, but if we are to believe that society had a perverse wish to do what Chessman did, and therefore killed him, we might as well believe that intellectuals perceived their own *mythos* in his condition, and therefore defended him. They made him into an intellectual (he was only a literate man trying to stay alive) and tossed him into the cockpit between Reaction and Truth.

The final stage in the evolution of Chessman as a culture hero was the translation from innocence to guilt. The early defenders were aware that there were good reasons for believing that Chessman had been falsely condemned. This was not the issue for some intellectuals on the further-out left; they memorialized him because his crime was a Reichian virtue. According to Tuli Kupferberg, the truths of underground sexual life were conveyed to the American public by Chessman's act—and in any case oral rape was hardly of that much seriousness.[20] Gregory Corso's "On Chessman's Crime" validated the point:

> It's all *abnormal*
> The virgin is sick!
> The whore is sick!
> The cocksucker the cuntlapper, sick!
> The sodomist the normalist, sick!
> The celibate the cocksman, sick!
> Yes! every man & woman who ever fucked, sick!
> The fucked and the fuckers
> The unfucked and non-fuckers, SICK!
> To the gas-chamber with all of them! [21]

Robert Wilson's essay in *The Realist* makes a great transition between Chessman as criminal and Reichian hero, and an equally important connection between culture and criminality. That it takes a political position is inevitable. The piece is in the form of a letter to a woman who has herself written in favor of the execution:

> Do you want a definition of fascism, little American mother-of-two who has never had an orgasm? Fascism is all the values that you consider American and Christian . . . all your cute little doilies and café curtains and the incredible bullshit that your magazines—*Life* and *Time* and *Look*—tell you every week.
> Do you know why you want to kill Caryl Chessman? . . . It's not because you love your daughters and want to protect them. Actually, little simpering woman out there in California, you hate your daughters. You hate their flesh, as you hate Chessman's breath-

20. Tuli Kupferberg, "Death and Love," *Kulchur*, III (1960), pp. 29–30. Used by permission of the author.
21. Gregory Corso, "On Chessman's Crime," *Yugen*, 7 (1961), pp. 29–30. Used by permission of the author.

ing flesh and want to destroy it, as you hate all flesh. . . . That is
what fascism is, little blood-thirsty PTA secretary. It is hatred of
the flesh, hatred of life.[22]

The crime is that of the culture; the criminal alone is innocent. By
this point Chessman has become the Reichian hero in full panoply,
the man who has escaped repression and finally made the break-
through into full humanity. The crime (it is assumed that he is
guilty) was a Reichian release from the hang-up of civilization
through the function of the orgasm. In order to perform it Chessman must have been superior in the sexual and moral sense to the
impotent society around him. I remarked on the inevitability of the
fascist routine—Chessman is of course a political hero. All Reichian
heroes are. If he has been used by liberals to attack the great
American masses he has been used by anti-liberals to attack the
concept of the social itself.

Diana Trilling noted that ours is an era of cases—Hiss, Oppen-
heimer, the Rosenbergs, Eichmann, Chessman.[23] Her essay on the
right of Stephen Ward to be considered in this group shows in
some detail the literary and political tangencies of sexual heroism.
To begin, Ward stood in a false relationship to society, which had
made a promise of moral relativism to all those who are of the
times. "Sexual enlightenment no less than political or cultural enlightenment" was the essence of modernity. In acting as a pimp
Ward was an acolyte of the modern:

> His urgent art or, we might put it, his urgent therapy was sex, per-
> haps chiefly in its perverse aspects. Ward was thus in social effect
> if not in precise legal fact on trial for his choice of dedication.

He simply lived out the demands which for the rest of us remain
psychiatric or literary. Perhaps the right word for it is "commitment."

The cultural attachments of Ward are quite plain. His mode of
sexuality has been validated by literature in the sense that "the chief
value that attaches to sex in our advanced literary view today lies

22. Robert Anton Wilson, "Negative Thinking," *The Realist* (May,
1960), pp. 4–6, 15. Used by permission.
23. Diana Trilling, "After the Profumo Case," *Claremont Essays*
(New York, 1964), pp. 1–19.

in its opposition to society, in the individual freedom it celebrates."
Ward is then, by definition, on the left; his life connects to dominant attitudes of contemporary thought. In order to arrive at this
position the literal has had to give way to the existential: it is clear
that so far as fact is concerned, Ward serviced the very rich and
was singularly unideological. But in dealing with culture heroes
fact becomes increasingly extraneous. This is not a sarcasm on my
part—Mrs. Trilling herself stresses the incongruities. She notes too
the electric sense of relationship between Ward and a group of
writers on the left. These writers were intuitively conscious of resemblance; the bond between Ward's death and "the enterprise of
modern literature" was acknowledged by their sending a wreath
to his grave. As for those who shared in Ward's life,

> There was implicit in the style of life this varied group had elected
> a shared freedom in matters of morality such as nowadays most
> readily translates itself into a progressive politics, or which at least
> opens the path for a steady erosion of the cultural foundations of a
> conservative politics.

Quite. It turns out, not surprisingly, that the real villain is Harold
Wilson, who exploited the moral aspects of the case and thereby
held back the Brownian revolution. It turns out, more interestingly,
that the true political dimensions of the case were these: The Labor
Party, which by definition was expected to speak for freedom, betrayed all liberals by this moralism. I should agree with Mrs. Trilling
that the life of reason has its difficulties right now, but on somewhat different grounds. Her canonization of Ward is almost un-
believably theoretical. Given the accident of a pimp servicing
politicians, we end by finding the great moral of modernity: In
the present political situation all those faithful to the spirit of enlightenment are hounded by the forces of the superego. It is only
those intellectuals careless of their own well-being who stand between the idea and middle-class *schwarmerei*. My own opinion is
this: Ward, like Chessman, was neither an intellectual nor a political
person. He was converted to both so that intellectuals could transfer their anxieties from art to life.

I will direct attention to one other man who is both a criminal
and a culture hero. He happens to be his own creation, but that

does not make him less of a representative figure. He is Eldridge
Cleaver, a Negro evidently under the influence of Genet—and of
many others. His story is certainly cautionary, if only because of
its effect on the pallid idea of "literary influence."

Cleaver became a rapist partly because of his reading list—it is to
be hoped that the librarians of the Birch Society never get hold
of his autobiography. He began with *Native Son*, graduated to
Rousseau, Paine, and Voltaire, and concluded with Marx. After
Bakunin and Nechayev he ascended to LeRoi Jones, whose "black
dada nihilismus" expressed exactly his moral position:

> I became a rapist. . . . It seemed to me that the act of rape was an
> insurrectionary act. It delighted me that I was defying and tramp-
> ling upon the white man's law, upon his system of values, and that
> I was defiling his women—and this point, I believe, was the most
> satisfying to me because I was very resentful over the historical
> fact of how the white man has used the black woman. I felt I was
> getting revenge. From the site of the act of rape, consternation
> spreads outwardly in concentric circles.[24]

Our criminals get better educated all the time. He has been through
Genet, Calvin Hernton, Nat Hentoff, Sartre, a whole library of
existential apprenticeship. Tell it not in Glenview, say it not in
Fort Worth.

Cleaver is an appealing person, apart from the crimes he committed—and apart even from the repentance he has for them. He
has combined that repentance with literary criticism, so to speak,
and dropped Jones as an exemplar. But he has stuck to his guns, at
least as far as American culture heroes are concerned:

> I'd like to leap the whole last mile and grow a beard and don what-
> ever threads the local nationalism might require and comrade with
> Che Guevara, and share his fate, blazing a new pathfinder's trail
> through the stymied upbeat brain of the New Left, or how I'd just
> love to be in Berkeley right now, to roll in that mud, frolic in that
> sty of funky revolution, to breathe in its heady fumes, and look
> with roving eyes for a new John Brown, Eugene Debs, a blacker-
> meaner-keener Malcolm X, a Robert Franklin Williams with less

24. Eldridge Cleaver, "Sorties in Mad Babylon," *Ramparts* (August,
1966), pp. 16–26. Used by permission.

rabbit in his hot blood, an American Lenin, Fidel, a Mao-Mao, A MAO MAO, A MAO MAO. . . All of which is true.

Paraphrase would be superfluous. Like any normal man he needs heroes, and he will take those he can get. Cleaver is better than he looks—it isn't every man who can be so accurate without a university education. He has picked the right models for the right reasons. Through intuition, reading, association, in some variety of ways he has seen the ideal form: the criminal as sociological hero; the crime as retribution; the existential act as the moral act; the politics of sexuality; the role of art in life. There is some poetic justice here—after all that mileage the intellectuals have gotten out of the ideological criminal, Cleaver reveals that he is going to be a writer. I wish him luck. We all ought to.

# INDEX

# INDEX

McCarthy, Joseph, 84
McCarthy, Mary, 197
McClure, Michael, 215
Maccoby, Michael, 42, 47, 175, 179
McCord, William, 95–96
McCormick, John, 225
MacDonald, Dwight, 4–5, 62, 64, 124
McMahan, Ian, 174
McNamara, Robert, 117
McReynolds, David, 114, 170, 267–268
Mailer, Norman, 8, 15, 74, 106, 107, 112, 121, 129, 131, 169, 206, 207, 208, 209, 211, 212 f., 218, 219, 229, 234, 247 f., 261–262, 268, 271 f.
Malamud, Bernard, 237 f.
Malcolm X, *see* X, Malcolm
Manganotti, Donatella, 220
Mannheim, Karl, 11, 21, 25, 40, 183
Marcus, Steven, 207
Marcuse, Herbert, 121, 122, 124 f., 130, 168–169, 170
Mascall, Eric, 65, 66
Maurras, Charles, 112–113
Meier, August, 80
Merton, Robert, 10–11, 22, 34
Meyer, Frank, 5, 192
Miller, Arthur, 235, 236
Miller, Henry, 16, 123, 211, 218, 262
Miller, Warren, 268, 269
Mills, C. Wright, 2–3, 15, 25–26, 32, 87, 115 f., 121, 136, 159, 184–185, 268, 269
Milosz, Czeslaw, 30–31, 33
Minogue, Kenneth, 184, 190–191, 192–193
Moberly, Sir Walter, 68
Morgenstern, Oskar, 70

Morgenthau, Hans, 29, 38, 39, 174, 202–203
Morris, I. I., 157
Moses, Robert, 81
Moynihan, Daniel Patrick, 49–50, 73, 74–76, 83
Mphahlele, Ezekiel, 246
Murray, John Courtney, 68

*New Leader*, 204
Newman, William J., 116
*New Radicals*, 149
*New University Thought*, 200–201
Nicolson, Marjorie, 23
Niebuhr, Reinhold, 50, 54, 55–56, 58, 59, 70, 147, 171, 190, 192
Nisbet, Robert, 40–41
Nixon, Richard, 84
Nolte, Ernst, 112, 126
Nomad, Max, 24, 31
Novak, Robert, 177

Oakeshott, Michael, 187, 190–191
Oglesby, Carl, 117–118, 120
Oliver, Revilo, 178
Orlovsky, Peter, 212

Palmer, R. R., 26
Palmer, Stuart, 274
Parenti, Michael, 86, 87
Parker, Michael, 97
Parry, Stanley, 192
*Partisan Review*, 197, 203, 204
Payne, Bruce, 128
Percy, Walker, 81
Petersen, William, 128
Petras, James, 158, 165
Petuchowski, Jakob, 62
Philips, William, 64, 235
Pickus, Robert, 133, 165
Pilisuk, Marc, 201